LETTS FILM

THE FILMS OF
PETER WEIR

DON SHIACH is the author of *The Movie Book* and *The Hollywood Movie Quiz Book*. He has taught cinema for many years and is currently teaching a course in American cinema at Sussex University. He is working on an extensive study of the career of Vincente Minnelli as a 'test case' director in terms of authorship within the institution of Hollywood cinema. Among his other titles are *The Critical Eye, From Page to Performance* and numerous other books intended for use in English and drama in secondary schools.

THE FILMS OF
PETER WEIR

Visions of alternative realities

DON SHIACH

CHARLES LETTS · *Letts* of London® · FOUNDED 1796

First published in 1993
by Charles Letts & Co Ltd
Letts of London House,
Parkgate Road,
London SW11 4NQ

ISBN 1 85238 359 3

A CIP catalogue record for this book is available from the
British Library

'Letts' is a registered trademark of Charles Letts & Co Limited

Cover picture: *Witness*, Harrison Ford (courtesy of Paramount
Pictures)

Printed and bound in Great Britain

Pictures were reproduced by kind permission of the following:

The Mosquito Coast © 1986 The Saul Zaentz Company. All
rights reserved.
Picnic at Hanging Rock © Picnic Productions Pty. Ltd.
Witness © 1985 by Paramount Pictures. All rights reserved.
Peter Weir portrait © Paramount Pictures. All rights reserved.
Last Wave © J. McElroy Holdings Pty Limited
The Cars That Ate Paris © J. McElroy Holdings Pty Limited
Gallipoli © Robert Stigwood Organization Ltd
Dead Poets Society © Walt Disney
Green Card © Walt Disney

Contents

Acknowledgements   vii

Introduction: Peter Weir,
            an Australian *Auteur*?   1
Themes and style   7
Starting out   15

The Films

The Cars That Ate Paris   31
Picnic at Hanging Rock   37
The Last Wave   59
The Plumber   77
Gallipoli   83
The Year of Living Dangerously   99
Witness   121
The Mosquito Coast   143
Dead Poets Society   163
Green Card   183

Conclusion   199
Notes   203
Filmography   205
Bibliography   209
Index   211

Acknowledgements

This book is dedicated to my wife, Jean.

Thanks also to Fiona Boyd of Film Australia, Jeanine Seawell of Seawell Films, and Penny Simpson and Cortina Butler of Letts.

Introduction
PETER WEIR, AN AUSTRALIAN AUTEUR?

I think the word 'auteur' has become devalued and we probably have to put it aside.

(Peter Weir)[1]

Film directing is the most overrated profession in the world.

(Orson Welles)

In the darkness of the cinema, we watch a man, aged about thirty with a bandage over his left eye, half-run towards an aeroplane waiting on the runway for take-off. He signals to the airport workers to put back the steps leading up to the plane's compartment. As they do so, his pace slows and he takes in a gulp of fresh air as if in relief. There is a half-smile on his face; he closes his eyes and throws his head back. In long shot we watch him unhurriedly mount the stairs. At the top of the steps a woman waits for him. They hold each other in a long embrace. He is safe, he is where he ought to be, he has chosen.

That is a description of the closing sequence of one of the best films of the eighties, *The Year of Living Dangerously*, a seriously underrated movie. The lovers who are reunited in a kind of reversal of the ending of *Casablanca* (1942) are played by Mel Gibson and Sigourney Weaver. The director of the movie was Peter Weir. In this final scene Weir in his *mise-en-scène* encapsulates what the whole film is about: the struggle between the demands of worldly ambition and love, between moral choice and amoral opportunism, instinct versus mundane rationality—all recurring themes in

Weir's films. Each film Weir now directs has the pre-credit 'A Peter Weir Film', an accolade that is now routinely awarded to average directors. But with what degree of accuracy can we talk about the body of films that this relatively young Australian director has directed as being by Peter Weir? That is one of the questions this book will have to address.

The question of authorship has haunted serious film criticism ever since the earnest critics of *Cahiers du Cinéma* produced their *Politique des auteurs* in the fifties. The essence of the *auteur* theory is the identification of a consistent vision or style (or both) in the body of films directed by an individual director. To qualify for *auteur* status there has to be a personal signature attached to a director's movies, for example, consistent thematic concerns or stylistic motifs that instantly mark them down as having been authored by, say, Hitchcock or John Ford. In the heady early days of the *auteur* theory, all sorts of dim Hollywood directors were resurrected by the French critics and granted *auteur* status. The theory reached its nadir when some ardent *auteur*ists even claimed Jerry Lewis as an *auteur*. Minor Hollywood figures such as Budd Boetticher, Edgar Ulmer and Joseph H Lewis were suddenly feted, and, much to their own astonishment no doubt, it was discovered that they had incorporated a world vision in their B movies. Other better-known American directors had their periods of worship when no film they made, however meretricious, was deemed unworthy of very serious consideration. Thus, Howard Hawks could make *Hatari* (1962) and *Man's Favorite Sport* (1963) and still be lauded by Hawksians on the premise that even flawed movies made by a master were of much more interest than the routine products made by those who were not *auteurs*. But the *auteur*ists were prone to modishness and directors rapidly fell in and out of favour. Otto Preminger, for example, could do no wrong at one time in the eyes of *auteur*ists; now is there anyone willing to speak up for the director of *Laura* (1944) and *Advise and Consent* (1962)?

Indeed, the *auteur* theory in its most extreme form has largely been discredited. Evidence has mounted about the compromised role of the director in the classical mode of production in the Hollywood studio system, evidence that points to the collaborative nature of film-making and the institutional and generic determinations that shaped the final movie product. Clearly the position of contemporary Hollywood directors is different from the experience of the studio slaves of the old Hollywood system. In addition, it is undeniable that individual art movie directors such as Ingmar Bergman or Akira Kurosawa have much more artistic control over the movies they make than most of those labouring away in the commercial film-making context.

Thus, it must not be assumed that the *auteur* theory is completely irrelevant to contemporary criticism. However, post-structuralist theory has led many critics to unseat authors in literature and the other arts, including the cinema. There has been a move towards discussing individual authors as merely fulfilling an author-function within the rhetoric of the text; post-structuralism talks about the 'notional figure within the rhetoric of the text' in an attempt to move away from the idea that the individual work of art is a matter of personal expressiveness and that it is the individual author who gives meaning to the text. Post-structuralism puts the emphasis on reading a text rather than receiving, as a passive reader, a given meaning from it, on what the text is actually saying as well as what it is not saying within what kind of discourse, and on how meaning is signified, rather than who is saying it.

As cinema is aimed at a mass audience using formulaic structures (genres) and conventional means of signifying meaning (the style of generic movies), it is hardly surprising that much contemporary film criticism has aspired to a scientific objectivity in deconstructing the movie-making process in order to lay bare the means by which Hollywood in particular creates its products and its ideologies. Much of this work has been invaluable and no serious film criticism can afford to avoid analysing movies within their historical and sociological contexts and against the background of conventional signifying practices within the movie industry. But the effect of post-structuralist analysis is finally reductive and repetitive. It also pretends to a scientific objectivity that it cannot attain, because individual critics are not unprejudiced scientists (there is no such animal) dissecting works of art and exposing the underlying structures and practices in a dispassionate and totally objective manner. They bring their own ideological prejudices to bear and are as shaped by class, gender and racial factors as anyone else.

My reading of Peter Weir's films will be affected by many factors including my maleness, my nationality, my age and my ideological stance. But one thing I can promise: I will be looking at the figure of Peter Weir as an individual and not as a critical construct. He will not be seen by me as a dehumanized figure performing a director-function within the discourse of the film text. At the risk of being accused of bourgeois individualism, I will be approaching this study of his career as though he were an individual who has been shaped by his own personal experiences and affected by the times he has lived through. I will not be looking at him or his career outside the historical circumstances in which he has made his films, or as though his movies are uninfluenced by the history of cinema itself, its conventional practices, its commercial and ideological pressures and the specific circumstances of the film industries (Australian and American) he has worked in. It may seem strange to have to stress this humanist approach, but so much informed and influential contemporary film criticism is imbued by a mixture of neo-Marxism and Lacanian psychoanalytical theory, that the impression is given that the individual artist is no longer important, indeed that the whole idea of the *self* has been exploded by Marx and Lacan, particularly by the latter. For those of us who still believe in a humanist tradition, who still see individuals as having control over their lives and careers, it is important to claw back this reality from those who would deny the importance of the individual and who claim that there is no such thing as the unified ego or indeed the individual.

Having made that emphatic point, however, it is still possible that in the particular case of Peter Weir, we are not considering a director of *auteur* status at all. He may just be a craftsman with a certain degree of technological know-how, a journeyman director who brings what talents he has to bear on the scripts he is handed. However, the fact that Weir is a writer-director is an important point. He mostly has worked on scripts he has either written himself or on which he has collaborated closely with the screenwriter(s). When we get to the Hollywood phase of his career, there are three movies for which he does not get screen credit as co-writer: *Witness, Mosquito Coast* and *Dead Poets Society*. The issue then is what relationship he, as director, has to the final movie product. In those films, has he merely been a director of someone else's vision, a craftsman who knows how to turn a screenplay into a movie but who brings very little of himself to the project? And even if we discern recurring thematic concerns in all of his movies, even those he did not originate in script form, that does not mean those movies have some inherent value *per se*. A director can deal with recurring themes in the movies he or she directs and still turn out trash. That was one of the weaknesses of the original *auteur* theory—that the very process of identifying directorial obsessions or repeated stylistic touches in a director's canon meant, according to the theory, inevitably those movies had some intrinsic worth.

What has also fascinated me in writing this book is the way in which Peter Weir's career has taken shape. One outstanding trait of the man is that he has controlled how his directing career has evolved. Peter Weir, it is accurate to say, is his own man. But equally it can be stated that his early career evolved out of the renaissance in the Australian film industry in the early seventies. In a sense he came from nowhere to become the leading Australian film director. As will be analysed in the next section, the Australian film industry suddenly opened out opportunities for those who had the talent and the initiative to take advantage of them. Peter Weir was one of those individuals who decided to go for it, seizing his opportunities with enthusiastic commitment. But he has never claimed to be interested in making movies for a relatively small art house audience. Weir wants to make movies for a mass audience and the country which dominates the world film market is America; inevitably, if he were to become an international film director, he had to go Hollywood. A key issue about Weir's *oeuvre* is how much the films he has directed in America have been diluted by the institutional and generic demands of the film industry there with its commercial imperatives and classical mode of film-making.

Themes and Style

Weir has not originated all of the movies he has directed: that is, he has not always found the original source material or created the original screenplay as a writer or co-writer, yet I would argue that even with his Hollywood movies, there are pronounced, recurring thematic concerns. I would describe those concerns as visions of alternative realities.

In all of his movies, the given reality that faces his protagonists (the school, small-town life, dessicated middle-class existence, a vulgar and materialistic society, various forms of oppression) is opposed by a vision of an alternative reality, almost always a reality that demands of the individuals that they allow their dreams to inform their lives and that they follow their instincts, which will lead to their liberation in one way or another. However, included in this vision of alternative realities is the realization that the path to self-fulfilment, and replacing our view of reality based on rationality and accepted values with one that allows our spiritual and creative sides full play, is a very difficult and treacherous one and society will do its best to defeat you.

This vision, then, has its dark side and Weir's protagonists do not always make it to the other side. And the alternative reality too is not all sugar and spice and all things nice: basic human instincts such as the sexual one unleash powerful and sometimes destructive forces. In *Picnic at Hanging Rock* and *The Last Wave* the visions of an alternative reality experienced by the main protagonists do not inevitably lead to peace of mind and transcendence. The Billy Kwan character in *The Year of Living Dangerously* may have a vision of an alternative reality, but he is incapable of adapting that vision to his own situation and so he is destroyed. Similarly with Allie Fox's vision of an alternative

America which he builds in a Central American jungle. He is blind to the innately destructive forces he is unleashing. The alternative reality that John Book encounters in *Witness*, the Amish community, idyllic as it may seem on the surface, depends on its own kind of oppression. In all his films Weir expresses a strong dissatisfaction with the status quo, whether it be the oppressive establishments of Appleyard College and Welton Academy in *Picnic* and *Dead Poets Society* respectively, the brutalizing influence of the army in *Gallipoli*, the male bonding of the Philadelphia police force in *Witness*, the deadness of middle America in *Mosquito Coast*, the supposed cosiness of small townships in *The Cars That Ate Paris* or New York trendy life in *Green Card*.

Weir does not offer political solutions to society's ills, nor advocate collective action. There is a significant emphasis on the value of the individual and the need for the individual to take control of his or her life and to forge a vision that will allow the whole person, not just the educated, civilized and rational self, to be present in a world of their own making.

Present-day civilization and its socializing agencies are represented in Weir's films as being in the grip of a deep malaise. In Weir's movies, the opposition to civilization is a primitivism or, at least, a culture that is still in touch with its dreams and its soul. Thus, the Hanging Rock in *Picnic* represents primitive forces that defeat rationality, the dreamtime of Aboriginal culture overcomes the surface order of the lawyer's life in *The Last Wave*, the influence of the mysticism of the shadow puppets affects the life of the ambitious protagonist in *The Year of Living Dangerously*.

Weir has been accused of sentimentalizing primitive cultures and of regressive attitudes in seeming to long for cultures that allow superstition and myths full play. For those who look to revolution or other political solutions as cures for society's ills, Weir's films might well seem reactionary. But what he seems to be saying is that contemporary urbanized and educated man has lost his way; our so-called rationality has led us to ignore the promptings of our bodies and our souls and we can only rediscover ourselves through getting in touch with our dreams and sustaining myths. It is no surprise that Weir has professed a strong interest in Jungian psychology, because his movies do place an enormous importance on dreams and visions, myths and archetypes. A psychic reality replaces the given, overt reality and then his individuals can attempt to lead the lives they are truly capable of. Their shadow sides can be rediscovered and they can once again be in tune with the unseen forces of life, those belonging to the spiritual and nature, to the hidden and the unrevealed.

When we discuss a director's style, we inevitably run into some problems. Some directors such as Von Sternberg, Ophuls and Minnelli have been labelled stylists because the elements of their *mise-en-scène* seem to outweigh greatly in importance the more literary aspects of the movies they directed. By *mise-en-scène*, I mean all those elements that are inserted into the screen space by the director, and his or her collaborators; these include use of framing, screen space, sound, colour, music, costumes, iconography, acting and editing among other things. *Mise-en-scène* means, in essence, staging events for the camera. The term comes from the theatre and there it means the act of staging. Now it is almost unknown for any one single director to have absolute control over all the elements of *mise-en-scène*, outside, say, independent, non-commercial film-making where an individual film-maker might act as his or her own cinematographer, designer, editor, sound recordist etc. In the world of commercial film-making, there is always a body of specialist experts on hand to take responsibility for, say, the design elements or the photographic process. Nominally, at least, in charge of all these specialists is the director, who usually has a producer to lay on resources and people for him or her.

Von Sternberg, who directed movies such as *The Scarlet Empress* (1934), *Morocco* (1930) and *Shanghai Express* (1932), was reputed to be uninterested in the stories he made; he was primarily devoted to the visual elements of the medium, the use of setting and decor, the play of light on people, particularly fetishized female stars, and on objects. Since the stuff of the movies Von Sternberg directed with Marlene Dietrich as the obsessive focus of his camera was melodramatic trash, critics seized on the stylistic motifs of the films, the elements of *mise-en-scène*, to justify taking Von Sternberg's movies seriously. But it is a matter of aesthetic judgement, of personal evaluation, whether the stylishness of Von Sternberg's *mise-en-scène* rescues the films he directed from being merely high-flown kitsch and elevates them to the status of serious art or whether they remain essentially meretricious film artefacts despite the dressing-up they receive at the hands of a director who is more of a designer than a story-teller. For those who hold to a style-is-meaning critical stance, then Von Sternberg's *mise-en-scène is* the movies. The story and characters are merely necessary appendages on which to hang a display of style, which in its turn becomes the essential meaning of the movies.

Peter Weir is not a stylist in the Von Sternberg or Ophuls mould. He is basically a story-teller whose medium happens to be film. As a writer, he clearly values what could be classed as the literary elements of movies: narrative, characters, themes. There is a definite change from a form of narrative that is less linear and classical in his early Australian films to narrative structures that are decidedly linear in his American movies, using linear in the sense that the films obey rules of causality, time and setting and that there is a structure of opening exposition, development of story, climactic scenes and resolution and closure. But then that raises the central issue of how far those narrative structures are determined by generic and institutional demands. In other words, did Weir in directing variations on generic forms of the American cinema have to employ conventional structures at the behest of the producers as the representatives of the studios who backed the movies?

Weir is certainly not a showy stylist, but he does help to create startling visual effects when these will help the narrative and make a point forcefully in cinematic terms. I have in mind scenes such as the first view we have of the Gallipoli shore in *Gallipoli*, when the soldiers on the boats see the lights in the dark like the illuminations at a fairground, or the shots of the Amish in *Witness* walking through the fields towards a funeral service for one of their number. Weir does not, however, see style as something extraneous to the whole, as though it can be applied with a trowel to embellish the story. Form, style and narrative are welded together and when elements of self-conscious imagery creep in, it is when Weir has forgotten that *mise-en-scène* should be used to serve the story, not as a prettifying element or as a self-conscious attempt to create stylistic effect.

One of Weir's strengths is his ability to suggest the uncanny, the other-worldly, the unknown, the psychic. He does this by mixing elements of his *mise-en-scène* (camera angles, use of screen space, music and sound, for example) to produce unsettling effects. He is consciously or unconsciously influenced by fantasy/ horror generic traditions, but by asserting that, I do not mean to detract from the originality of his imaginative vision. A skilled director borrows from film-making traditions and adapts them to his own needs. It also has to be stressed that Weir has not remained the same director throughout the nearly twenty years of his career. His handling of narrative structures, his creation of rhythm in a film, his techniques with the camera – all these have changed from movie to movie. Some would argue that his style has become more bland and unadventurous since he started making films in America. But that may be a case of his having to deal with blander and less adventurous material in the commercial market-place; the style of these later films reflects the type of narrative and the more conventional projects that they are.

Weir almost certainly sees himself primarily as a story-teller. That does not mean, however, that we need to perceive him like that. He is a story-teller who has something to say about the grand themes, the big issues: life and death, why we are here, freedom versus imprisonment of one kind or another, the spiritual side of life. His willingness to take on large themes is one of Weir's stylistic signatures. Most of his films deal with fundamental questions of human existence – what then must we do? what meaning can we give to life? what kinds of moral choices face us? Even when he takes on the limited canvas of romantic comedy in *Green Card*, Weir tries to inject some higher significance into the narrative. Thus, he has left himself open to the charge of pretentiousness and naivety, a charge that is not always easy to rebuff. But in his willingness to take risks, to go after significance, he is signalling one of the characteristics that make him a director worthy of consideration for *auteur* status. He may fail at times in his movies, but at least he is attempting to give substance to the narrative. He is not content to make hollow, superficially entertaining films that you forget about the minute you leave the cinema.

Most Weir films have a resonance that stays with you

and yet he would almost vehemently deny that he was any kind of intellectual. Indeed, he is frequently on record as saying he despises pedagogues and academics and is very wary of the academization of cinema. Despite this, there are ideas at work in his movies and an ideology that is very consciously produced. 'A Peter Weir Film' does mean something specific; it is more than just an industry device to help promote the selling of a product by identifying the name of the director, an element in a process of product differentiation. We have come to expect something rather unusual from a Peter Weir film. That in itself, in these days of endless sequels and bland, mindless entertainments, is something to treasure in a contemporary director.

Starting Out

It was an incredibly exciting period for Weir . . . the air was electric . . .

(David Stratton)[1]

Born in Sydney, Australia in 1944, Peter Weir passed through his early adult years in the sixties and was as influenced by the social and historical changes of that famous decade as any other young person finding themselves at that time. His background was fairly standard middle-class; his father was an estate agent. His great-grandparents on both sides had emigrated from England, Ireland and Scotland. The Celtic influence was probably the strongest, which may in part explain Weir's interest in mythology, legends, the mystical and the uncanny. Weir, by his own admission, did not seem to prosper at school or university (he is not fond of academics or academia and schools, generally, in Weir's films are portrayed unsympathetically). He dropped out of Sydney University after one year and went to work as an estate agent with a view to working with his father. After two years however, he had saved enough money to finance a trip to Europe.

Non-Australians like myself may have to remember how distant many Australians feel from the rest of the world, even in these days of fast travel. This sense of isolation is a state of mind for many Australians whose families emigrated from Europe or other places. There seems to be a strong need among many young Australians to see the countries where their families came from, to explore the wider world, to come into contact with older cultures, to leave their country, situated at the edge of the world as it were, and feel more in the centre of things. At the age of twenty, Peter Weir chose that option.

Weir took a passage on a Greek ship bound for **Peter Weir** Piraeus, the port of Athens, During the trip, Weir helped organize a ship's revue using the closed circuit television system they had on board. The length of the journey to Greece and subsequently to other countries in Europe helped Weir understand how far Australia was from the rest of the world not only in terms of distance, but also perhaps in terms of culture. As the descendant of British immigrants, he felt how far away he was from the culture that had shaped his family. 'It struck me very strongly that I was a European, that this was where we had come from and where I belonged,' he has said about that trip. This is in no way an expression of cultural inferiority, but an acknowledgement of the deep roots he felt in Europe. Indeed, this trip probably helped him define what it is to be an Australian, an issue that would surface later in his Australian films.

Weir spent nearly a year in London, taking casual jobs, like many young Australians of the time, to help pay for his trip. It was 1965 and the swinging London myth was being manufactured and sold. It was the era of the Beatles, the Stones and rock music in general, flower power and youthful rebellion. The Vietnam war was becoming the major tragedy of the decade, arousing virulent opposition among the young people of Europe (and America, of course). For many young people, the sixties signified a throwing off of old shackles, repressions and ideas. The post-war period and the grimness of the fifties were finally over. Abundance was in the air, not only in terms of material goods but in the accessibility of the good things in life—love, friendship, freedom and pleasure. The feeling that anything was possible, especially for the young, may have led Weir to reassess his future when he got back to Sydney. The profession of an estate agent and the image of flower power are almost polarities, so it is perhaps not surprising that Weir decided to leave that stage of his life behind and try to break into the world of entertainment as a writer or as an actor.

Very few people decide to be a film director and immediately become one. Many, many young people dream about making their own films but their dreams are never acted upon. Others try but come up against the hard fact that very few of those who set out on that path ever finally reach the pinnacle of being given the responsibility of making a commercial film. In the heyday of the Hollywood studios, or even during the thirties and forties in the British film industry, it was possible to serve your time as an apprentice film-maker, working your way up to editor or cameraman status and finally being given the job of feature film director. Nowadays, with the demise of the studio system, directors come to feature films via different routes: through television, the stage or even occasionally through their own writing (e.g. the writer, David Mamet, who now directs his own films). In the mid-sixties in Australia, there was certainly no indigenous film industry for Peter Weir to work his way up in. But there was Australian television and this is the route that would eventually lead Weir into making feature films.

But jobs in Australian television were not all that easy to come by in the mid-sixties, especially perhaps for a young man who had dropped out of university and had not proved himself in any aspect of the entertainment industry. While he was waiting for an opportunity to present itself, Weir increased his credibility by producing a revue in a church hall during Christmas 1966. Then the call from Channel 7 in Sydney came, but the offer was for a job as a stagehand. However, from small beginnings great things grow and humble as his initial position was, it was clearly important for Weir to find any niche in this world of entertainment, however remote it might be from the creative control he ultimately had in mind. To prosper in the entertainment industry, whether as a performer, producer, writer or director, a person usually has to have a single-mindedness, a toughness, a clarity of purpose and vision, a certain talent for self-promotion and for spotting the opportunities. Forget Hollywood biopics with their sugary sentiments about show people pulling together and giving each other a helping hand; the entertainment industry is imbued with a profound competitiveness and a survival of the fittest ethos. Very often, success depends on knowing the right person, choosing your collaborators and supporters with care and being in the right place at the right time. Very few people are discovered, à la Hollywood, by a famous producer who stumbles across their talent.

Weir decided to make his own luck. While producing a staff Christmas revue he decided, or was given permission, to make a short film, *Count Vim's Last Exercise*, a fifteen-minute comic exercise. Obviously, this first attempt was greeted with some enthusiasm (although *Count Vim* was turned down for showing in the 1968 Sydney Film Festival), because Weir was able to make another film in 1968, *The Life and Flight of the Rev. Buck Shotte*, which was a spoof of religious cults. Having had *Buck Shotte* accepted for showing in the 1969 film festival, he refused to allow it to be screened because of the official banning of the showing of a Swedish film, *I Love, You Love*. Amateurish as these efforts may have been, they were impressive enough for his bosses at Channel 7 to promote him to the task of directing film clips for a popular show of the time, *The Mavis Bramston Show*. He worked for a year on the film clips before the show was taken off the air. During that time he had not received a salary rise and when the programme was cut, he was told he was to go back to being a stagehand. Weir showed courage in resisting this demotion and resigned. He had no job and few prospects, but he had the feeling that things would work out for him. There was an energy in the air, youth was in the ascendancy, anything was possible.

About three months later, Weir got his first big break: he was employed as a trainee director by the Commonwealth Film Unit. A considerable amount of lobbying had been going on for an indigenous Australian cinema during the previous few years. To all intents and purposes, there was no film industry in Australia at the time. This was partly due to the virtual monopolistic control over the distribution and exhibition functions enjoyed by major cinema chains. American films dominated in the cinemas because there was no incentive for exhibitors to take the chance on Australian movies, when the public seemed to yearn to see only Hollywood films or the occasional British film. By showing only foreign films, there were economic advantages for the major chains of cinemas: production costs were borne by other countries and they could choose to show films that had already proven their box-office worth in America or Britain.

In the thirties, it had been a different story with Cinesound Studios (owned by the major distribution company, Australasian Films, and its exhibition arm, Union Theatres) producing seventeen features between 1932 and 1940. Cinesound was set up as a Hollywood-type studio and its products were mainly movies of the bushranger variety (in a sense, the Australian equivalent of westerns), hayseed comedies (comic tales about poor rustics, including a series about the Rudd family) and films about diggers, notably a series starring Pat Hanna (*Diggers, Diggers in Blighty, Waltzing Matilda*). Cinesound production facilities were closed down after the Second World War, with the merger of Greater Union and Rank. From then until 1969, hardly any Australian features were made with the exception of Charles Chauvel's *The Rats of Tobruk, The Rugged O'Riordans* and *Jedda*. British productions using Australian settings, actors and personnel included *The Overlanders* (1946) and *The Shiralee* (1957) whilst Hollywood weighed in with *On the Beach* (1959) and *The Sundowners* (1960).

However, towards the end of the sixties, the restitution of a national cinema became almost a political issue. John Gorton's government took the decision in 1970 to establish the Australian Film Development Corporation. This move towards creating an indigenous film industry has to be seen as part of the cultural renaissance that Australia experienced in the sixties. The theatre led the way with writers such as Bob Ellis, David Williamson and Ray Lawler. Television with its home-grown products, however unsophisticated, had established that it need not be entirely dependent on American and British programmes. The huge anti-Vietnam war demonstrations in Australia, including mass protests in Melbourne and Sydney in 1970, helped to shape a sense of Australian-ness, with young people questioning Australia's role in the wider world and its relationship to America and the mother country, Britain. This identification of what it is to be Australian is a process that continues to this day with the current pressure to turn Australia into a republic by severing ties with the British crown. A strong indigenous film industry is one of the ways a nation can find its sense of nationality and undoubtedly the upsurge in film production in Australia in the seventies reflected the country's move towards throwing off a sense of inferiority and its colonial heritage. For thirty years prior to 1970, only a handful of Australian feature films were produced; in the decade that followed, over two hundred Australian feature films were made. Peter Weir was in the right place at the right time to benefit from what was happening around him.

Thus, at the Commonwealth Film Unit, Weir was favourably positioned to take advantage of the new impetus the Gorton government had given to the Australian film industry. The CFU had had a history of turning out dull but worthy documentaries, but amidst this feeling of excitement about re-establishing a fully-fledged home film industry, it branched out into feature films. In 1969, Weir was given the chance to direct one section of a three-part film on contemporary youth, a project which reflected the youth culture of the era and the new-found emphasis on listening to what the Australian younger generation were trying to say. The film was *Three to Go* and Weir's section was entitled *Michael*.

Weir is given writing and directing credit for *Michael*, but in fact the writing element was relatively small, certainly in terms of the amount of dialogue used in the half-hour segment. Screenwriters have to do more than write dialogue, of course, they have to describe scenes in terms of what the camera will record. Screenwriters have to think in cinematic terms and dialogue is only one of the means by which a story can be told on screen. Weir's contribution as a writer to *Michael* was the original story, the shaping of the various scenes and the decision to handle certain thematic concerns in the course of the short movie. He has since admitted that the prevalence of rock music on the soundtrack was a kind of substitute for dialogue:

> We didn't know how to write dialogue for Australians and the actors were frightened of saying it. The sound of the Australian accent in films was totally unfamiliar. So I pulled a lot of tricks to have minimal dialogue in the picture.[2]

Weir's statement to Sue Mathews in an interview for her book on five Australian directors is very revealing about the state of Australian films and culture at this juncture. Australian popular culture was dominated by American products and theatrical and literary culture was dominated by the British. Australian actors were not accustomed to talking in their native accents on stage, on television or in films. Weir's admission is an honest statement about a sense of cultural inferiority that Australians felt in the late sixties. It was a state of mind that numerous Australian artists had to break free from if they were to find their own voice in their chosen medium.

We are now very accustomed to hearing authentic Australian voices on film, so it may be difficult for us to realize just how difficult it was for Australian artists to make the breakthrough twenty years ago. Australian writers had to find their own voice and realize they were just as good as the Brits. Since the increase of immigrants from southern Europe and the growth of the republican movement, the umbilical connection with Britain has been loosened and indeed the significance of Commonwealth ties well-nigh obliterated. That sense of cultural inferiority has fortunately been considerably lessened, although the British still indulge in patronage of the Australian cultural scene, an attitude that is given some kind of respectability by self-inflicted wounds from Australian artists, such as Barry Humphries with his horrific creation, the Australian cultural attaché Les Patterson, Australia's own superstar, Dame Edna Everage, and the series of *Barry Mackenzie* films.

In 1969, however, it was a problem to have his Australians talk as Australians. Weir's solution, the playing of Beatles songs and those of other contemporary rock bands to underscore the action on screen, now seems clichéd and superficial. It should be remembered, however, how prevalent that technique was in commercial movies emanating from Hollywood and Britain at that time.

Hollywood film companies interested in selling record albums of soundtracks flooded their movies with accompanying rock songs. Outstanding examples of films of the era that did this are *The Graduate* (1967) and *Easy Rider* (1969). British films such as *Here We Go Round the Mulberry Bush* (1967) and *Georgy Girl* (1966) imitated this trend. Thus, Weir was probably consciously or unconsciously influenced by the dominant commercial cinema of the time when he used so much rock music on the soundtrack of *Michael*. Indeed, it would have been surprising if a new, young film-maker making his first commercial film had not been influenced by what was then current on the commercial cinema scene.

As well as the use of rock music on the soundtrack, Weir used fast editing techniques and cross-cutting between images that are meant to be significant, a sort of less assured use of similar techniques used by British director John Schlesinger in *Midnight Cowboy* (1969). Just as that movie made some simplistic and superficially significant points by juxtaposing oppositional images (contrasting images of poverty and wealth, of plenty and scarcity, underscored by relevant

21

songs by Simon and Garfunkel *et alia*), so *Michael* contrasts the world of the suburban middle class with the culture of the hippies with similarly superficial effect. This superficiality has been retrospectively admitted by Weir, who now finds much of the film embarrassing.

The eponymous hero of *Michael* is a middle-class young man living amidst the suburban conformity of his family but attracted to the youthful rebellion of his generation. The film opens with scenes of urban militia (intended to represent revolutionary students dressed in Ché Guevara-type dress) in battle with the army. These scenes are shot in a documentary style much in the style of Godard's *Les Carabiniers*. The soldiers are represented as being rather incompetent; the student rebels wipe out a lorry-load of them. It is never very clear whether these scenes are meant to represent actual reality, in that these scenes of armed conflict are actually happening in the city, or whether they are a projection in the mind of the main protagonist of what might conceivably happen in the future. After these opening scenes, the rest of the film seems to paint a much calmer portrait of everyday life in Sydney, although rebellion is in the air.

We see Michael at a club with his respectable, straight-laced fiancée, Judy. Around them are posters asking the question: 'Rebellion: could it happen here?', which seems to reinforce an interpretation of the opening scenes as projections of a possible future, rather than the present reality in the narrative of the film. We then see the recording of a television programme *Youthquake*, in which a panel of bumbling experts pass pronouncements on the current rebellion of youth. At his family home, Michael is subjected to the mindless and trivial chatter of his mother. We then see him queueing for the bus with three other conventionally-suited business-men. On his way to work, he passes a vox pop street interview by the *Youthquake* programme. The young people being interviewed are told to be angry and the presenter claims to be taking a fresh look at the phenomenon of youthful rebellion. Michael is seen arriving at his dull office and then at lunch-time quarrelling with his girlfriend at a trendy dress shop festooned with icons of the rock and youth scene of the time, including posters of John Lennon and James Dean. The film cuts back to the television panel who are self-consciously answering questions on the sexual attitudes of the young. In a pub after work, Michael is bored by the talk of his stockbroker colleagues and deliberately strikes up an acquaintance with an alternative culture young man. He attends a revolutionary meeting where various students announce that revolution in an advanced capitalist society is possible.

At home later in the evening, Michael is shown slumped in front of the television with his family and then at church next day with his mother and fiancée. Bored and restless with the family barbecue afterwards, he leaves and goes to the pad of his new hippie pal he had met in the pub. He seems relaxed and happy among his new friends. He takes two of the flower children to his fiancée's twenty-first birthday party, thereby offending his intended in-laws, his fiancée herself and his mother, who demands an explanation from him for the offence he has caused. Michael takes the next day off work, spends it having fun with his hippie friend and plucks up his courage to phone home to say that he will be late as he is out with his alternative friends. At the hippie's pad, however, he feels isolated among the gathering of people whom he realizes he may not have that much in common with. He wanders away from the party and the last shots of the film are of him walking in the street, looking lost and unhappy. Michael seems to be caught between two worlds: the world of his respectable family and job and the new alternative culture. He seems to fit in with neither.

Michael is a film very much of its time, as it is intended to be. Weir's embarrassment about its superficialities and rough techniques is understandable, because in many ways it *is* superficial and naive. However, making allowances for the fact that this was the work of a very young director feeling his way in the medium, there are definite signs of talent in these thirty minutes of film. The film obeys one of the first laws of motion pictures: it moves. The quickly-changing scenes, the rapid cutting techniques, the juxtaposition of images, all help to reinforce the idea of a society in the throes of change and upheaval. Some scenes are expertly staged. Even the scenes of armed rebellion at the beginning of the film have a certain raw authenticity, whilst the scenes staged in Michael's home more than adequately represent the stultifying boredom of the suburban milieu.

Other scenes, such as the birthday party where Michael offends everyone by bringing along his hippie friends or the scene at the hippie's pad, are stiff and unconvincing.

In these representations, the writer-director Weir has not given his actors enough to work on either in terms of dialogue or convincing action. The repetitive montage sequences where revolutionary icons such as Guevara and Lennon are used to reinforce the representation of youthful rebellion become tedious, as does the repeated use of rock music on the soundtrack. The scenes of Michael having fun with his hippie pal at the seaside have a certain forced gaiety about them. The film, like many first films, attempts to squeeze far too much into a very limited time framework so the director is forced to turn to ready-made clichés to make his points about society. Not surprisingly, the film seems dated today, but it retains an interest because of its portrait, however clichéd, of aspects of Australian life of the period.

For those interested in Peter Weir's career as a film director, *Michael* has an added interest. Despite its flaws, Weir shows himself to have a real feel for the cinema and what it is capable of communicating. It shows his willingness to take on big themes. There is the concern for the individual and the refusal to endorse fashionable remedies for the ills of society. The hippies and alternative culture are sympathetically portrayed in the movie, but there is no rubber-stamping of alternative life styles as being the only recourse for a young person stifled by routine and dullness. On the other side, the snobberies and restrictions of respectable society are shown to lead to repression and joylessness, a recurring feature of later Weir films. The indecisive ending where Michael is represented as being directionless is perhaps an early example of Weir's refusal to invent closed endings to his films to satisfy ready-made audience expectations. *Picnic at Hanging Rock, The Last Wave, Witness* and, to a certain extent, *Green Card* are others of his movies that break orthodox cinematic rules by avoiding conventional closure of the narrative.

Michael was written *and* directed by Weir, so it can certainly be claimed as his film. The thematic concerns are almost certainly his. His main collaborators were the producer, Gil Brealey of the CFU, and the editor Wayne Le Clos, who helped Weir, according to Weir's own testimony, to paper over a lot of the cracks in the shooting script. What comes over more than anything in the film is the passion of the film-maker, his commitment to his subject. He reveals the passion in the way he realizes his themes in a rather pell-mell style, rough-edged and unsophisticated. Weir has always struck me as a romantic in the sense of his willingness to address large thematic concerns, his concern for the individual, his interest in mystery and the unknown, and his sensitive focusing on love of one kind or another. His films talk of the limitless possibilities of life, whilst rejecting pat solutions and happy endings. Some of these aspects of Weir's future work in cinema are very much present in *Michael*.

Michael won the Grand Prix award from the Australian Film Institute, establishing Weir as a talent to watch in the re-emerging Australian cinema. *Three to Go*, the complete film, was transmitted on Channel 7 in February, 1971, and aroused considerable comment. However, it was to be *Homesdale* that would help Weir decide that film directing was to be his métier. Again, *Homesdale* is a very personal film: it was shot in a mysterious, old rented house that Weir and his wife lived in for a while at Church Point on the Barrenjoey Peninsula north of Sydney, and the idea for the story came from Weir's recollection of a weekend stay he had made with some friends at a guest house called Homesdale in the Blue Mountains. Most artists use what they can from their own lives as material for their work. Weir is interesting in that he clearly notes small incidents or events in his life and stores them away for future reference, expanding the small event on the screen into something larger and more significant. It is almost as though he has a drive to make life more meaningful, more intense; the films he directs are his expression of that need. The figures in his narratives are always striving towards intensity of feeling, attempting to break through society's oppressions or their own inhibitions. An artist has to have the talent to select from his experiences what can be used as raw material for artistic expression. In writing and directing *Homesdale* Weir was embellishing past experience and using what he had at hand: this mysterious colonial-style house that he just happened to have rented and a memory of a stay at a guest house where he and his friends had behaved somewhat outrageously.

Homesdale was funded by the Experimental Film

Fund. His co-writer was Piers Davies. With the help of Richard Brennan from the CFU, Weir received enough money to make the movie. The narrative is set in the Homesdale Hunting Lodge, a kind of retreat where the guests are encouraged by the unctuous manager to indulge in togetherness. However, the guests or inmates are guarded by men in white coats, so the question is raised whether Homesdale is really a guest house, a mental institution or a prison. This kind of ambiguity was a familiar element in theatre of the absurd and in plays such as *The Birthday Party* by Harold Pinter, where the audience is never sure if the characters are who they say they are or whether anything is what it appears to be, so *Homesdale* is a cinematic version of the kind of absurdist drama much in vogue in the sixties in Europe. With its black humour and grotesque characters and events, it also reminds one of Polanski's movies *Repulsion* (1965) and *Cul de Sac* (1966). Again, it would be surprising if a young film-maker such as Weir were not influenced by what was going on in the arts around him.

At Homesdale, guests are encouraged to act out their fantasies in a treasure hunt and in a revue. The black comedy consists of the parodying of therapy and religious services. The treasure hunt involves the guests facing up to nature's dangers, again an early representation of a recurring theme in Weir's films, one that was to surface later in *Picnic at Hanging Rock, The Last Wave* and *The Mosquito Coast. Homesdale* exploits intimations of the irrational and the macabre (there is a reference to the shower scene in *Psycho* (1960)) and one of the characters ends up decapitated. The Homesdale Hunting Lodge is portrayed as an oppressive, authoritarian institution despite its encouragement to the guests to explore their fantasies. It is like all schools, institutions, organizations and communities in Weir's films in its attempt to enforce conformity and submission on its guests. Thus, once again, in this early and raw exercise in absurdist comedy can be seen some of the themes that will be handled in Weir's major films.

Once more, a film directed by Peter Weir won the Grand Prix at the Australian Film Institute awards. When it was shown at the 1971 Sydney Film Festival, it had a very enthusiastic reception from audiences. However, Weir had left Australia for an extended visit to Europe and the Middle East. Clearly, Weir had been marked down as a young man with great potential because he had been awarded a study grant from the Interim Council set up to explore the possibility of setting up a film school. He returned to England and found his way on to feature film sets at Pinewood and Elstree (in those not-so-distant days, feature films were still being turned out in England). He also wrote a lot and from this trip emerged ideas that would be the springboards for three Weir-directed films: *The Cars That Ate Paris, The Last Wave* and *The Plumber*.

The Commonwealth Film Unit had become Film Australia by the time he returned. He made two documentaries, *Incredible Floridas* and *What Ever Happened to Green Valley?*, in 1972 and 1973. But for a young man of 29, with two minor successes behind him, the lure was to direct a fully-fledged commercial feature film and the opportunity was just around the corner with *The Cars That Ate Paris*. From the time of his first efforts in 1969 (the short films produced for the staff social at Channel 7) to the start of production of his first commercially-backed feature film (October, 1973 with *Cars*) only four years had passed. In comparison with the kind of apprenticeship would-be directors would have had to serve in America or Britain, Weir's rise to that eminence was meteoric. That is a reflection of his innate talent, which people in a position to help him were able to recognize. But this rapid promotion also reflects what was happening in Australia at the time in the arts scene and, perhaps, in society as a whole.

The convulsions of the sixties and the early seventies had shaken up cultural assumptions and helped to erase feelings of cultural inferiority. Many young Australians were throwing off the oppressions of the older generation and questioning old allegiances. A sense of national identity was being sought and new immigrants from southern Europe did not look to the mother country for sustenance or cultural inspiration. In the midst of these changes, the Australian film industry was struggling to be reborn. Michael Powell, the British director, had directed two films set in Australia, *They're A Weird Mob* (1966) and *Age of Consent* (1969), but Tim Burstall's *2000 Weeks* (1970) became Australia's first truly indigenous film for years. Canadian director Ted Kotcheff made *Outback* in 1971 and Nicolas Roeg made *Walkabout* in the same year. Brian Kavanagh's

A City's Child and Burstall's *Stork* were produced also in 1971 and two ocker comedies presenting an image of raw Australian maleness and crudity, *The Adventures of Barry Mackenzie* and *Alvin Purple*, were successful in 1972 and 1973 respectively. *Sunstruck* (1972) was the first movie funded by the newly-formed Australian Film Development Corporation to be released in cinemas. Things were on the move. An Australian film industry could now be seriously discussed, although no single new Australian feature had yet made a major breakthrough in terms of box-office returns *and* artistic success in the world market.

It would be a film directed by Peter Weir, *Picnic at Hanging Rock*, which would make that breakthrough for Australian films, but first he had to cut his teeth on a lesser project but still a movie that would gain him the kind of attention a young and ambitious director needed. Up to this juncture in his career, Weir had largely made his own opportunities with some help from Channel 7 and the CFU. Now if he were to make it in the world of real movie-making, he would have to enlist the help of experienced professional wheeler-dealers, producers who knew how the movie world operated and how to put together a package that made sense for the creative personnel involved *and* the money people. Peter Weir had already shown himself to have the determination and stamina to start and finish projects he had largely initiated and created. When the hugely collaborative nature of film-making is considered, it is clear that a director has to have something of the business-man and the politician about him or her. A film director, as has already been pointed out, also has to have a single-mindedness about the task in mind, especially if it is his baby in terms of the original concept and script. While other young people had fantasized about being film directors, Weir had gone out and done it. He had made his own luck, his own opportunities. This devotion to the projects he believed in would be one of his strongest characteristics as his career in the cinema took shape.

The Cars That
Ate Paris

. . . at that point in my life, I don't know for what reason, I was dealing with the overwhelming normality of things, the ordinariness that could sometimes choke you.

(Peter Weir)[1]

Like most Australian directors, Weir has not yet shown himself markedly an actor's director and there is some fairly rudimentary characterization here for which his own script must bear some responsibility.

(Brian McFarlane)[2]

Australian cinema was in the middle of a renaissance that would catapult it to prominence on the map of world cinema and Peter Weir was destined to be the Australian film industry's most famous director. However, despite this boom time, and his two local successes with *Michael* and *Homesdale*, the producers of his first feature, Jim and Hal McElroy, still found it difficult to raise the money for *The Cars That Ate Paris*. Eventually, The Australian Film Development Corporation came up with half the $220,000 budget and Royce Smeal Productions furnished the other half.

Weir got the idea for *Cars* while travelling in Europe. He tells of a time when he was driving in France and was diverted from the main road on to side roads and had to pass through some isolated French villages which began to look rather sinister. Later in England he saw newspaper headlines about suburban shotgun killings and fifteen people dying in a major pile-up on the M1. He got down to writing the screenplay in Tunisia and went through endless draft scripts, co-operating with Keith Gow and Piers Davies along the way, before submitting it to the McElroys.

Synopsis: *Arthur and George Waldo, while driving through the New South Wales outback, are diverted off the main road towards the isolated outback township of Paris. Arthur (Terry Camilleri) is at the wheel and sudden lights in his eyes force him to lose control of the car and caravan and they have a bad crash. George is killed and Arthur is treated for shock in the local hospital. While recovering from this traumatic experience, Arthur is befriended by the town mayor (John Meillon), who invites him to his home for dinner. Too frightened of driving to leave town, Arthur gets to know the local community. He is shown the 'veggies', the victims of other accidents who are now in a vegetable state in the town hospital. The town itself is terrorized by a gang of young people who drive around in souped-up cars that resemble monsters. It dawns on Arthur that the town's economy is entirely based on the scavenging from accidents that have been caused deliberately by the townspeople. The Mayor asks Arthur to stay and become part of his family. He later warns him that no one ever left Paris. At the mayoral fancy dress ball, the veggies are present and the Mayor makes a speech about the town's potential. However, the tensions between the middle-aged townspeople and the young gang members come to the boil. The gang attacks people and buildings in an orgy of hate and Arthur is forced to defend himself, killing one of the gang members. The town is wrecked and several people are killed before Arthur is able to drive away from Paris.*

The Cars That Ate Paris employs a structure very similar to many a Hollywood horror film: a stranger in an isolated part of the country is forced to take refuge in a sinister small community, which gradually reveals its horrifying secrets. Peter Weir has taken that basic recipe and shifted the locale to outback Australia, using that setting to satirize Australian small-town cosiness and to comment on a materialistic society that had participated in the Vietnam war. The movie has something of the *Mad Max* series about it and it also resembles

Peckinpah's *Straw Dogs* (1971). In the latter, Dustin Hoffman plays a rather timid academic who is terrorized by local louts in a Cornish village before he rouses himself and kills them off one by one after his wife has been raped and his home attacked. *Straw Dogs* ends with a shot of Hoffman's smiling face as he realizes that he has stood up to fascism and won through. Similarly Arthur, the main protagonist of *Cars*, is shown smiling in triumph as he escapes from Paris.

Whether it is fascism Weir has in mind in his portrayal of the outwardly normal Australian community of Paris or not, he definitely creates a picture of a nasty, predatory and amoral town that is meant to represent Australia as a whole. The Vietnam war caused great social unrest in Australia with mass demonstrations against the country's involvement in what was perceived as an American disaster. What Weir shows in *Cars* is the seething violence and innate corruption that lie just below the surface of genteel Australian-ness. The kitsch gentility of the home of the Mayor exactly represents the false, hypocritical values of many Australians who could ignore the injustices in their society (eg to the Aborigines) whilst indulging in wholesale materialism. The town of Paris depends on exploitation of the most blatant kind (the proceeds from deliberately-staged accidents), but the worthies of the township attend church and mouth platitudes about the town's future. The young are largely alienated and join destructive gangs who ride around in monster cars and terrorize the respectable citizens. A society that lives by violence spawns violence, the film seems to be saying, and so the eruption of destruction and killing at the end of the movie is a metaphor for how violence will inevitably turn in on itself. The grotesque cars that the young use against their elders are the progeny of a society that has itself lived off car wrecks. The violence that respectable society has condoned and encouraged rebounds on that society and finally destroys it.

It would be a mistake to try to pin down an exact sociological or political meaning to *The Cars That Ate Paris*, but the film has to be seen in the historical perspective of Australia in the early seventies, a time when the country was torn by dissension and the young were rebelling against the moral certainties of their parents. *Cars* continues the themes Weir had dealt with in *Homesdale* and *Michael*. In *Homesdale*, he had portrayed the nastiness lurking behind the ordinariness of the institution, just as the tastelessness, vulgarity, and respectable religiosity of Paris hides the reality of the means by which the town prospers. In *Michael*, he had shown a society seemingly on the edge of violent revolution; in *Cars* the violence is ever-present but clandestine until it finally erupts. Indeed, Weir had wanted to give the movie a fuller texture by representing Australia as a society in turmoil and with anarchy just around the corner. If he had managed to represent the township of Paris within that wider context, the film might have acquired more overall conviction. As it is, Paris is represented as a weird, isolated example which Arthur can drive away from into safety just as the horror movie hero and heroine can escape from the deserted mansion or Dracula's castle.

The final sequence of the movie seems to condone the use of violence to confront violence. Faced with the mindless mayhem of the gangs, Arthur brutally kills one of the members and takes some satisfaction from the fact that he has met fire with fire. Weir does not take the easy option here: he does not set up the elders of the township as grotesque hypocrites and killers so as to glamorize youth by contrast. The elders have created the young they deserve: ruthless, mindless and alienated. His earlier hero, Michael, had also been caught between the respectability of suburban life and the superficiality of the alternative world and had settled for neither. Here again we see Weir refusing to back either the old or the young, the respectable or the rebels. Arthur remains an individual and Weir, the writer-director, endorses neither the status quo nor the rebellion against it. In *Cars* there is no right side. Arthur has to kill to survive; he has to escape from Paris, but his escape is engineered by himself and he has to fight both sides in the conflict. Weir shows a society in chaos, but he does not take sides.

'A plague on both your houses' might sum up the general philosophy embodied in the movie. At the heart of all Peter Weir's movies is the concept of the individual, who has to win freedom for himself or herself through their own efforts and by following their instincts rather than what their rationality tells them to do. Arthur at the end of *Cars* has acted instinctively (by defending himself against murderous attacks) and retained his individuality despite the attempts of the community to turn them into one of them.

The horror behind the normality, the representation of dark forces beneath a surface of order, civilization and barbarity—these motifs will be constants in Weir's movies. *The Cars That Ate Paris* was a very interesting first feature for any director to have made, but a *Citizen Kane* it is not. There is a certain crudeness in the realization and enactment. Characterization is generally of the simplistic and uncomplicated variety and much of the acting, with the exception of Meillon and Camilleri, is equally crude. To be enjoyed, and the movie is primarily entertainment, *Cars* has to be accepted on the pure fantasy level. If issues of reality enter into the discussion, then the fact that Paris has managed to escape retribution for its murderous exploits seems hard to swallow. Why too does Arthur not become one of the many veggie victims of the township's predatoriness? If Weir had followed through on his intention of showing Australia as a whole in a state of imminent chaos, then these details would have seemed more believable.

However, that critical approach is in danger of applying naturalistic criteria to what is basically a fantasy. The movie is best interpreted as a metaphor for Australian society in the seventies. However, that does not mean it has nothing to say to us in the nineties. The historical perspective enables us to see where the movie came from, but it does not define or limit its meaning. It is a film that uses the conventional elements and structures of the horror and fantasy genres in order to mirror Australia back to itself, but, in the process, the film-makers have made a movie that is of interest and import to non-Australians as well. Peter Weir would make finer, more challenging films than *Cars*, but this movie marked him down as a writer and director who was willing to take on big themes and who could, through his *mise-en-scène* (the staging of scenes for the camera), create a vision of the world. Weir's alternative vision in this movie is not a comforting one. The only real comfort offered to the viewer is that Arthur manages to escape the horror of Paris in the time-honoured tradition of the horror genre. Weir, in his later movies, would go on to create alternative visions of reality that offered more hope, although the path to attaining that alternative reality is never portrayed as easy.

35

Picnic at Hanging Rock

Picnic is about an outing at the edge between innocence and experience, where the starched white linens end, the earth begins and romance encounters passion.

(Robert Winer)[1]

The best Australian film I have ever seen and the most unusual in its distillation of youth, summer and tragedy.

(Helen Frizzell, *Sydney Morning Herald*)

Although *The Cars That Ate Paris* did not actually make the producers any money and had mixed responses from audiences, nevertheless it did provide Weir with his first opportunity to direct a commercial feature, albeit on a very restricted budget. *Cars* did not denote the big time, but it was a useful staging post along the path to creating the kind of career that every aspiring director dreams of. Inevitably, this book about the films of Peter Weir has to accept that he is not only a creative artist communicating his vision through the films he directs, but a career professional subject to the same ambitions, career moves, business politics, wheeler-dealing and setbacks as anyone else operating in this megabucks, highly-visible industry of manufacturing films for mass markets.

The business side of film-making was very much an element of the next film Weir was asked to direct, *Picnic at Hanging Rock*. The first business issue was, as it is for any movie project other than for a very few cast-iron certainties, whether enough money would be found to

Anne Lambert

finance it. The source material was a novel of the same name by Joan Lindsay, first published in 1967. Pat Lovell, who was a well-known presenter on Australian television at the time, read the novel and decided that Peter Weir was the man to direct the movie version on the strength of seeing his handling of the uncanny themes of *Homesdale*. Lovell bought an option on the novel in 1973; she also got Weir's agreement to direct if she could find the financial backing for the project. Although Weir did not initiate the project, it was a novel he admired and he was very enthusiastic about the idea of filming it. David Williamson, one of Australia's new wave of playwrights who emerged in the sixties, was approached to write the screenplay but he was committed to other projects, so Cliff Green was commissioned to write a draft screenplay aided by a small initial grant from the Australian Film Development Corporation (AFDC). Hal and Jim McElroy were then bought into the project because it was thought they had the requisite experience of raising money in the film industry. But the AFDC (despite their initial enthusiasm) rejected the project when it was presented to them with detailed costing because it was felt that the film was too expensive. That the project did not fold there and then was almost certainly a tribute to Lovell and Weir's tenacity and their faith in the commercial and artistic viability of the material. Unlike most other international directors (as he has become), Weir nurtures one project at a time and sees that project through to completion. Even though he was not the initiator of *Picnic*, once he was on board he became committed to the enterprise and the worth of the material as a vehicle for exploring his own obsessions. Weir's career is distinguished by just such commitment to the kind of films he wants to make. He is no journeyman director willing to turn his hand to any available script. It is clear that he has to be committed to the concept of a film before he will devote his time and energies to the enterprise.

Lovell invested some of her own money to help pay Green's fee for writing further versions of the screenplay and signalled her dedication by devoting herself full-time to the project, resigning from her television duties. Gradually, the finance needed was assembled: the AFDC agreed to supply one-third on seeing a final draft of the screenplay; BEF, the distributor arm of the Greater Union Organisation, supplied a further one-third and the newly-formed South Australian Film Corporation (SAFC) pitched in with the final third with the agreement that John Graves of the SAFC would act as one of the executive producers. The credits for *Picnic* list Hal and Jim McElroy as producers, Patricia Lovell as executive producer and John Graves as executive producer for the SAFC. Fingers in the pie, indeed. However, a company, Picnic Productions, was formed with Lovell, the McElroys and Weir equal partners in the venture.

Casting problems were the next hurdle to face. Eventually, twenty girls were cast in the film from among the hundreds Lovell and Weir looked at. Weir has said that they were after a kind of pre-Raphaelite look for the young women and for the overall visual impact of the movie. This made sense in terms of the period of the narrative—1900—and because the pre-Raphaelite aesthetic movement wedded spirituality with sensuality in a sometimes uneasy, unsettling and not altogether healthy mixture, which reflects the confusion of adolescent romantic yearnings and adult sexuality that the young women of Appleyard College in the movie are experiencing. What Weir was after, according to Sue Mathews' interview with him in *35mm Dreams*, was a kind of innocent or serene quality. For some reason, most of the girls finally cast were from Adelaide in South Australia; Weir linked this with the way of life they led in that part of Australia. However, as the agreement with the SAFC had stipulated that the production would use a maximum of South Australian locations and facilities and as Graves of the SAFC was on the spot as executive producer looking out for SAFC interests, it may also have been politic to cast as many young women from that state as possible.

Other casting difficulties centred round the roles of Michael Fitzherbert, the young English aristocrat who becomes obsessed with Miranda, one of the girls who disappears on the rock, and Mrs Appleyard, the principal of Appleyard College. Weir was conscious of the danger of portraying both key figures in the narrative as stereotypical characters: one the la-di-da public schoolboy, the other the repressive villain of a headmistress. Eventually, Weir cast Dominic Guard who had been so effective as the boy in Joseph Losey's 1970 film, *The Go-Between*. Weir perceived something intrinsically melancholy in Guard, a characteristic he hoped the camera would pick up. In the event, Weir was right to cast Guard. In both *Go-Between* and *Picnic*, Guard plays an observer, fascinated by sexuality and frightened by it as well. In both films he plays a character who is drawn into a chain of events that ends in the destruction of ordered lives. There is something hapless and passive about Guard (on-screen) that made it right for Weir to cast him as Michael Fitzherbert. As Mrs Appleyard, Weir originally cast Vivien Merchant, but the difficulties she was going through in her own life (difficulties that doubtless contributed to her premature death in 1983) made her unable to fulfil her obligation. At the last moment and after all the scenes at Hanging Rock itself had been shot, Rachel Roberts was cast. By a strange irony, Roberts too would die prematurely by her own hand at the age of 53 in 1980. Roberts specialized in two types of roles: sensual working-class women as in *Saturday Night and Sunday Morning* (1960) and repressed, bitter types as in *This Sporting Life* (1963) and *Murder on the Orient Express* (1974). Clearly, Roberts called on reservoirs of bitterness in herself (perhaps a legacy of a stormy and unhappy marriage to Rex Harrison) to fill out her role as Mrs Appleyard.

Casting is clearly one of the key functions of a director. With *Picnic*, Weir cast with a perfect eye. Although he has not acquired a reputation for being an actors' director in the sense that he is able to provide performers with amazing insights into how their roles should be played, he nevertheless must be given credit for the fact that under his aegis, numerous actors, including Guard and Roberts, but also Mel Gibson, Sigourney Weaver, Linda Hunt, Kelly McGillis, Robin Williams and Gérard Depardieu, have given some of their best performances.

The movie begins with these words on the screen:

> On Saturday the 14th of February, 1900, a party of schoolgirls from Appleyard College picnicked at Hanging Rock near Mt Macedon in the state of Victoria.
> During the afternoon several members of the party disappeared without trace.

This legend leaves the impression that the narrative of the movie is to be based on actual events, that these young women did in fact just disappear in 1900 and that no explanation was ever established to unravel this mystery. In fact, these events never took place except in the pages of Joan Lindsay's novel. When I first saw the film in London, I assumed that the movie *was* based on some such real-life incident in Australia around the turn of the century. This assumption was shared by numerous other people I discussed the film with at the time. However, exhaustive enquiries by Australian reporters found no evidence whatsoever of any such event. Thus, in a sense, the film starts with a kind of con trick on the audience, inviting them to believe that the events which are to be represented on screen are based on actuality.

Rober Winer in his essay on Peter Weir's films in *Images in Our Souls* states that it is uncertain whether the disappearance is a historical reality.[2] In the absence of any concrete evidence it has to be assumed that this incident did not actually take place. That is not in any way to invalidate the movie or its representation of *its own* reality. The film raises the question of reality, juxtaposing a kind of psychic version with the representation of everyday reality. The film masquerading as faction also inevitably dips its toe into the muddy waters of what is fact and what is fiction. Weir's interest in the material surely did not depend on the historical veracity of the story, but much, much more on a vision of an alternative reality that the movie represented on screen. Just as Weir had represented an alternative reality in *The Cars That Ate Paris* (the predatory small town as the alternative reality beneath the surface respectability), so in *Picnic* he was intent on creating another more positive alternative reality, this time a psychic reality in opposition to the oppressive college and bourgeois family life represented in the movie. The alternative reality of *Picnic at Hanging Rock* consists of a world of the unknown, created out of the liberated desires of the young people in the narrative, as they break free, under the influence of the rock, from the stranglehold that adult life and institutions seek to impose upon them.

Synopsis: *The narrative begins on February the 14th, Valentine's Day, 1900. We see the volcanic formation of Hanging Rock emerging from the mist and in voice-over we hear a girl's voice say 'What we see and what we seem are but a dream. A dream within a dream . . .', which in a sense cuts across what has been written on the screen about the historical reality of the events we are about to see represented. The ideas the movie*

seems about to juggle with are to do with dreams and reality and the confusion of the two. Under the opening credits we see the girls of Appleyard College showing one another the Valentine cards they have received. Edith, a plump girl, counts hers as trophies rather than evidence of how much she is loved. There is a certain atmosphere of competitiveness around these Valentine cards. An outing is planned to Hanging Rock, a volcanic formation at Mount Macedon, a sacred place to the Aborigines. However, one of the pupils, the intense and troubled Sara Waybourne, has been forbidden to go on the picnic by the repressive and repressed headmistress, Mrs Appleyard. There is a suggestion that Sara has a crush on the pretty Miranda, who tells her: 'You must learn to love someone other than me, Sara. I won't be here much longer.' Mrs Appleyard warns the girls of the dangers of Hanging Rock (snakes, poisonous ants) and asks them not to behave like tomboys but like ladies of the college. The girls depart for the rock with Miss de Portiers and Miss McCraw, the mathematics teacher, who is dressed severely in dark brown, in charge. The girls are told that the rock is 350 million years old and that it was formed by lava pushing up from below the surface of the earth. When the girls arrive at the rock, they are observed by an aristocratic English family picnicking nearby. Observing the girls are Michael, adolescent nephew of the elderly Englishman and his wife, and Albert, the family coachman, a young Australian. Michael particularly admires Miranda; whilst Albert talks in rather more crude terms about the girls' legs, Michael compares Miranda to a Botticelli angel. Michael is warned by his uncle that there might be snakes on the rock, an echo of Mrs Appleyard's warning to her charges. Back at the college, Mrs Appleyard has set Sara some poetry to learn by heart, but Sara has written her own poem 'Ode to St Valentine', which Appleyard stops her saying. Sara repeats to herself the names,
'Bertie . . . Bertie . . . Miranda.' At the rock Albert's watch stops dead on noon as does the watch of the mathematics teacher. A group of four girls approach the rock. Edith, the plump girl, complains that 'it is nasty here.' The girls remove their stockings and shoes. Miranda mysteriously says that 'Everything begins and ends at exactly the right time and place.' The girls fall asleep. There is the beginnings of a thunderstorm. We

see Miss McCraw looking at a mathematics volume. The girls are awake and Edith complains that she feels awful. The rest ignore her and the three of them climb the rock further, this sequence shot in slow motion. Back at the college Mrs Appleyard appears to hear the screams of the plump girl. We also see Minnie, the college maid, in bed with her boyfriend, Tom, the gardener at the college. Minnie says how sorry she feels for the girls. Alarm grows at the lateness of the return of the party from the rock. It transpires that three girls and Miss McCraw have disappeared. Edith tells of passing Miss McCraw on her way back from the rock: 'It was a cloud. It was red. Just after I passed Miss McCraw. She was funny. She had no skirt on, just drawers.' Mrs Appleyard has confirmation from the school doctor that Edith has not been molested, that she is indeed intact. At a garden party given by his uncle and aunt, Michael tells Albert of his obsession with Miranda and the rock; he says he wakes up every night in a cold sweat and that he wants to go back to the rock. He sees Miranda as a swan in the lake. Returning to the rock, he seems to hear the voices of the girls. Later Albert finds Michael on the rock in a kind of stupour clutching a piece of lace from a dress. He also finds Irma, one of the girls who went with Miranda; she is intact but is wearing no corset. We discover that Albert is Sara's long lost brother (Bertie). Sara is told that she will have to leave the college as her fees have not been paid. Meanwhile, other girls have been withdrawn by their worried parents. The strain begins to tell on Mrs Appleyard who is increasingly unpleasant to her staff and more and more dependent on alcohol. Michael and Irma remember nothing of their experiences on the rock, but the event becomes something of a media circus. Irma is clearly attracted to Michael, but he is too obsessed with his vision of Miranda. Sara says that Miranda knew lots of things (secrets) that other people didn't know and that she had hinted that she would not be coming back. Irma seems far more mature now and on the day that she leaves the college, she is dressed in a red hat and cloak. The other girls become almost hysterical in their attempts to force the truth out of her. Mrs Appleyard is gradually going to pieces and we learn that there may have been some deeper relationship between her and Miss McCraw: 'How could she have allowed herself to be spirited away?' Sara's body is found in the *greenhouse; she has committed suicide. In the following month, Mrs Appleyard's body is found at the foot of Hanging Rock.*

Picnic at Hanging Rock is a mystery with no solution. Perhaps Weir and his collaborators were taking a risk by telling audiences at the beginning of the film what amounts to a summary of the plot. Some of the narrative suspense might thereby have been dissipated. Another risk is taken by not providing any solution to the mystery. The girls disappear, Appleyard College begins to disintegrate, Sara and Mrs Appleyard die, but there is no explanation of what happened on the rock. Irma, the survivor of the disappearance, refuses to divulge what occurred and Michael seems to have no memory of his experience.

Picnic has been compared to Antonioni's *L'Avventura* with its plot of the mysterious disappearance on an island of a woman, whose lover and friend search for her without success. In that movie, too, there is no explanation given and Antonioni discards the plot device of the disappearance in favour of exploring the relationship of the searchers. Weir and his screenwriter do not narrow their focus in a similar way, but show the effect of the strange events on a whole range of characters—Michael, Mrs Appleyard, Sara, the rest of the pupils and the wider community. The lack of narrative closure, a feature of post-modernist fiction, helps to sustain a reading of *Picnic* as being more interested in the atmosphere it creates and the ideas it floats than in meeting audience expectations. Part of the appeal of the movie is that it remains a mystery. Those spectators who feel cheated by the lack of explanation and who are left with the feeling that the film has promised more than it has delivered are perfectly justified in responding in this way, but the film-makers seem to have made a deliberate choice to distract the viewers' attention away from the everyday details of the investigation into the disappearance and on to a more mystical, ethereal level where linear narrative and logic are to a certain extent jettisoned. *Picnic at Hanging Rock* was a film made for a mass market, but it can be seen as a popularized version in the medium of the cinema of the kind of magical realism of contemporary novels, where writers feel free to reject conventional narrativity and causality in their works.

What are these themes or ideas, then, that *Picnic* deals with and are they recognizable as personal obsessions of Peter Weir analysed in the context of the body of films he has directed? In *Picnic* there is a surface reality and there is a psychic reality. The surface reality is the girls' existence at Appleyard College with its rules and routine, its allegiance to the ordered world of society and its assumptions about proper education and moral standards. The psychic reality is represented by the missing girls' attraction to, and absorption by, instinctual forces symbolised by Hanging Rock. The college imposes rationality and order; the rock appeals to the girls because it smashes those norms of oppression and puritanism. The college allows the harmless exchange of Valentine cards as a form of sublimation of sexuality into acceptable romantic substitutes; the influence of the rock unleashes the repressed sexuality of the young women and Michael. The rock itself had been formed by hot lava forcing its way up from the earth's crust; the submerged natural and innate desires of the young people find their expression on the rock and they are consumed by it, except for Edith, the young girl who counts her Valentine cards and thinks that the rock is 'nasty'. The rest of the school party, mindful of Mrs Appleyard's warning, do not actually venture on to the rock, but Miss McCraw, a seemingly repressed and rational mathematics teacher, does. McCraw is reported by Edith to have taken off her skirt and the missing girls also disrobe to a certain extent by taking off their stockings on the rock. Irma, the returnee, is shown to have matured into a woman, presumably as a result of her experience on the rock, and when she leaves the college, she is wearing red in stark contrast to the pure whiteness of her dress when she visited the rock. Thus, the film represents the rock as a primeval, mysterious influence that provides a gateway to adulthood and sexuality for the girls.

However, such is the power of these primitive instincts that chaotic forces are released which the norms of society are relatively defenceless against. The oppression of Mrs Appleyard, turned inwards against herself and outwards against her students, leads to the virtual destruction of her proud college and her own mysterious death. Time itself stops, the very measure of our everyday existence. The police are 'baffled', as are the media in the face of the inexplicable. Normal order

45

is shown to be fragile and however benevolent and liberating the influence of the rock may be, the resultant chaos in the lives of the humans touched by the tragedy is substantial. The implication could be that sexuality is a dangerous and disruptive thing when released, but a more positive reading would foreground the liberation that Miranda, Irma and Michael feel as a result of their experiences. It is not that natural instinct and our connection with nature and the mystical have to continue to be repressed, the film seems to be stating, but that our society in its institutions, such as the family and schools, is repressive and unhealthy, leading to widespread neurosis and unhappiness.

Appleyard College and Michael's lifeless English family are further examples of Weir's disenchantment with the established institutions of society and their agents. Similar examples in Weir's earlier films have been Michael's family in *Michael*, Homesdale Hunting Lodge in *Homesdale* and the small-town environment of *The Cars That Ate Paris*. *Picnic* represents in its narrative the oppositional forces of rationality and instinct, outer and inner reality, conformity and liberation, order and disorder, the visible world and the unseen and unknowable. These elements would become increasingly characteristic of Weir's obsessions as he continued his directing career.

Another feature of Weir's films is that usually at the heart of the narrative there is one charismatic figure who affects the other characters and who symbolizes or embodies the thematic concerns or value systems of the particular film. Miranda is just such a figure in *Picnic*, although she is less central to the narrative than other catalyst figures in future Weir-directed films, such as Chris Lee (Gulpilil) in *The Last Wave*, Max (Ivar Kants) in *The Plumber*, Billy Kwan (Linda Hunt) in *The Year of Living Dangerously*, Allie Fox (Harrison Ford) in *The Mosquito Coast*, John Keating (Robin Williams) in *Dead Poets Society* and Georges (Gérard Depardieu) in *Green Card*. Not all of these charismatic characters have beneficial interactions with the other main protagonists, but they figure as catalytic forces in the narrative and are all outsiders refusing to conform to society's rules and norms. Miranda is the most important figure among the young women at the college. Most of the major characters react to her strongly and their lives are influenced by her example: Michael, who falls in love with her image and becomes obsessed by her disappearance, Sara, who seems to be in love with her, Miss de Portiers, who seems to be drawn to the mystery of the rock and Irma. Mrs Appleyard is the antithesis of Miranda, shutting down on her sensual nature, severe in her appearance and manner and having a controlling effect on those around her, whereas the example of Miranda liberates others. Towards the end of the film, we see Appleyard obsessively searching Miranda's room. Weir's camera privileges Miranda, giving her centrality while she is still an actual presence in the narrative. Even when she disappears, she is still a presence through her overwhelming impact on others, especially Michael. She is given obscure lines to say such as 'Everything begins and ends at exactly the right time and place', which reinforce her special significance in the narrative. What exactly the significance of this particular utterance is, is difficult to say, but it may refer to Miranda's realisation that the child-woman life she has lead at the college has now to come to an end and she must enter a new dimension of life, it being the right time (Valentine's Day, 1900) and the right place (the mysterious Hanging Rock) to do so.

It is interesting to note that in three of Weir's American movies (*Mosquito Coast, Dead Poets Society* and *Green Card*) the catalyst figure is the chief male protagonist. The tradition of Hollywood films is to create these central 'star' parts for the male lead, the individual with whom the audience is invited to identify and sympathize. However, the figures of Allie Fox, John Keating and Georges could be seen as the natural extension of this characteristic and charismatic figure that appears in most of Weir's movies.

This emphasis on the individual is also a characteristic of Weir's films. It is an emphasis very often on the individual placed in a particular closed community. Weir is in the romantic tradition, in the sense that romanticism emphasizes the importance of the individual as opposed to the group and society. However, Weir is also a romantic director in the more popular and narrower meaning of the word. Not all of Weir's films deal directly with love (romantic or sexual), but several of the most important do: *Picnic, The Year of Living Dangerously, Witness* and *Green Card*. Two of his movies deal with variations of male bonding (*Gallipoli* and *Dead Poets Society*). Running through much of his work is the assumption that a close man—woman relationship is central to life. In *Mosquito Coast* Allie Fox (Harrison Ford) addresses his wife (Helen Mirren) as Mother, hardly the basis for a romantic attachment, but she is the linchpin of his life. *Picnic* is romantic in the importance given to the yearnings of the girls and Michael. Romantic love is shown to be inseparable from sensual love—Miranda and Irma are not content with the sentimental effusions of Valentine cards. They want to be fully-fledged women, just as Michael in his stumbling, repressed public schoolboy way wants to enter into the world of sensuality. In *Picnic*, romanticism merges with sensuality, the adolescent dream becomes some kind of reality on the rock, the purely spiritual is left behind and something more earthy and basic enters the lives of the girls, as the figure of Irma encapsulates.

Naturally this leads to an examination of the charge of voyeurism that has been laid at the door of Weir and his collaborators, particularly in relation to how the young women are observed by the camera. Mathews in her interview with Weir put that point: ' . . . the film's point of view was that of an outside observer—almost a voyeur looking at schoolgirls, rather than coming in any way out of a schoolgirl's sense of herself.' Weir's response somewhat deflected the charge of voyeurism: he replied that the way the young women were photographed was meant to be a simple and emotive series of images. He also makes the valid point that the film is viewed very differently now from when it was first shown (1975).[4] It is undoubtedly true that our consciousness about the cinema's tendency to objectify women and treat them as decorative parts of the general *mise-en-scène* has been raised substantially in the last twenty years. However, bearing the historical perspective in mind, it has to be admitted that the young women are viewed voyeuristically, especially in the opening section of the movie.

In a very real sense, all cinema is voyeuristic. The viewer is there in the darkness spying on these giant figures on a white screen. The camera becomes our eyes and although we need not remain merely passive spectators, there is something of the dream about the cinema experience where events (as in a dream) seem to be out of our control. Cinema spectators can interact emotionally with the action and the characters, can even distance themselves from the narrative through a conscious act of will or through boredom, but the film is a finished artefact produced by technological means in a way that, say, a theatre performance is not. Much post-structuralist film criticism seems to recommend informed film spectators to sit in the cinema darkness defending themselves from the emotional and identification ploys of the film they are viewing. But a viewing strategy like that shuts off a whole person response by which viewers can respond without inhibitions or self-censoring to the experience being offered. It is possible to have a strong emotional response to a film *and* retain an ideological detachment from the values that seem to be embodied in the text. You give yourself (the whole person) to the total experience of viewing the movie and, at the same time, are aware of the values that are being propagated by the movie, some of which you might highly disapprove of. Indeed, it is possible to be totally involved emotionally with a movie and yet realize how your emotions are being manipulated by the film-makers.

To take an example from a fairly recent film: *Fatal Attraction* (1987) is a powerfully manipulative melodrama which pulls the spectator into identification with the husband and wife figures (Michael Douglas and Anne Archer) of the narrative, who are defending themselves against the demonic revenge of the spurned lover (Glenn Close). The film almost forces you to side with the need to destroy this wholly irrational threat to the family. However, some part of the viewer may well realize that the movie, in its representation of the Close character, is being grossly unfair to that character and what she represents. In an overall assessment of the movie, your enjoyment of it as a powerful melodrama may well be tempered by the consciousness of how your emotions have been manipulated by the film-makers. However, if individuals sit in the cinema taking only a politically correct stance, denying themselves an emotional response to what is happening on the screen, then surely that is a wholly different concept of viewing films and one which is sadly deficient.

This argument has relevance to the style and content of *Picnic*. Viewing the film now, yes, it is possible to identify a definite tendency to objectify the girls, for the camera, as Mathews points out, to observe them in a voyeuristic manner, but that need not interfere with our appreciation of the film, unless, of course, a rigorously pure line is taken. In fact, the pre-Raphaelite look of the young women underlines one of the deficiencies in the movie: given that it appears to deal with burgeoning sexuality and the breaking free from the puritan restraints of society's agencies (family, school, parent figures), the film almost totally lacks any correlative to represent actual sexuality, apart from the brief scene of the servants in bed with one another and Albert's rather crude admiration of the girls. Actual sexual contact is restricted to the lower classes with their presumably less repressed instincts. We have to take the sexual maturing of Miranda, Irma and Michael on trust, as it were, because there are no sexual scenes involving them. Thus, the ethereal air of Miranda (and the camera lingers on her more than any of the other girls) is not disturbed by overt sexuality, although it is strongly implied that something of a sexual nature has happened to her.

The scene where the girls take their stockings off on the rock is as close to eroticism as the film gets. However, it can be argued that any attempt to represent actual sex would have dissipated the mystery and would have been too direct and conventional an approach. Yet the film seems to posit sexuality as the force that disturbs the equilibrium and causes the wholesale destruction of lives. It is almost as though the stylistic prettiness the film attains to, the monochromatic, muted pastel look that makes it appear the figures are being photographed through gauze, imposes its own limitations. Introduce raw sexuality into that approach and the mood would have been broken. Another film that *Picnic* has been likened to is the Swedish *Elvira Madigan* (1967), directed by Bo Widerberg. It is also, in part, a study of burgeoning adolescent sexuality and it too represents it in a voyeuristic and tasteful style, underscored by Mozart.

Looking at the body of Weir's films, there is very little direct representation of sex in any of them. The only directly erotic scene in any of his films is the scene in *Witness* where John Book (Harrison Ford) sees Rachel (Kelly McGillis) washing herself in a state of semi-nudity. Once again, it is a scene where there is a strong voyeuristic element (the naked woman is looked at by the male protagonist and by us, the audience). In other Weir movies, people go to bed with one another but there is no insistent emphasis on eroticism. The director seems far more interested in the romantic attachment between men and women.

Picnic seems to aspire to the status of an art house movie and the comparisons with *Elvira Madigan* and even *L'Avventura* (1959) are not unfair. Another film it has been compared with is Nicolas Roeg's *Don't Look Now* (1973) which tells a mystery story about guilt and death. Like Roeg, Weir and his collaborators obviously wanted to make a resonant film with taste and restraint yet one that would appeal to a broad spectrum of the cinema-going public. However, the tastefulness of the photography and the prettiness of the design of the film do give it a self-conscious air. It is perhaps too controlled, too languorous. More energy, more pace in the narrative and fewer lingering shots of the girls and the rock would have helped to give the movie more variety and impact without necessarily destroying the atmosphere of mystery it works so hard to establish. The narrative also introduces plot strands and social issues that are superfluous or left dangling unsatisfactorily. For example, the sub-plot of the brother and sister lost to one another, Sara and Albert, seems a mere adjunct to the main story, and the class dimension is touched upon lightly and left. Mrs Appleyard is clearly from lower-class origins than her students; Michael and Albert, the family coachman, have stilted conversations until they exchange some kind of sexual confidences; the servants at the college have a hidden sexual life under the noses of their employer. Disappointingly, these class issues are not consistently dealt with in the movie.

An important sub-text, however, is the clash of cultures symbolized by the British-style Appleyard College and Hanging Rock, supposedly sacred to the Aborigines, which has been there for millions of years. This sub-text struggles to emerge among the other concerns of the screenplay by Cliff Green, but it is present. The movie obliquely raises the issue of colonial heritage and, indeed, the question of what it is to be an Australian. Appleyard College, with its emphasis on British culture (Mrs Appleyard forces Sara to learn a poem by Mrs Felicia Hemans, 'one of the finest of our English poets'), clearly is an agency of the Empire and the educational objective seems to be to produce marriageable young ladies who would pass muster at a garden party in Tunbridge Wells. Culture means English culture; the mores of the school seem to be based on English girls' public schools—gentility, appearances, social graces and discipline. The culture of the school, and by implication, British culture, is portrayed as deadening to individuality; the aim is to produce young women who will jump through society's hoops and never rebel against their pre-ordained roles in the class system and as wives and mothers in a male-dominated world.

To reinforce this view of Australia's colonial heritage, Michael's aunt and uncle, the Fitzherberts, are represented as bloodless, half-alive aristocrats, almost as stereotypes of their class and nation. The rebellion of the girls, their disappearance, could be read as their wish to escape the shackles of British imperialism and oppression. After all, they disappear on Hanging Rock with its associations with native Australians, the Aborigines, a place which the very British Mrs Appleyard warns them is dangerous. It is dangerous because it is not subject to British rule, it cannot be tamed or colonized. It has an ancient knowledge that British rationality and organisation cannot imprison. Michael's obsession with Miranda and the rock could also be seen as his unconscious desire to escape the influence of his moribund relations and his British-ness. He is shot sitting well apart from his aunt and uncle at the rock. Although their relationship is not one of equals, he would much rather talk to the very Australian Albert. Sara's longing for her lost brother, who turns out to be Albert, could also be read as her yearning for her real self, an Australian young woman free from the imposition of foreign and subjugating influences. This thematic concern of Australian-ness is one that Weir, with different screenwriters, was to return to in varying degrees in the next three major films he directed: *The Last Wave*, *Gallipoli* and *The Year of Living Dangerously*.

Another important aspect of Weir's *mise-en-scène* is his use of music. Most of his films from now on would have emphatic underscoring, at times even overwhelming. Indeed, *Picnic* suffers from too much tasteful music on the soundtrack. Bruce Smeaton, the composer and arranger, decided with Weir on the use of *Pan's Pipe* by Gheorghe Zamphir and the second movement of Beethoven's Fifth Piano Concerto. The flute music helps to create an appropriately ethereal tone associated with nature, whilst the slow movement enhances the dreaminess and languid atmosphere. However, the underscoring does become intrusive at times and the use of the Beethoven, especially, reinforces the argument that the film reaches for artistic status rather too self-consciously. Having stated those reservations, however, it needs to be stressed that the flute accompaniment generally adds to the impact the film has on audiences and it is an element of the *mise-en-scène* that many people remember from the movie.

It is important to remember the source material from which *Picnic* emerged, the novel by Joan Lindsay. She was in her sixties by the time she wrote it. The movie version undoubtedly emphasizes the sexuality theme much more than the novel, but it cannot be said Lindsay's fiction is merely the catalyst for the film. Much contemporary film criticism is too dismissive of the importance of source material in discussing movies, as though once a screenwriter and director have taken over the material, the relevance of the original source is negligible. Film professionals themselves, however, rarely make that error and Weir in interviews about *Picnic* acknowledges the worth of Lindsay's novel and how much he admired it. Nevertheless, Weir's film is much more than a straight version of the novel.

Another key individual in the creation of the movie was Cliff Green, the screenwriter. Weir worked with Green on the adaptation of the novel to the screen, but did not have a co-writer screen credit. It is almost impossible to divide credit for a screenplay in the circumstance where a talented director co-operates closely with a creative screenwriter. Hitchcock worked closely with almost all his writers, perfecting the screenplay into a form that would enable him to explore his obsessions within the format of the thriller genre. Something similar almost certainly happened on *Picnic* with Weir and Green. It would be unjust not to acknowledge Green's contribution to the overall artistic success of the the movie.

The director of photography was Russell Boyd, who would work with Weir several times in the future. Martin Sharp, an Australian artist, was also employed as artistic assistant to the director and seemingly played an important role in throwing ideas around in relation to the look of the film. Vincente Minnelli, the MGM director, always used to have voluminous files of prints and photographs on set with him, which he would show to his cameramen to suggest the visual effect he wanted them to capture. Minnelli-like, Weir admits to collecting all kinds of visual stimuli before the shoot to help him identify the overall style he is aiming for. However, Boyd's contribution to *Picnic* should not be underestimated; he is clearly a creative lighting cameraman, a key worker in the Weir ensemble and a colleague with whom Weir worked in close tandem.

However, at the core of the film-making process that manufactured *Picnic* was Peter Weir, who was much more than just an organizing figure. If another Australian director had eventually directed the film of Joan Lindsay's novel, say, Gillian Armstrong or Fred Schepisi, the movie would undoubtedly have turned out quite differently. That seems a truism, but in fact there are many film directors whose work is largely anonymous or so derivative that their hand in the making of the film cannot really be distinguished. Weir is a presence in the film because of the thematic concerns it chooses to deal with and the style of the *mise-en-scène*. Weir cannot be said to be the author of the film, because there are too many competing factors to attribute authorship to any one person. *Picnic* is also a film of its time, the particular historical juncture when it was produced. One of the reasons it did so well with audiences and critics is that it symbolized an aspect of the Australian cultural renaissance of the seventies. In its tastefulness and aspiration to seriousness, it somehow encompassed something about that drive to break free from a cultural inferiority that had been imposed on the country by years of subservience to the mother country. With *Picnic* Australian cinema found its own voice to a certain extent; this can be stated despite the fact that, as I would claim, it shows strong influences from European art films of the time, some of which have already been mentioned. Its theme of liberation and opposition to conformity and rationality marks it down as a late example of sixties philosophy. The Michael of the *Three to Go* has become the Michael of *Picnic*, psychically and obsessively connected with the forces of rebellion. However, the rebellion in *Picnic* has no real significantly political overtones, except in the sense of personal politics. This would be an increasing feature of Weir's films as the sixties became more distant – the protagonists of his films are politically neutral and stand for individual liberation rather than the liberation of a class or other sections of society.

Picnic became one of the most profitable Australian films of the seventies. It attracted a large audience in Australia itself and did equally well in Britain. Its American release was delayed until 1979 after the success of *The Last Wave* in that country. The critics in Australia, Britain and America all received it enthusiastically and the consensus opinion was that this movie had forced people to take Australian films seriously. Despite its flaws – its self-conscious artistry, its at times meandering narrative techniques, its frequent lack of focus – *Picnic* is a considerable achievement. It is not just a good Australian film; by any standards it is a worthwhile film. It is also the kind of film that will, I am sure, stand the test of time and win new admirers as time passes, because it deals with important themes and it is also very much a film of its time, albeit the setting of the narrative is the turn-of-the-century. It will also have an enduring aesthetic appeal; people will almost certainly always admire it for how it looks. All these aspects are important for our appreciation of the movie, but its outstanding characteristic for me is its realization of the theme of individual liberation, its implicit warning of the dangers of conformity and repression and its overall humanism.

There are few out-and-out villains in Weir's films. He is not a director looking for handy figures in the narrative to blame for the state of the world. There are forces and vested interests that individuals such as Mrs Appleyard or the headmaster in *Dead Poets Society* are misguided enough to back and defend, but audiences are seldom invited to hate any of these repressive or destructive characters. There is a gentleness at the heart of Weir's films, a relatively rare quality in the world of the cinema. He is a director who allows his feminine side to emerge and, although he has his strong likes and dislikes, he rarely allows his distaste for the repressive forces in society to force him into the cul-de-sac of hatred.

Thus, after the film's enthusiastic reception on three continents and its huge box-office success, Weir was in a position to launch himself as an international director. He had proved that he could weld difficult and diverse themes into a cinematic form that appealed to more discerning cinema-goers and mass audiences alike. And he was commercial. His film had made big bucks by Australian standards and those of the movie business, that is the bottom line. His directing career had taken shape in a remarkably short time. Opportunities had come his way because of his innate talent and because the Australian film industry was undergoing a rebirth. Things could scarcely have turned out better for the young man who seven years previously had been wholly uncertain about what direction his life should take.

The Last Wave

Strange, foreboding and brilliantly different from any film ever made in Australia, The Last Wave *is time past, future and present, a mingling of Aboriginal Dreamtime, Revelations, Doomsday predictions and the Deluge.*

(Helen Frizzell)[1]

Nandjiwara put in all the lines about the law and the law being more important than the man, and that is really the heart of the film.

(Peter Weir)[2]

When a director has a major success on his hands with his second commercial film, as Weir had with *Picnic*, then the problem becomes what to do next to capitalize on the prominence that this success has brought. Peter Weir is a director who chooses his projects carefully and who has to care about the material he is working on, but he is also a professional film-maker who has to consider the commercial viability of material he either originates himself or which is suggested to him; he may also have to evaluate his next project within an overall vision of what he might want his career to be. After *Picnic*, Weir had a considerable reputation in Australia and Britain. His name would only become known in America after the release of his next film *The Last Wave*, which led to the showing of *Picnic* in the States. International success as a film director or for a film depends largely on success in the huge American market. That eluded Weir with *Picnic*, but *The Last Wave* would, to a certain extent, make up for that and launch Weir into a truly international directing career.

Richard Chamberlain, Gulpilil

Weir turned down numerous offers of projects after the success of *Picnic* and spent much of his time reading novels and other material to find the source for his next film. Eventually, the idea for *The Last Wave* came from his own experience and imagination. One of the measures of directors must surely be how much they are involved in the creation of the screenplays and how much they depend on their own creative faculties to generate ideas for their movies. On that count, Weir rates highly, certainly as far as his Australian movies are concerned. However, directors who play little or no part in the origination of the material, who do not choose the source material or do not participate significantly in the writing of the screenplay, can still make a major contribution to the overall film by their stylistic presence or the conscious use of cinematic techniques to slant the material to suit their interpretation of the semantic content. An example of a director who might be said to have done that is Douglas Sirk; the melodramas he directed for Universal in the fifties (*Magnificent Obsession* (1954), *There's Always Tomorrow* (1956), *All that Heaven Allows* (1955), *Written on the Wind* (1956) and *Imitation of Life* (1959)) are basically Hollywood schlock, but Sirk managed to use the clichés embedded in the script in an ironic and distancing style so that the films can be read in different ways. When we come to discuss Weir's American movies where he did not originate the material or was not closely involved in the writing, then we have to discuss whether Weir transformed the basic material of the screenplay into a Weir film.

The Last Wave had its origins in a small event with psychic overtones that Weir experienced when he was travelling in Tunisia in 1971. Weir visited a preserved Roman city where he 'was suddenly seized with this strange feeling that he was going to find something'.[3] Weir claims that he even foresaw what he was going to find: a carving of a child's head. He allowed the experience to digest for a number of years, mentioning the incident to Gulpilil, the Aborigine actor, who expressed no particular surprise at the psychic nature of the experience and told Weir stories from Aboriginal lore that fascinated him so much that he wove them into a story that used the Tunisian experience as the starting-point. Weir then co-operated with Tony Morphett, an Australian writer, who made a considerable contribution to a draft screenplay, which was later polished and perfected by Petru Popescu, a Romanian expatriate whom Weir met in Los Angeles.

An important part of the financing for *The Last Wave* came from the American company, United Artists (absorbed by MGM in 1981). They put up $350,000 towards the cost of the production in return for distribution rights over all English-speaking territories. In terms of Weir's career, this has to be seen as a fairly significant factor. An American film company, for the first time, was investing real money into a film that he was directing. International financing (the production was finally financed by Australian, American and West German investment) perhaps inevitably led to international casting. Richard Chamberlain was cast in the leading role of David Burton. Although Chamberlain had starred in some notable films, including *Petulia* (1968, directed by Richard Lester) and *The Music Lovers* (1970, directed by Ken Russell), he was still better known for his television roles and was not a major star in the cinema. Still, he was an international name and his participation in the film ensured that it would gain more attention than if an actor with no international reputation at all had starred.

Synopsis: *Under the credits we see an Aborigine dressed in conventional contemporary clothes painting on the roof of a cave. The symbol he is painting consists of three concentric circles with four dots in the middle. The scene then changes to a small town in the Australian desert. Suddenly torrential rain and hail pour from a cloudless sky. The film then moves to Sydney where the city is enduring a remorseless downpour, which causes chaos. David Burton, a corporation lawyer, finds sanctuary in his home in the suburbs with his wife and children, but is disturbed by the sound of running water inside the house, which turns out to be no more than an overflowing bath. However, David is disturbed by a dream in which he sees an Aborigine holding a stone towards him. We then see David attending a barbecue at the home of his clergyman step-father. David mentions his bad dreams and his step-father recalls that he (David) used to have terrible nightmares as a child and had been convinced that 'When you go to sleep, people come and steal your body.' We then see a young Aborigine, Billy, in* underground caves near the city sewers, the location of tribal grounds, from which he is stealing sacred stones. He is pursued by four Aborigines. An old Aborigine points a bone at him and Billy is killed. David is asked to defend the Aborigines and recognizes one of them, Chris, as the figure in his dream. He learns from them that they are tribal Aborigines, whereas he had been assured that there were no tribals in Sydney. The Aborigines tell David that Billy had been killed for stealing tribal artefacts: 'He knew things. He had things. He could be rich.' Chris comes to dinner with Charlie, the man we have seen painting the cave at the beginning of the film. Charlie has magical powers, it seems, and can transform himself into an owl. The Aborigines tell David that he may be descended from an ancient South American tribe who, according to tribal lore, had visited Australia in prehistoric times. He may be a spirit from the Dreamtime, which is more real than everyday reality. Whatever happens in Dreamtime establishes the values, symbols and laws in Aborigine society. It is explained to David by an expert on Aborigines that a race of spirits from the rising sun, the Mulkrul, have the ability to contact the Dreamtime. David also learns from his step-father that as a child he had predicted the death of his mother. The weather turns even worse and the rain falls as a kind of oily sludge. David's garden is covered with a plague of frogs, as an owl watches from the tree. David sends his family away to the country. At the trial Chris and the others plead guilty. Chris leads David to secret caves under the city (part of Sydney's sewerage system). He sees wall paintings that depict a coming apocalypse, a tidal wave, which will lead to an era of spiritual regeneration. Charlie arrives in the caves and attacks David for discovering tribal secrets. David appears to kill Charlie and finds his way back to the surface via the sewers. On Bondi Beach, he either sees an actual tidal wave or imagines, through his power to predict events, the coming apocalypse.

Thus, once more, Weir had chosen difficult material to juggle with. *The Last Wave* contains now familiar elements of his thematic concerns: dreams and reality, clash of cultures, the uncanny and the psychic, the intimations of chaos beneath the surface of a seemingly ordered society, the individual with special charisma or powers and the opposition of rationality and the intuitive. *The Last Wave* is not an easy film and once again, as in *Picnic*, it may raise more ideas and issues than it can properly deal with in a two-hour movie. However, yet again it shows Weir as a director willing to, and capable of, dealing with large themes within the genre of the fantasy or horror film. It reinforces the analysis of Weir's films as having recurring themes and obsessions, which can safely be identified as stemming from the director, because he is the one constant factor in the creation of *Cars, Picnic, Last Wave* and his earlier films. It needs to be stressed, though, that in making these films, Weir was working within a certain genre of movie, a type of movie that audiences would have certain expectations of: the horror or fantasy film with its departures from logic, its treatment of the horror of the unknown and the inexplicable, and its playing on the nightmarish fears lurking in our unconscious. However, Weir has taken some of the conventions of the horror film and used them, like all truly imaginative directors, to explore his own personal obsessions. *The Last Wave* has (once more) been likened to Nicolas Roeg's *Don't Look Now* in which the central protagonist foresees his own death and is brought into contact with psychic powers. But the movie also in some ways reminds me of Val Lewton's series of horror movies for RKO in the forties: *Cat People* (1942), *I Walked with a Zombie* (1943) and *The Leopard Man* (1943).

The Last Wave is another Weir-directed film without a definite closure. In talking about this movie, he has said he was not interested in neat endings: 'There are no answers; there is no ending. We did at one stage consider making another, quite separate, film to come at the end, which would take you into the water – but there was no money to do it.'[4] For Weir, the film was a voyage: 'It was a curious experience of using film as a means of discovery.'[5] He admits to altering the script on set according to the promptings of the tribal Aborigines (notably Nandjiwara, who plays Charlie) involved in the making of the film and that he himself never wholly understood what exactly he was dealing with in the film. The unsettled feelings that an audience may well experience after seeing *Wave* is a reflection of the director's own confusion. The lack of narrative closure, the fragmented narrative style itself, the playing on subconscious fears and an atmosphere of the uncanny all help to create this unsettling quality.

It is possible to interpret *The Last Wave* as a film made by people imbued with something that could be categorized as a sixties philosophy. Once more, rationality is represented as inadequate to deal with the forces of nature, both physical and psychic. For example, when David is in his car in Sydney and the city is being enveloped by the unnatural torrential rain, the car radio tries to explain the phenomenon away by saying it is an unusually widespread low-pressure trough. Earlier, the schoolteacher tries to demystify the savage hailstorm by telling the children that it is only nature at work, but the children are highly excited by the event and initially react joyfully to this break in normality. David Burton (Chamberlain) complains to his clergyman step-father: 'You stood in that church and explained away mysteries.' The anthropologist, Dr Whitburn, explains the significance of the Aboriginal Dreamtime to David, but does so in a scientific, detached manner; she is an observer, not a participant or a believer. In placing in opposition to one another the mystical and the explained world, the child's intuition and the adult's rationality, the inexplicable and the comfortable assurances of religion, the film takes on some of the prevalent beliefs of the alternative society of the sixties. Many of these ways of thinking and feeling about existence have evolved into New Age philosophies. The positivism of New Age philosophies is absent from *The Last Wave*, but in its searching for profound truths that go beyond science and reason and its premise that modern, rational man has lost touch with his dreams and his intuitive side, *The Last Wave* seems like a very contemporary movie.

It is ironic that a movie which takes an overtly liberal attitude to the place of Aborigines within Australian history should have been picketed by militant Aborigines during its making. But it is entirely understandable. The movie does not deal with the problems of contemporary Aborigines in Australia directly, although it does show the inadequacy of liberal, and less than liberal, attitudes to Aborigines. David's legal colleague who brings him in to defend the Aborigines operates under the delusion that there are no tribal Aborigines in the city, because 'We've killed their songs, dances and laws.' This admission of white Australian oppression is undercut somewhat by his blindness to the reality that there are indeed tribal Aborigines in Sydney, as David quickly discovers, and that their laws are very much in existence, witness the killing of Billy Corman for the stealing of tribal artefacts. The court case shows white man's law being administered, with the tribal Aborigines being judged according to rules that have nothing to do with the tribal beliefs which they recognize as their true law.

The film evades the issue as to whether the murder of Billy Corman by pointing the death bone at him is any less reprehensible than any other kind of capital punishment. It is content to underline the culture clash intrinsic to the imposition of white Australian law on people who obey quite different laws. However, some of the opposition to the making of the film on the part of Aboriginal activists stemmed from the feeling that here were white Australian film-makers colonizing Aboriginal culture, or an aspect of it, to make an entertainment for the world film market and, in the process, representing Aborigines as looking to the past and obeying ancient tribal laws rather than taking up political cudgels to deal with the problems facing the Aboriginal people in contemporary Australia. In some ways, a case could be made for *The Last Wave* being a regressive film in the values it seems to espouse and the representation it offers of contemporary Aborigines. It seems to support the thesis that white Australian society has done its best to destroy Aboriginal culture and driven it underground (literally in the movie, because the sacred places are below the surface in underground caves), but fails to represent any contemporary Aborigines who want to do anything about the injustice suffered by their people other than in terms of retreating to the mysticism of the Dreamtime. The movie wears its liberal colours on its sleeve, but seems to end up in quite a conservative stance *vis-à-vis* the question of Aboriginal rights. Weir has said that 'the heart of the film' is the idea that 'the law is more important than the man,' the law referred to being tribal Aboriginal law. That seems a strange position for Weir to take up given his general view of conformity and established order. However, it is Aboriginal law that is in question, so the same questioning of the 'law of the fathers' does not seem to be required. This may well be an example of the liberal confusion that the film is guilty of, a kind of sentimentalization of Aboriginal tribal culture and beliefs involving an evasion of the implications of harsh judgements and punishments and the imposition of a conformity that may be just as restricting as that imposed by white society.

However, is this a case of criticizing the movie for not being a different type of movie, of a kind of contentism criticism that withholds total approval because *Last Wave* fails to come up to ideological scratch? Certainly, Weir's interest is in the uncanny and the mystical rather than the political and contemporary reality. Once more, a kind of alternative reality is set up into which the Aborigines escape, a reality that is hidden to the white Australians who have become cut off from their dreams. Dreams are real and prophetic to the Aborigines. David Burton, however, as a descendant of the Aborigines who travelled across the sea from South America to visit Australia, gradually recognizes who he is and his association with the Dreamtime. His dreams become alive again, but they are not comforting dreams. They are nightmarish visions which foretell the destruction of society as we know it through a gigantic tidal wave. However, for the Aborigines, this apocalyptic event will be part of the cycle of evolution and the disaster will lead to a kind of regeneration. The implication is that the best Aborigines can hope for is the destruction of white society. The film points backwards into time and tribal culture and represents Aborigines clinging to what could be interpreted as superstitions, when perhaps an argument could be made that what present-day Aborigines need to do is to confront white Australia with the reality of its racism. Just as in *Picnic*, political issues are touched upon and then passed over in favour of the mystery elements in the narrative. The depoliticization of Weir, as worked out in his movies, is taken one step further in *Last Wave*. And yet again we have the emphasis on the individual and the individual's power to change events. David Burton as played by Richard Chamberlain may not be a charismatic figure, but he is represented as having special intuitive and psychic powers. He fights a lone battle against the prejudices and ignorance of white society and eventually has to fight the tribal Aborigines as well in the person of Charlie. He is caught in the middle between white Australian society from which he becomes increasingly estranged and the alternative reality associated with the tribal Aborigines and their culture and Dreamtime.

There is no sense of collective action in *Last Wave*, other than the silent resistance of the tribal Aborigines in the face of the white man's law.

Picnic at Hanging Rock dealt to a certain extent with the question of what is meant by what it is to be an Australian. Similarly, *The Last Wave* touches on the question of Australian identity. Whereas *Picnic* showed the repressive influence of British colonialism and its cultural imperialism, *Last Wave* shows how Australia has deliberately buried its native Australian roots. If David Burton is a direct descendant of prehistoric travellers from South America, the film seems to be hinting at the mixing of racial elements that go to make up contemporary Australia. Implicitly, it seems to challenge the racial purity of white Australia, reminding its audience that the image of Australian-ness that is usually projected is an incomplete picture. The fact that Sydney is built on top of the underground caves where the sacred Aboriginal symbols are kept is a metaphor for this collective burying or amnesia. White Australia hides realities from itself, consigning unsettling questions of racial mixing and genocide to the underground places, the unconscious. David Burton, in climbing up from the underground caves and sewers into the light where he sees his vision of the apocalypse, is freeing himself from that amnesia and coming in touch with not only his dreams (which in terms of Aboriginal Dreamtime are real) but with his origins as an Australian.

It has to be said that David Burton as played by Richard Chamberlain seems an unlikely figure to be in possession of such psychic and visionary powers. The gradual breakdown of his ordered world, his belief systems, his family, his middle-class life style and his sense of identity is not represented in strong enough terms in Chamberlain's performance. As one Australian critic put it, Chamberlain 'goes through everything looking mildly startled'.[6] It is true that for a man with an apocalyptic vision whose whole identity and way of life are being turned upside down, Chamberlain does not show enough signs of unravelling. But it is too easy to blame the actor. Chamberlain showed he could play a neurotic character coming apart at the seams in Russell's *Music Lovers* and he can also play nasty as he showed in Lester's *Petulia*. An actor can only play what he is required to play, so if the Burton protagonist does not show sufficient alarm at the destruction of his everyday, safe, bourgeois existence, then the fault lies with the director and the screenwriters. Chamberlain is a very underrated actor; he has never quite been able to throw off his television *Dr Kildare* role or that he is seen as very handsome, a fact that seems to disqualify him, particularly among male critics, from being taken seriously. He brings a kind of dignity and seriousness to his better roles that can be an asset to a film, but psychic powers, the ability to foresee apocalyptic events, are not readily associated with his rather controlled and smooth screen persona. If at the heart of *Picnic at Hanging Rock* there is the lack of an objective correlative, in *Last Wave* what is missing is the emotional intensity rather than the objective correlative, which is there in the form of all the events and interactions that Burton/Chamberlain experiences.

The Last Wave is much less widely known among the general public than *Picnic at Hanging Rock* and the balance of professional criticism came down on the side of the earlier film. However, the movie shows Weir progressing in the craft of film-making. The pacing of the film, for example, is better than in *Picnic*. A film's rhythm, the manner in which scenes are juxtaposed with one another, the length of scenes, the way in which the film is edited, all these interlinked structural elements are clearly crucial to the overall tone and atmosphere it achieves. I have already mentioned that the pace of *Picnic* is perhaps just a shade too slow and lingering. The subject-matter of the movie demanded a kind of languorous rhythm, certainly in the first half of the movie till the disappearance. *Last Wave* is dealing with apocalyptic events, foreshadowed by the unnatural weather conditions in Australia that are represented right from the opening scenes. These events are more dramatic, even melodramatic, so the film's pacing has to reflect that. But there are other signs that Weir as a director is learning his craft in this movie: he knows how to juxtapose scenes, how long to make them, how to edit in such a way as to help the narrative along at the same time as unravelling the mystery behind the story. Not that things are made easy for the audience. The narrative technique employed is not linear nor causal, with that kind of seamless narrative quality of Hollywood commercial movies in which we are told something about characters who then do something in keeping with their psychology, actions which cause certain clearly-defined developments in the narrative (cause and effect, in essence). *Last Wave* demands more of its audience than that. For example, the opening sequences of the movie are puzzling to an audience and are intended to be; essentially this is another mystery story Weir is telling us. Under the credits we see an Aboriginal painting on the roof of a cave. Then there is a sudden cut to a small town in the Australian desert; we see a group of Aborigines sitting in the heat surrounded by a few meagre possessions. Children playing are suddenly drenched by torrential rain and then hail ('There's no clouds, miss,' one says); the schoolteacher herds them together in the school, but the hail shatters windows and some of the children are hurt. The film then cuts to Sydney with a scene of an Aborigine drinking from a water-fountain. Burton/ Chamberlain, leaving his office building, is handed a yellow pepper by the caretaker and Burton comments on its peculiar colour. The city is enduring a ferocious downpour, which causes chaotic traffic jams and people to lose their tempers. There is a close shot of a leopard in an advert on a bus. At home with his wife and family, Burton's domestic idyll is interrupted by the dripping of water from upstairs. Someone has left the bath running. Burton sees the figure of Chris outside his house.

The audience is given the task of piecing together these disparate elements without much help from the director. The mystery has been set up and the connections between these people and these events will gradually become clear, although the audience will have to work hard to make sense of it. Indeed, there is perhaps no complete sense to be made of it, as Weir has implied when he said that he was dealing with things he never really understood. Again, in a post-modernist sense, the style of the film is its meaning. Allusive, undefined, wrapped in obscurity, the style used by Weir and his co-writers spells out the meaning of the movie: that there are no certainties, no cosy rationalities that can ease our existentialist nightmares, that the accepted dimensions of time and place are but illusions. In these opening sequences, Weir introduces or alludes to most of the central themes of the movie: the alternative reality of the tribal Aborigines existing beneath Sydney, the chaos that nature brings and the helplessness of human response, the intuition and joy of children (the pupils in the schoolyard and their excitement, plus the Burtons' kids) and the attempts at rational explanation by adults, the intimation of psychic powers associated with the Burton figure and the fusion of dream and reality. The juxtaposition of these scenes is skilfully put together; they are just long enough to make their point and tell astute spectators what they need to know, but they leave a lot of questions unanswered. What is the connection between the Aborigine painting in the cave and the hailstorms? What is the significance of the strange-coloured pepper and why include the joke of the bath overflowing? A close analysis of these scenes shows that there is a narrative cohesion to them: the Aborigine painting reflects the continuing presence of tribal culture in the city despite the blindness of even informed white Australians to it; the cut to the dispossessed, poor Aborigines makes a point about the oppression Aborigines suffer; the rainstorm is the first allusion to water imagery in the film and the shot of the Aborigine drinking from the fountain links this water imagery with the Aborigines; the water motif continues in the scenes in the Sydney streets and in the domestic scene where the menace is undercut by revealing that the source of the water is the bath, but it is quickly built up again by Burton's vision. The joke of the overflowing bath is taking a risk with audience expectations, but in another way it helps to reinforce the cosy family domestic scene where things like that are everyday occurrences, only to show how that very cosiness is fragile and vulnerable to unseen forces. The water motif, of course, culminates in the gigantic wave that ends the film. These opening scenes are richly allusive and detailed; one or two touches are, perhaps, rather over-determined, such as the shot of the leopard on the bus which hints at the power of raw nature and man's unavailing attempts to control it, but generally the scenes show Weir and his collaborators in full charge of their material, presenting in cinematic terms the mysterious story they have to tell. As a story-teller, both as a writer and a director, Weir has acquired a strong sense of how to put scenes together, how to build up an atmosphere and a narrative scene by scene and how to underline thematic concerns with individual shots or cryptic pieces of dialogue.

But, there are faults in the film too. It seems that Weir perhaps felt that the movie was being too allusive, too mysterious, so there is some heavy-handed exposition to make up for it. For example, when Chris and Charlie come to dinner at David Burton's house, Annie, Burton's wife, says, 'I'm a fourth generation Australian and I've never met an Aborigine before.' The same point (the gap between white and Aboriginal Australia) has already been made more visually and allusively, and this kind of explicitness jars. Similarly, the legal aid lawyer who brings David into the case has an explicit scene where he says how white Australia had killed off Aboriginal culture and accuses David of a patronizing middle-class attitude to the blacks. It is almost as though, by putting this argument in the mouth of this not very sympathetic character, the film-makers are signalling something important to the audience: no, they are not guilty themselves of patronizing attitudes to the Aborigines. All through the film, the audience (by implication a white Australian audience, at least initially) is encouraged to see the events through David Burton's eyes and, therefore, identify with the star of the movie, Chamberlain. In doing this, the film-makers are employing the standard Hollywood practice of using the star of a film to embody certain values they may wish, consciously or unconsciously, to communicate and to iron out any inconsistencies in ideology. The effect of having a Hollywood star name is that the star brings a star persona with him into the film and by privileging the star's role in the narrative, the film-makers can manipulate the audience's viewpoint and sympathies by their identification with, and foreknowledge of, the star.

To use an example from classical Hollywood film-making, in *High Noon*, the star presence of Gary Cooper provided the archetypal good Joe star: honest, incorruptible, gentle but tough when necessary, a man incapable of brutality, callousness or cowardice. This star persona had been established in films such as *Mr Deeds Goes to Town* (1936), *Beau Geste* (1939), *The Westerner* (1940), *Meet John Doe* (1941), *Good Sam* (1948), and *The Fountainhead* (1949) and many others. By using the likeable Gary Cooper, with his persona of honesty and quiet determination, as the beleaguered marshal in *High Noon* (1952), the film-makers were exploiting a well of audience sympathy and identification that had been built up over many years. In addition, the standard Hollywood practice was to encourage audience identification with the central figure of the narrative, usually a hero or heroine figure, whatever the standing of the star playing that role. Thus, *Last Wave* prolongs this tradition, although Burton/ Chamberlain is not an heroic figure. Chamberlain's star persona is one of decency and integrity; even when he plays a character who is not at all admirable (such as the psychopath he plays in *Petulia*), there is a sense that the film gains from the fact that it is that nice Richard Chamberlain playing the role, thereby enhancing the badness of the character by contrast with the star's usual persona. I have already paid tribute to Chamberlain's acting in the film: he is very effective within the limitations imposed by the script and the demands of his usual star persona. However, the film might have been given an added dimension had a different actor been used, someone who could have communicated more moral ambiguity, for example, or an actor whose screen persona encompassed darker elements. Casting is a very important element in film-making. On the one hand, Weir was fortunate in having an able star like Chamberlain in his film; on the other, his screen persona of a bland integrity works against suggesting moral ambivalence or deeper dimensions in the figure of David Burton. Imagine if Albert Finney, Harvey Keitel or John Cassavetes, for example, had been cast in the central role. These stars would certainly have altered our reading of the film. These actors are not mentioned because I think they would have been ideal casting, but are used to illustrate how star actors bring their own meaning to movies, a concept we will have to return to, especially when we discuss Weir's Hollywood films.

Another problem with the film is the rather peremptory ending. After all the emphasis on apocalyptic visions, what we actually see is stock footage of a tidal wave, which has to represent David's apocalyptic vision or, depending on how you read the film, the last wave itself. Weir and his collaborators had intended to film the wave enveloping Sydney, but the money ran out, partly because of picketing by Aborigine activists, which slowed the progress. Thus, the small-budget limitations of *The Last Wave* do weaken the ending. Indeed, Weir had considered a quite different ending which would have taken the audience into the water, but again lack of resources denied him the opportunity. Film-making, or at any rate commercial film-making, cannot be divorced from material circumstances. The realities of budgeting affect what artists can do. Weir's Australian movies were all produced under tight budgets. In itself that does not imply that less artistically successful films are made in those circumstances (think of film noir B movies of the forties, such as *Out of the Past* (1947) or *Crossfire* (1947)), but in matters of production values, when big scenes or elaborate effects are required, it is not always possible to paper over the cracks and such is the case with the final scene in *Last Wave*. Perhaps too much is left to the imagination of the audience by using the stock footage that ends the film.

Unlike *Picnic*, Weir originated the idea behind *The Last Wave*. He wrote the first draft of the screenplay and co-operated with Morphett and Popescu in fashioning the final script. However, it is clear that Weir allowed the dynamics of the set to affect the development of the film. He was particularly open to suggestions from Gulpilil and Nandjiwara. His own Celtic lineage played a part in the exploration of the uncanny in the sense that he discussed Celtic mythology with Nandjiwara and that he wanted to 'show the contrast between the European without the dreaming and the tribal person with the dreaming'.[7] It is clear that Nandjiwara exercised considerable authority on the set and suggested lines of dialogue, particularly in the dinner scene with the Burtons. However, Weir took what he needed from the Aborigine actors and shaped it according to his own artistic needs. He had been interested in Heyerdahl's theories that 'the sea is a highway and there have been many groups and civilizations who have crossed to other countries and perished or stayed briefly or whatever.'[8] Weir welded this theory to the concept of the Mulkrul, which seemingly was a word that Gulpilil, but not Nandjiwara, used to describe other white people who had come here before the Europeans.

In some ways, *The Last Wave* can be read as a more personal film than *Picnic at Hanging Rock*. Directing it was clearly a matter of exploration for Weir, not only in terms of his development as professional film-maker, but also as himself, the whole Peter Weir. And that is one of the strengths of Weir as a director. In his films, there is a strong sense of an individual artist at the centre of things exploring ideas, beliefs, possibilities, the unknowable, the unseen, the big questions, what, indeed, Robert Winer calls 'Weir's penchant for the Major Arcana'. For Winer, *The Last Wave* 'evokes late adolescence' with its 'achievement of ego continuity – the adolescent's construction of himself as an historical being with a past, present and future'.[9] The film seen through this psychoanalytical perspective has to do with Burton's (and therefore by implication Weir's) reconstruction of himself: where he came from (South America), who he is now (a lawyer or a mulkrul with psychic powers) and what the future has in store (an apocalyptic event)? However, the tendency of all psychoanalytically-based film criticism, whether based on Lacan or on other gurus in the field, is to reduce all films to the same explanation. It is open to critics such as Winer to use psychoanalytical theory to write about films, but the process is deterministic in that the theory can be applied to a whole body of films made by different people and the end result will be the same. It robs the film-makers of individuality, of their uniqueness, and perhaps it needs to be stressed that no serious artist, whatever their sphere, is ever wholly indistinguishable from other artists, because no individual's experience of life or consciousness can ever be exactly the same as any other human being's. We are all unique in that sense. What Lacan and other post-Freudian psychoanalyists attempt to do is question the notion of self. If there is no self, then that allows us to talk about individual writers, artists or film directors as contructs or notional figures, even things. The opposite side of that critical coin is the divine spark, the individual genius type of critical analysis, which I do not ascribe to either. Yet Peter Weir, the real Peter Weir, not the critical construct, whatever that may be, cannot be ignored. Though we might not want to return to the days of the romantic tradition, whereby critics wrote about individual artists as the sole creator of the work of art, without reference to history or the industrial circumstances in which the artefacts were produced, there is certainly a pressing need to stress the importance of the individual creator, whether or not he/she may be working on a collaborative basis, instead of distancing oneself from the humanity of the artist and applying post-structuralist concepts, which have the effect of deflating the artist and inflating the critic and of denying aesthetic judgements and pleasure in the reader/viewer/consumer. The pleasure we can take from *The Last Wave* has to do with the unfolding of this uncanny tale, its suggestions of an alternative reality, its skilled mixing of diverse elements, its narrative pace and the convincing entactment of incident. The film cannot be summed up by an analysis of its themes. Weir's *mise-en-scène*, what he actually puts into the frame, shows an assurance and an awareness that helps to give *The Last Wave* its frightening dimension. Yes, the movie does achieve a frisson or two, for this writer, at least, and that is another point about film criticism that needs to be stressed.

Those of us who write about film or consider ourselves to be informed spectators cannot somehow divorce ourselves from the visceral and emotional effect of film, or, put another way, from the pleasure principle. We surely cannot be disembodied intelligences sitting in the dark watching a film dispassionately. Much of contemporary film criticism seems to posit a model of the critic doing just that very thing. If that model is an accurate one, then the film critic is not sharing the same experience as the vast majority of viewers. I believe that the critic must come as the whole person to the viewing of films. Certainly, critics must scrutinize film texts, but they should also allow themselves to admit to whatever it is they felt when seeing the film in question. Perhaps, for some critics, it is more a matter of allowing themselves to feel anything at all, because so many seem to resist at all costs the manipulation of the film-makers, as though that would corrupt the critical process itself. Critics cannot place themselves as 'objects' in the viewing state and hope to respond to cinema in any meaningful way. Such a critical stance leads to aridity, to rigid academization, to so-called scientific objectivity which is very distant from the creative energy that went into the creation of the artistic artefact in the first place. A film such as *The Last Wave* requires viewers, and critics, because in essence critics are viewers like anyone else, to view it with their whole person, if necessary suspending their disbelief (yes, that old concept!) and allowing the film's form and atmosphere to take you where it will. After the viewing, it is open to the critics to tear it to shreds, but that can only really be justified if they have moved towards the film with some kind of openness in the first place and not with the closed-down attitude of the dispassionate observer, who is somehow different from the rest of humanity, a kind of intellectual in the stalls. If you allow *The Last Wave* to take you along with it, if you are open to its exploration of the uncanny, as Weir was in the actual making of it, then it can be a rewarding, if disturbing, experience. If Weir is not the sole author of the movie, and he isn't, at least he can be clearly identified as the key player in the creation of the movie. The film relates to other films dealing with the uncanny and unseen world and there were also several other key collaborators important in the making of it, but when we look at the body of Weir's work, we can identify recurring elements that establish him at the heart of the creative process.

The Plumber

The Last Wave brought Weir a measure of commercial success in America, the market-place that really counts in the film business. It mainly showed in art houses, but it brought his name to the attention of both people in the business and informed cinema-goers. Its comparative success led to the release of *Picnic* in the States, but many preferred *Last Wave*, which achieved a kind of cult status. Despite this commercial success, Weir's next work would be a film made for transmission on the Channel 9 television station in Australia, although the production was funded by the South Australian Film Corporation.

The Plumber can be seen as an interlude in Weir's career before he went on to the major achievements of *Gallipoli* and *The Year of Living Dangerously*. Weir has said that he wrote it because he needed the money, but that certainly does not need to imply that he put less of himself or his talent into the project. But it was a modest production, shot in 16mm with only a few actors and located in the claustrophobic setting of a small apartment in Adelaide. In essence, then, it was a script that Weir developed with the television medium in mind: small-scale, domestic, focused on a basic situation that could be represented as having significance beyond the transparent meaning of the narrative. With *The Plumber*, we have Weir operating again as the sole writer-director, not adapting material from other sources and not collaborating with other screenwriters. Thus, Weir has (ostensibly, at least) stronger claims of authorship over *The Plumber* than for *Picnic*, for example, where he worked on Cliff Green's script which had been adapted from a novel by another hand.

Synopsis: *Jill Cowper, a post-graduate student of*

anthropology, lives with her husband, Brian, in a large impersonal block of apartments owned by the University of Adelaide. They have just returned from New Guinea where Jill has been studying the primitive tribe, the Niugini, and has also had an unsettling encounter with a native who came into her room and performed some kind of ceremony, whereupon, in her fear, she tipped some milk over him. Brian is remote and obsessed with getting a job with the World Health Organization. A young man, Max, arrives at the apartment one day claiming to be the university plumber and saying he has to check the pipes in the apartment. His behaviour is very strange: he takes a shower in Jill's bathroom and claims to be a convicted rapist, which he later denies. His work on the plumbing seems to be getting nowhere and Jill becomes increasingly agitated by his presence. Her husband and her neighbour, Meg, dismiss her misgivings. Meg even suggests that Max's presence in the house is really a bit of a turn-on. Her husband is upset, however, when some scaffolding that Max has put up in the bathroom causes difficulty for the WHO guests he has round to dinner one evening. Max begins to sing Bob Dylan songs, which are contrasted with Jill's academic interest in primitive music. Max's authenticity is put into question when the bathroom pipes sprout leaks, which helps Jill make up her mind to break out of this siege. She plants a watch in Max's van, tells her husband that it is missing, who then calls the police. The watch is found in Max's van and he is arrested, screaming 'You bloody bitch' at Jill as he is taken away. At a celebratory dinner to mark Brian's appointment to a job with the WHO, Jill confesses that she felt she was in danger of losing control of herself vis-à-vis Max and his presence in her territory.

Some of Weir's recurring thematic concerns should be visible in this summary of the film's narrative. There is the challenge to order, especially that type of order symbolized by rationality and academic study, by primitive forces. Like the teachers in *Picnic* and the lawyer in *Last Wave*, Jill, the rational academic with her controlled interest in tribal culture and artefacts, has her world turned upside down by unexpected and uncontrollable primitive forces—Max's disturbing presence in her flat. Is he a would-be rapist or is she projecting on to him her own unconscious fears?

Another element in the movie is the class dimension, just as class had been an understated issue in *Picnic* and, implicitly, in *Last Wave*. The Cowpers' ménage and life style generally are middle-class. Their apartment is festooned with tribal works of art, which Max refers to as 'this boong stuff'. Jill's interest in tribal music is directly contrasted with Max's singing of Dylan songs. Here we have another clash of cultures, another clash between instinct and the controlling ego. Max represents something to Jill that she would rather do without in her ordered life, a chaotic life force that disturbs the seemingly even tenor of her life with her shut-down husband. But her marriage and academic life style offer her only a superficial peace, as we are shown at the beginning of the film when Jill tells Brian about her frightening experience with the native in New Guinea; she is nervy and he seems detached from her. Max can move into the empty space created by the limitations of their marriage and their academic sterility. Unconsciously, Jill may see Max as a repressed symbol of the kind of man she would prefer to her ambitious and academic husband.

Once again, sexuality is represented as the chaotic force, as it had been in *Picnic*. Basic instincts break through the veneer of civilized feelings, nurtured by education and middle-class culture. Jill, in her threatened state, needs to reassert her control and fights dirty by planting the watch in Max's van. As a middle-class person, she uses the forces of established order to defeat the lower-class interloper and to allow her to avoid facing up to her own desires. In her callous act of incriminating Max, she shows herself to be just as primitive as her enemy or the primitive tribe she studies with so much academic detachment. The fragility of the civilized way of life as represented by the Cowpers' academicism and tastefulness is once again exposed in a Weir-directed movie. The ambivalence that has been an essential element of *Picnic* and *Last Wave* is also present in *The Plumber* because we are never sure of how much of a threat Max is to Jill. It is never really established whether he is a plumber or not, and whether he intends some harm to her. The important thing is that he represents a threat to Jill herself and that enables Weir to explore her psyche and the theme of the vulnerability of normal life to the unexpected and the unclassifiable. On one level, *The Plumber* is a variation on the woman-in-peril sub-genre, but unlike most movies of that type, it never descends into representation of outright violence. Violence is very much present in the film, but it is a verbal and implicit violence, not the overt variety. Just as in *Picnic* and *Last Wave*, Weir suggests by nuance and implication, by hints and suggestions, the possibility of danger, just as Val Lewton had done over thirty years before in *Cat People*. Weir had learned that appealing to the audience's imagination and playing on their sub-concious fears can produce more chilling effects than a direct onslaught through enacted violence and visceral impact.

Film reviewers in Australia largely ignored *The Plumber* when it was first transmitted on Channel 9 on 20 June 1979, but that is the fate of most films made for television. However, the film did have a showing at Filmex in Los Angeles in March 1980, where it was well received. It is a small-scale production, fairly modest in its aims and realization, but it shows Weir applying his talents to a smaller canvas and working on obsessions that crop up in almost all his movies. As he was so much in control of the film both as a writer and a director, it would surely be perverse to deny his claims to authorship of the movie. However, the film text has to be seen in relation to other films of this kind. One that springs to mind is Kubrick's *The Shining* (1980); Kubrick was to play a part in opening up the possibility of Weir directing American films. Weir had always admired Kubrick's films and acknowledges that he is an influence on his work. Kubrick, for his part, had seen *Picnic* and *Last Wave* and admired them both. Warner Brothers wanted to film *Salem's Lot* from a Stephen King novel. Kubrick recommended Weir to Warners, but Weir decided that the project did not interest him. So here was this comparatively young director turning down a feature film which was to be produced by one of the Hollywood majors and this after being recommended for the job by a director of immense prestige and whom he himself admired greatly. The refusal of this offer reinforces the concept of Weir as a director of integrity who will only work on projects that he believes in. Perhaps Warner Brothers were impressed by his single-mindedness, because, despite his turning them down on *Salem's Lot*, they offered him a two-picture deal. Weir was now an international director, involved with one of the Hollywood majors. However, the first project Warner Brothers offered him under this new arrangement was an Australian subject, *The Thorn Birds*, a film version of the novel by the Australian novelist, Colleen McCullough. But after working with screenwriter Ivan Moffatt on the screenplay over a period of months, Weir finally turned the project down. This was another courageous move on his part because at that stage *Thorn Birds* was planned as a big-budget American movie with Robert Redford and Bette Davis as possible stars. It must have been a very difficult decision to make at the time, but, as it happens, it worked out well for Weir because it freed him to concentrate on two movies that were close to his heart and which would consolidate his reputation world-wide, *Gallipoli* and *The Year of Living Dangerously*.

Gallipoli

It was the birth of a nation.

(Peter Weir)

The film's mood is openness and enthusiasm, a sparky challenge to the deserts of Western Australia, Egypt and Turkey, boys measuring themselves against the world in rites of passage.

(Robert Winer)[1]

Gallipoli Day is a national holiday in Australia. It commemorates the massive defeat and slaughter of Australian and New Zealand troops in April 1915 at the hands of Turkish troops on the Gallipoli peninsula. Gallipoli represents several things to Australians: a sense of pride in the courage of the troops who died in the carnage, the forging of a sense of Australian-ness in the face of British imperialist attitudes and hence a focus of resentment at British duplicity and exploitation. Perhaps the tragedy of Gallipoli could be said to have undermined forever the trust Australians had in the fairness of the mother country. Indeed, in 1916, when a referendum was held in Australia on whether or not conscription should be introduced as a means of harnessing support to defend the Empire, a resounding no vote was recorded. The sacrifice of Gallipoli had left its scars. The colonial nation had rounded on Britain and made a statement of its independence. A second referendum confirmed the first verdict. Only volunteer Australian troops would fight Britain's wars for it.

Mark Lee, Mel Gibson The screenplay for *Gallipoli* was by David Williamson, one of the playwrights who had helped revive the Australian theatre (*The Removalists, Don's Party*). However, the writing credits record that Williamson wrote the script from a story by Weir and almost certainly he worked in very close tandem with Williamson. The funding for the film came from an association of Robert Stigwood and Rupert Murdoch, perhaps not as surprising as it seems because both these Australian entrepreneurs must have recognized the commercial appeal in the story of Gallipoli. In addition, the significance that Gallipoli has in Australian history and the anti-establishment feeling that the historical event evoked must have appealed to Rupert Murdoch in particular.

Synopsis: *The film is structured in three interlinked parts: the scenes in Western Australia and Perth, the section that takes place in Egypt and the final section on the Gallipoli peninsula in Turkey. The film opens on a ranch in the Western Australian bush. Eighteen-year-old Archy Hamilton is being trained as a sprinter by his Uncle Jack, who sets rigid training routines and disciplined goals for his nephew. Archy's model is Harry Lassalles, an Australian world champion sprinter. After endangering his chances of winning a big race by taking on a challenge to run barefoot across the bush only a few days before the event, lacerating his feet in the process, Archy does manage to win the race defeating Frank Dunne, a city boy, who is as cynical and worldly-wise on the surface as Archy is idealistic and naive. Archy takes the decision to try to enlist in the Light Horse, but fails to do so because Les, the stockman whom he had raced against in the bush race, exposes him to the authorities as being under-age. Frank and Archy strike up a friendship, even though Frank shows his total cynicism about joining up. Frank persuades Archy to go to Perth where he might have a better chance of enlisting. They board a freight train which lands them in the middle of the Australian desert. Archy leads the protesting Frank fifty miles across the desert, meeting a nomadic white man on the way who has not even heard that there is a war on. They spend the night in the home of a middle-class family, who are full of admiration for Archy's determination to join the Light Horse. The pretty young daughter's admiration particularly strikes Frank, who realizes that he might be able to use the war to better himself. As he explains to his father, he does not intend to die for the British*

Empire but to return an officer so that he won't be pushed around for the rest of his life. Frank's father is of Irish origins and reminds him that the British executed Frank's grandfather. Archy succeeds in enlisting in the Light Horse under the name of Lassalles, but Frank fails the riding test and joins the infantry with his mates—Barney, Snowy and Billy—whom he had previously worked with on the railroad. Archy and Frank part. We next follow the adolescent exploits of Frank and his mates in Cairo, playing Australian football in a grudge match between the Western Australians and the Victorians, causing mayhem in the bazaar, mocking English officers, buying prostitutes despite official lectures on VD from the army and taking part in ridiculous training exercises. During one laughable exercise, Frank is reunited with Archy, who persuades the Major in charge of his unit to allow Frank to transfer from the infantry, principally on the grounds that he is a fast runner. The Light Horse are shipped off to Gallipoli, where the Anzac troops are pinned down on a narrow strip of beach by the Turkish artillery. There is a supposed need for a diversionary attack by the Anzac troops on the Turkish lines to allow the British to land at Souvla. It is quite clear that the attack will be horrendously costly in lives, but the Colonel in charge of the operation is insistent that the British must be given every chance to land safely. Due to a failure to sychronize watches and British intransigence, the attack is a disaster and turns into a massacre. Earlier, Archy had turned over the position of runner between the front lines and the command post to Frank, whom he realizes is very scared at the prospect of the attack. Running back from command headquarters with a belated order to halt the attack, Frank hears the whistle that signals the third phase of the attack, the one that has Archy going over the top to his death. The last shot of the film is a freeze frame of the dying Archy.

Weir has called *Gallipoli* his 'graduation film'[2] and there are several ways in which this can be interpreted. Firstly, the movie involves a much larger canvas than any of his previous films. Weir here has to direct scenes shot in Australia and Egypt involving large numbers of extras. He also had the responsibility of a fairly large budget and of representing a significant event in Australian history. Secondly, the movie reflects his graduation to a sure command of film technique. Weir now felt he knew what he was doing, whereas before he had never quite understood why something he had done had worked on screen. Moreover, he was working with a linear narrative in *Gallipoli*, which follows a chronological story and obeys cause-and-effect rules. It is much more realistic than *Picnic* or *Last Wave* and it also has an identifiable transparent theme or themes, whereas with the two earlier films, there was ambiguity and ambivalence. That is not to say that the movie does not have sub-texts or that spectators have to accept the ostensible meaning as the only meaning of the film (no film text is ever closed in that sense), but there is little that can be identified as belonging to the uncanny or the unknowable in the movie. The story of Gallipoli is told largely through the figures of Archy (Mark Lee) and Frank (Mel Gibson) with Frank's mates and the Major as subsidiary figures. Through these representative figures, the film recreates an Australian tragedy, a nation's experience of loss, waste and defeat, out of which came something important, a sense of Australian-ness and separateness from Britain which the country is still struggling and identifying with in present times. In *Gallipoli*, the film-makers are recreating a significant event in Australian history but are, in addition, surely making a statement about present-day Australia.

The film also presents a picture of male conditioning and mateship. Male bonding in Australian culture is very much more prevalent and acceptable than perhaps it is, say, in British culture. This may reflect the days when men were often marooned together without women in the bush and out-of-the-way early Australian settlements. Mateship, the interdependence of male groups, often in opposition to other male groupings, is still a strong feature of Australian life. The emphasis on male friendships has its positive and its negative sides. It does provide support for individuals from other men, but too often it promotes intense competition, a cultural oppression, an overemphatic and insensitive masculinity and a disparagement of women. Most of those aspects of mateship form a sub-text in *Gallipoli*.

The theme of male conditioning is represented from the opening scenes of the movie. Archy is trained by his Uncle Jack, who continually asks him 'What are your legs?' to which Archy has to answer 'Steel springs'. The question 'How fast can you run?' receives the rote answer 'As fast as a leopard.' It is those words that Archy repeats to himself as he psyches himself up at the end of the film just before he goes over the top to his certain death. The film seems to be saying that the philosophy embodied in Uncle Jack's training routines (driving the body to extreme lengths, focusing on winning and the notion of heroic glory) leads ultimately to that kind of blind obedience that has Archy willingly go towards certain death because he has been ordered to do so and because he has been taught to believe that to shirk that order would be to show weakness. He still has to run as fast as a leopard even though he is running suicidally to a useless death. Uncle Jack is angry that Archy desperately wants to enlist in the Australian volunteers, because he sees that as a diversion from Archy's destiny—to be as great as their mutual idol, Lassalles, the great Australian runner. However, the conditioning that Jack instils in Archy cannot be divorced from the conditioning that results in Archy saying that he would be ashamed of himself if he didn't fight in the war. The silly challenge that Archy throws out to Les, the bone-headed stockman, stems from this competitive male pride as well and his determination to challenge himself to the utmost limit. Uncle Jack deplores the dissipation of Archy's energies in such frivolous activities, but his single-minded focus on achieving supreme performance for Archy helps to form Archy's view of life and his obligations. However, it is Uncle Jack who reads to the children from Kipling's *Jungle Book* about Mowgli crying and recognizing that he is human because of his tears. Mowgli deciding he must leave the jungle and 'go to men' is symbolic of Archy's leaving the bush and joining the army. Archy too will come to tears in the desert of Gallipoli.

Archy's friendship with Frank starts in fierce competition when he defeats him in an important race, which Frank initially sulks over. Frank is the cynical town boy, drifting from job to job, whilst dreaming one day of having his own bike shop. Frank becomes Archy's mentor, introducing him to the ways of the world but refusing to join him in his enthusiasm for joining the army. 'It's not our war,' says Frank, 'it's an English war.' This anti-English sentiment he has learnt from his father, who is outraged when Frank announces that he is joining up. Frank has been affected by the promise of advancement that the army offers, especially if he manages to join the admired Light Horse. Class issues feature again in a Weir film, but this time they are more explicitly stated and realized, almost certainly because of Williamson's hand in the script and because of the basically realist approach the movie takes. Frank symbolizes worldly values to Archy, whilst Archy represents Frank's class aspirations. However, Frank is taught a hard lesson when entry into the club that is the Light Horse is denied him by the disparaging officers, who see immediately that he is no horseman. Frank engineers Archy's acceptance into the regiment by forging his passport in the name of Archibald Lassalles. So Frank rejoins his railroad worker mates and forms close bonds with them when Archy leaves for training with the Light Horse. Later, he will betray his working-class mates by wangling his transfer to the Light Horse, but their mateship will be re-forged at Gallipoli under the threat of imminent death. Frank and Archy are seen parting from one another with much repressed emotion, Archy saying 'See you when I see you' and Frank replying, 'Not if I see you first.' Australian males can, it seems, allow themselves to show feelings towards one another only in this tone of defensive badinage. However, this first leave-taking scene hints at the emergence of what Weir has called the characters' 'feminine side': the caring for one another and the ability to express feelings.

We see the cheering crowds at the quayside as the troops embark for Egypt and then Frank and his mates playing an intensely competitive game of Australian football for Western Australian lads against the Vics. Billy admires the Pyramids which tower over the soldiers, but Frank dismisses them as a pile of rubble. He is much more interested in the rivalry between the troops from two Australian states than the Pyramids, which Billy says are 'man's first attempt to beat death'. On the whole, the behaviour of Frank and his mates in Cairo is shown to be loutish, insular and ignorant. They judge everything from an Australian viewpoint and anything that is different is suspect. 'You're dealing with Australians here, you know' says Snowy, the most bigoted and puritanical of the four, to an Egyptian shopkeeper as they terrorize him into returning some money to them. Frank, whilst looking at some dirty postcards, remarks that Egyptian women have no respect for themselves and it is the same in all foreign places. Nevertheless, he later buys a prostitute's favours. They also deliberately hire some donkeys so that they can mock two English officers, who are represented in a very stereotypical manner (monocles and braying voices). The friends wear imitation monocles and sing mockingly, 'If England needs a hand, well, here it is.' Here the film makes its sympathies very clear, but there is an ambivalence about the representation of the group's behaviour in these Cairo scenes: the film-makers observe their youthful gaucheness and crudity without judging them as characters. However, the representation of their naivety and unworldliness in the face of a foreign and closed culture reinforces the idea that they are just cannon fodder for some higher purpose, the needs of the British Empire. This is further emphasized by the representation of the laughably inadequate training the Australian troops receive in Egypt. In an exercise which pitches the infantry against the gentlemen of the Light Horse, class antagonisms surface again, but Frank and Archy's renewed friendship climbs above this. They express their feelings for one another by racing to the Pyramids, which they climb to scratch their names at the top. Frank has transferred to the Light Horse; this causes a break with his mates, who feel that he has betrayed them. Ominously, Snowy says that it's always bad luck for mates to break up in the middle of something they're involved in. Archy and Frank bluff their way into a dance for officers only and the sympathetic Major Barton (Bill Hunter) allows them to stay, partly because he knows they are embarking for Gallipoli the next day.

We then see the lights on the shore at Gallipoli from the viewpoint of the soldiers in the boats as they come into land. The lights make a pretty pattern in the night, creating an unreal fairground effect. The faces of the troops are strained and anxious; the games are over now, they are faced with the reality of war. They are under fire from the moment they step on shore. Archy is remorselessly cheerful because he thinks he has embarked on a great adventure; his *Boys' Own* view of the world is still intact and this is just one more challenge to him, something he must face and conquer just as his running had tested his courage and masculinity. Frank finds his cheerfulness grating and is clearly more anxious about what lies in store for them. Conditions are parlous; they are in constant danger as they are pinned down on the strip of beach and the food consists of biscuits covered in flies. When a group of them swim in the sea, there are some underwater shots that convey the peace of this safe underworld, until this haven is shattered by bullets from the Turkish guns which wounds one of the swimming soldiers. Frank is reunited with Snowy, Billy and Barney and Archy is made a honorary member of the group. Mateship wins out over jealousies and class aspirations.

The Colonel in charge announces that the Anzac troops have to charge the Turkish positions to divert their fire from the British troops landing at Souvla. The agreement is that the Turkish lines will be softened by an intense barrage of artillery fire before the Australian attack, but the officers fail to synchronize their watches properly, and the barrage ends too quickly, allowing the Turks to return to their positions in time for the attack. The Colonel is inflexible and insists that the suicidal venture take place despite Major Barton's protests. Archy has got Barton to accept Frank as the official runner instead of him, because he can see that Frank is windy about the attack. In a lull between attacks, we see Major Barton listening to his opera records and drinking whisky. Archy writes a letter home saying that they all think they are involved 'in an adventure larger than life'. He keeps his illusions to the end or perhaps what he writes in the letter is just for home consumption. The whole military operation is shown to be the result of the cynical employment of Anzac troops to protect the British forces arising out of incompetence that defies credibility, given that so many men's lives were at stake. The movie records this rather than hammering the point home; the only villain is the Colonel who is insistent that the need to protect the British overrides everything else. The waste of it all is summed up in Frank's despairing cry as he hears the whistle that precedes the final attack that kills Archy—he is running back with the order to stop the attack, but he is too late.

Thus, the film can be interpreted as an account of the Gallipoli operation presented from the perspective of a group of Western Australian young men. However, the central relationship between Archy and Frank provides the underlying structure and furnishes the narrative link that gives the movie its undoubted cohesion. Archy and Frank move from a standpoint of fierce rivalry to a relationship where one is prepared to sacrifice himself for the other (Archy's surrendering of the safe job of runner to Frank). Frank's last despairing cry as he realizes he is too late to stop the final phase attack is not only a cry of anguish about the slaughter of the many, but very much an expression of his pain at the loss of his friend. They have shared rites of passage together and have become almost one. Each has influenced the other: Frank has shown the world to Archy, however fallibly, and Archy has opened Frank's eyes to wider horizons (the Light Horse, the possibility of becoming an officer, the bike shop). They manage to negotiate the life-threatening initiation test of the fifty-mile trek across the desert, represented as a uniquely Australian expedition with its reference to the Burke and Wills expedition. Archy comes from the bush, conquers the desert and ends up in the city, Perth, where his joining-up allows him to test himself in two other deserts: the Egyptian and the Turkish. Frank is a city boy, who drifts into railroad work, meets Archy in a bush township, survives the desert and is shipped to two other deserts. He survives the final challenge, Gallipoli, whilst Archy, partly by his own choice, dies.

Frank throughout the movie is confident of his life skills, his ability to survive, but he is over-confident. He can manage some things (hopping on trains, forging passports, pressurizing army recruiting officials when they threaten to turn down one of his group, negotiating the Cairo bazaar), but without Archy he would have died in the Australian desert and it is only through Archy's influence that he can gain entry into the Light Horse. His attitude to the Pyramids betrays him as an insular and ignorant young man. Of the two, however, Frank is identified by the logic of the narrative as the survivor. Because of his Irishness he knows that the war is an English war. He has no intention of sacrificing himself for the British Empire and he does not see it, as Archy does, as a great adventure. He is drawn into the war against his better judgement by a mixture of emotions and ambitions; he reacts angrily when Archy accuses him of cowardice, he notes the admiration shown by young women to those who volunteer (his first exploitation of his new and glamorous Light Horse uniform is to chat up a young woman at the Pyramids), he feels a sense of loyalty and comradeship to Barney, Snowy and Billy so he joins up with them, and he sees the army as a chance to better himself so that he can become the small shopkeeper he aspires to be.

Archy, by contrast, is designated by the logic of the narrative to be the sacrificial lamb on the altars of patriotic duty, male conditioning and class allegiances. We see him studying the early newspaper reports of the Gallipoli operations, which construct a myth of 'a magnificent Australian achievement'. Just as Archy wants to become a great Australian sprinter like Lassalles, so he wants to be part of the Australian military glory that is supposedly the noble resistance at Gallipoli. Whereas Frank knows with his gut feelings that Australia is being used by Britain, Archy has only the vaguest notion of why Australia is in the war at all, contenting himself with the illusion that 'it was the Germans' fault' and that 'if we don't stop them there, they could end up here', which must be a deliberate echo on the film-makers' part of the argument put forward by those who supported Australian involvement in the Vietnam war. Archy moves away from a stance of competitiveness with other males (the races with Les, whom he encounters later on the battlefield just before the stockman goes over the top, and with Frank) to an emotional bonding that allows him to show affection to other men, albeit in a disguised manner. This development is partly spelt out in the routine exchange of male camaraderie. When Archy leaves Frank behind in Perth, he says the 'See you when I see you' and Frank in a defensively aggressive manner says 'Not if I see you first.' At this time, they are still bound by the rigid rules of male bonding. Any show of emotion about parting from your mates would almost certainly be thought of as suspect. When they part for the last time in the trenches, they shake hands and it is Frank who says 'See you when I see you' and Archy who says gently and not at all defensively, 'Not if I see you first', which brings a sad smile of recognition to Frank's face. The emotion is still submerged, they do not embrace as women friends would, but neither is able to, or wants to, disguise the emotions they are feeling. What Weir calls their feminine side has emerged. The journey that Frank and Archy have taken, rather than being from Australia via Egypt to Turkey, could be seen as from competitiveness to close friendship, from isolation to mutual support, from a driven kind of masculinity to a feminized maleness. Both are caught, however, in a trap from which there is no escape. Even Frank in his rebelliousness has to obey orders and can only do so much to change the course of the tragic events by leaning on the General to delay the final attack. Archy is caught in his own contradictions: a feeling young man, sensitive and caring, who still clings to the conditioned reflexes of what it is to be a man, the ideal of the hero and the supreme athlete inextricably linked in his mind.

How overtly masculine men can allow themselves to open out to their emotional and intuitive selves is a theme that will emerge more and more in Weir's films. This thematic concern is already there in *Picnic* through Michael and in *Last Wave* in the figure of David Burton. However, these two figures are not represented as symbolizing masculine traits (Michael is an uncertain teenager and David is a rational lawyer) in the same way as Archy, Frank and their mates are in *Gallipoli*, or as Guy Hamilton (Mel Gibson) and John Book (Harrison Ford) are in *The Year of Living Dangerously* and *Witness* respectively. The transition Archy and Frank go through takes them a few steps down the path towards new men status, where masculinity is no longer defined by toughness and lack of feeling but allows for weakness and show of emotions. Frank is the figure in the narrative of *Gallipoli* that represents this shift of perspective on what is acceptably masculine. Not only does he show feeling about Archy, but he is shown as being deeply affected when he visits Snowy on his death bed and by the death of Barney. Even Les, the macho stockman, is shown crying with fear before he goes over the top and Archy acknowledges silently the right of this overtly masculine man, who has derided running as something girls do whereas men box, to show his feelings. The film dispenses with the illusions of false heroics: these men are scared, but they are more frightened of the punishment and opprobrium that will come their way if they refuse to attack, so they assent to their own deaths. Undoubtedly, David Williamson, the screenwriter, is a crucial mediator in the handling of this theme in the movie. A critique of Australian masculinity crops up in *Don's Party* (1976) which he wrote both for the stage and the screen version and it crops up again in *Living Dangerously* which he also co-wrote. However, it is a theme that Weir, independently of Williamson, also comes back to, so it can be interpreted as a shared thematic concern in *Gallipoli*, where the standpoints of the writer and director seem to unite.

Screenwriters have traditionally had a raw deal from serious film critics, but it would be a nonsense to discuss *Gallipoli* without identifying David Williamson as a key figure in its creation. In its structure and detail, the movie clearly indicates an authorial hand or hands. It is related to other film texts – intertexts – but the screenplay has been shaped very deliberately to make statements about the events the movie depicts and the characters it uses as representative figures in the narrative. One of the movies it resembles in some ways is Kubrick's *Paths of Glory* (1957), which also dealt with a military debacle during the First World War. *Gallipoli* is a much less angry film, but it touches upon similar themes – the hapless victims of military blunders, the political manoeuvres that decide the fate of ordinary people, the camaraderie of ordinary soldiers and the basic decency that lies under a brutalized exterior. Both films avoid making explicit anti-war statements whilst exposing the intransigence and destructive pride of those who send men to their deaths in the name of military glory. We know that Weir has expressed his admiration for Kubrick, so it is possible that *Paths of Glory* was a conscious, or unconcious, influence on *Gallipoli*. Williamson's screenplay, of course, is not the film, just as a playscript is not a play. It was Weir's job to turn the screenplay into a film and this he does triumphantly. However, it would be possible to sit through *Gallipoli*, having shut your eyes during the credits, and not realize that this was a Peter Weir film. Only in a few scenes are there recognizable Weir traits in terms of stylistic signature. For example, two scenes that have already been referred to: the scene where the boats approach the Gallipoli shore and the underwater swimming scene. The bright lights seen from the soldiers' point of view look like the lights you might see in a seaside resort at night. The scene has an air of unreality, a dream-like quality which echoes scenes in earlier Weir films. Then the underwater scene where the men go swimming creates a silent world apart, a fantasy refuge from the noise and dangers of the real world, until bullets soundlessly plummet as symbols of the horrible reality that awaits the soldiers once they leave the sea. It is another example, too, of Weir's water motifs.

To say that the film for the most part lacks a

clearly-defined Weir signature is not intended to detract from his work on the movie. What he shows in *Gallipoli* is his ability to handle linear narrative, a story told with the skill of a proficient story-teller. Even if we attribute the script entirely to Williamson, Weir still had to bring his story-telling skills to the task of putting that story with those particular characters and events on to celluloid. That is perhaps what Weir means when he talks about *Gallipoli* being the first film where he understood completely what he was doing. In a sense, the material that was given to him (although the story originated with him), compelled him to use a disciplined craftsmanship. It would have been inappropriate to aim for the particular resonances he created in *Picnic* and *Last Wave*. Story-telling skills in the cinema are undervalued generally. Partly, this is because so much contemporary criticism looks upon narrative with a kind of disdain as though the blandishments of the story have to be resisted so that the underlying structures that signify meaning can be revealed. Yet our collective need for stories is one of our deepest instincts and a film that tells a good story is always likely to attract a large audience. Too much modern criticism undervalues the power of narrative and the gift of cinematic story-telling. Ford and Hitchcock knew the value of a good story and were expert story-tellers. Most famous directors are more than efficient story-tellers; they may use the narrative as a means of exploring their own obsessions, but if they lose contact with their story while doing so, it is at the expense of their film and their audience. When Weir talks about *Gallipoli* as his graduation film, he may have in mind his graduation as a story-teller of the cinema. His ability to stage action scenes and other scenes involving large groups of people is also tested in this movie. There is the scene of the big race with its crowd and recruiting soldiers; there is the scene where the cheering crowds see off the ship of departing troops; the throngs in the Cairo bazaar and the ridiculous training exercise further test Weir's ability to handle large numbers of people on screen and there are, of course, the scenes of warfare themselves. Probably budgetary restrictions limited the extent of these latter scenes. There are just enough of them to suggest the reality of the Gallipoli disaster, but they do not begin to compare with the scope and intensity of the attack depicted in Kubrick's *Paths of Glory*, but then that is comparing Weir's attempts with some of the most compelling reconstructions of warfare ever put together for a fiction film. From a career point of view, Weir must have felt reasonably satisfied that any American studio seeing his handling of action sequences in *Gallipoli* might well mark him down as a director capable of handling large scenes and numbers of people. Considering how many American movies rely heavily on scenes of action and spectacle, this is an important aspect of a director's skills, if he is to move into directing within the American film industry.

All the films Weir directs are to a greater or lesser extent personal films. Clearly, recurring thematic concerns from his previous movies re-surface in *Gallipoli* and no doubt these concerns stemmed from Weir's story outline. Yet it is difficult to avoid the conclusion that Weir has less claims to authorship of *Gallipoli* than he has for *Last Wave*, for example. But he displays enough directing skills in making the movie to strengthen his claims to being an outstanding director, a director whose name above the title can almost guarantee an interesting and entertaining time in the cinema. However, there are some criticisms that can be made of the movie that need addressing. Firstly, it is an almost entirely male-dominated film. The excuse that the subject justifies that is a trifle thin, because Gallipoli was an Australian experience that touched both genders equally. Yet women play next to no part in the narrative, except as playthings or trophies to be won. Indeed, a charge of misogyny might even be levelled at the movie: of the few female figures in the narrative, some are used to suggest that women expected their menfolk to go to war ('The women of Australia expect') and the others are Egyptian prostitutes, who are disparaged. There is no doubt that male figures dominate in Weir's films. In his defence, if defence is needed, one of his concerns is to portray men who are able to show their feminine side, their emotions, their imaginations, their souls. Weir is a product of a country where women, by and large, are not encouraged to challenge men's dominance and where gender roles are still rigidly imposed. Weir shows a consciousness that this must change, that men must break free from their male conditioning and be open to new roles and new experiences. It would be a rather unforgiving political correctness that would ask Weir to condemn the chauvinist actions of characters in *Gallipoli*, given that he was recreating a particular period in Australian history when such attitudes were taken for granted.

The other criticism that could be levelled against the film is that it is transparent—in other words, there is a given meaning that the film-makers hand down to the audience, a message that is all too clear and explicit. It is a matter of judgement about how heavy-handed the movie is, but it is open to any member of an audience to reject this given meaning and reinterpret the movie according to their own lights. In my analysis I have foregrounded the theme of male bonding and the feminization of the main narrative figures, but for many others the movie will be about quite different things. In essence, the movie is about many things and there is no one fixed meaning. It is not a text, however, that has endless resonances as perhaps *Picnic* and *Last Wave* do. There is a realist aesthetic at work here in its thematic treatment of its apparent subject and the style in which it is put together. In some ways, it is the cinematic equivalent of a good read, a narrative about recognizable characters involved in a historical event, and that brings it back to its story-telling qualities. This is not a post-modernist film; it follows a clear and logical narrative, it does not switch viewpoints, it tells its story through two central characters and there is a definite narrative closure—the death of Archy. In other words, it obeys the rules of the classic narrative fiction film. It holds few surprises for its audience and for those who like their Peter Weir films more off-the-wall, improvisatory and unsettling, *Gallipoli* may have seemed something of a disappointment. But an artist cannot go on endlessly repeating himself without running the risk of becoming a parody of himself. This movie shows Weir moving on in his career and his artistic development, a move that inexorably brought him closer to making movies in Hollywood, that mecca for most film directors who want to break out of the straitjacket of national cinema or experimental film. There will be many people for whom Weir's best films will always be the early films he made in Australia before the commercial world got hold of him, but Weir could not go on making remakes of *Picnic* or *Last Wave*, much as many people might have wished him to do so. He had to move on and *Gallipoli* was an important staging-post on that path to an international career.

The Year of Living Dangerously

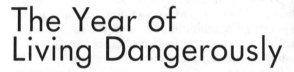

'We're divided men. Your father an American, mine Chinese. We're not certain we're Australians. You and I, we're not quite at home in the world.'

(Billy Kwan in *The Year of Living Dangerously*)

Like most men who live alone, and have reached their maturity single, Hamilton had done so by numbing his feelings at crucial times and turning to action for relief.

(from the novel *The Year of Living Dangerously*)[1]
by C J Koch

In 1978, Weir bought the rights to C J Koch's book, *The Year of Living Dangerously*, but it was not until 1981, post *Gallipoli*, that he exercised his option and started filming. Here is Weir once more working on material from another medium, a novel, as he had done with *Picnic at Hanging Rock*, but he clearly was excited by the subject-matter and invested his own money in the project from the outset. Eventually, MGM-UA became the major financiers and distributors, which, in terms of Weir's career, was a significant development. The McElroy brothers again produced with James McElroy as the line producer. Weir's partnership with David Williamson was resumed and he, Williamson and the author of the novel, C J Koch, eventually shared the screenwriting credits.

The eighties would see a rash of films in which journalists are the main characters who become involved in the violence and politics of Third World **Mel Gibson,** countries. Films such as *Salvador* (1986) *Under Fire* **Sigourney** (1983) and *The Killing Fields* (1984), set in El Salvador, **Weaver** Nicaragua and Cambodia respectively. Additionally, there had been portrayals of journalists-as-heroes or guardians of liberty in Alan Pakula's *All the President's Men* (1976) and *The Parallax View* (1974), paranoiac parables based on conspiracy theories about the nature of power in the state. The British movie, *Defence of the Realm* (1984), also represented journalists as bastions against the machinations of secret and ruthless powers that manipulated the information channels and institutions to maintain the power status quo. *The Year of Living Dangerously* can only be fully interpreted in relation to this sub-genre of the journalist-in-extremis. In *Salvador, Under Fire* and *The Killing Fields*, the journalists, played by James Wood, Nick Nolte and Sam Waterston respectively, find themselves in the midst of grotesque terror and abuse of basic human rights. They themselves are threatened with death for carrying out their journalistic duties and each is radicalized by his experiences. They cast off the traditional journalistic non-involvement and take sides. This is an important difference from *The Year of Living Dangerously* where the main protagonist, played by Mel Gibson, chooses to walk away from his journalist's duties and does not choose a side to support. Perhaps this can be interpreted as another stage in Weir's progression away from political involvement to an emphasis on the personal and the individual. Michael from *Three to Go* has become Guy in *Living Dangerously* who is no longer even tempted by the possibilities of political action, but finally pins his faith on personal relationships. Weir had used the public event of *Gallipoli* to explore the relationships between men; now in *The Year of Living Dangerously*, he uses the political events in Indonesia in 1965 to represent a love affair between a man and a woman and along the way tackles the big issues of the nature of love, what is really important in life and what we can do to make things better in the world.

Synopsis: *The year is 1965. The place is Jakarta, the capital of Indonesia. President Sukarno has dubbed 1965 'the year of living dangerously' because he wants to end Indonesian dependence on the West. For twenty years he has balanced the forces of the Communists, the Muslim right, Western Imperialism and the poverty-stricken masses of the country. Guy Hamilton (Mel Gibson) arrives in Jakarta as the foreign correspondent* of the Australian Broadcasting Service. It is his first overseas posting and he is desperate to be successful in it. The other foreign correspondents, notably Curtis of the Washington Post and Wally O'Sullivan of the Sydney Morning Herald, greet him warily as a new competitor, but Hamilton is befriended by the diminutive half-Chinese, half-Australian Billy Kwan (Linda Hunt), a photographer who knows his way round Jakarta and has acquired many useful contacts. Billy gets Guy a scoop interview with the head of the Indonesian Communist Party, which enhances Hamilton's reputation as a correspondent. Billy senses a potential in Guy and wonders whether he could be his 'unmet friend'. He also idolizes President Sukarno, at times dressing like him; he admires Sukarno's ability to balance forces and his desire to do something for his people. To Billy, Sukarno is the great puppet-master, which links him with the shadow puppets of the Wayang. In the Wayang, no final solutions exist, there are no right or wrong answers as there are in the West. He explains to Guy that the shadows of the puppets on the screen are their souls. He introduces the puppet characters of the Prince (a hero with the potential to be selfish and fickle), the Princess (beautiful, but proud and headstrong) and the dwarf (he serves the Prince). He takes Guy into the slums of Jakarta and poses Tolstoy's question, 'What then must we do?', the title of the book the Russian novelist wrote after going into the Moscow slums and giving his money away to the poor. Billy introduces Guy to Jill Bryant (Sigourney Weaver), an attractive Englishwoman who works at the British Embassy. It is clear he wants to bring the Prince and the Princess together, despite the opposition of Colonel Henderson (Bill Kerr), an attaché at the Embassy, who has what appears to be a fatherly relationship with Jill. Billy has adopted a poor Indonesian woman and her baby; he gives them money and advice about medical care. Billy explains this to Guy: 'We must give with love to whomever God has placed in our path.' After a reception at the British Embassy, Guy and Jill drive through a road-block and survive the gunfire levelled at the car by Indonesian soldiers. They become lovers, but Jill, who has to leave Jakarta shortly and has tried to keep her feelings for Guy under control because of that, receives a posting to Saigon. She receives top secret information about an arms shipment coming from

Shanghai for the Communists. She fears that, if the Communists take power, there will be a massacre of Westerners. She tells Guy about the arms shipment because she wants him to leave, but Guy sees this as an opportunity for a major story. Jill protests that she told him in confidence and that when the story breaks, everyone will know his source, and he replies that she knew he was a journalist. Jill, and Billy Kwan, see this as a betrayal of their trust on Guy's part, who seems to be retreating from commitment to Jill into devotion to his journalistic career. He goes into the country with Kumar, his assistant, and Kumar's wife, both members of the PKI (Communist Party), to find evidence to confirm the arms shipment. Kumar tells him that he (Guy) is on the party's death list. Returning to Jakarta, Guy has a drunken evening with Curtis, who is overjoyed that he has a posting to Saigon. Billy's disillusionment with Guy, the Prince, is quickly followed by his loss of faith in his other hero figure, Sukarno. The child of Ibu, the Indonesian woman whom he has adopted, dies and he starts to blame Sukarno for making empty speeches and building monuments to his vanity while his people starve. He reviles Guy for having betrayed his trust. Billy takes a room in a large hotel where Sukarno is due to make an important speech and hangs a banner out of the window: 'Sukarno feed your people.' Sukarno's bodyguards toss him out of the window to his death. Guy asks Jill when she is leaving Jakarta — the next day — and tells her to be certain to be on the plane. However, when he hears there has been a military take-over, he decides to go to the Presidential palace instead of to the airport. He receives a rifle butt in the eye when he breaks through the line of guards around the palace. He is taken to Billy's bungalow and a doctor warns him that he has to have ten days' rest if he is to save his detached retina. Kumar arrives and tells him that the Communist coup has failed and that he (Kumar) is facing certain death. Guy decides to go to the airport despite the danger to his eye and the assurances of Kumar that things are safe for him now and that he can stay and write all the stories he wants. They have to bluff their way through road-blocks, passing firing squads executing people involved in the coup. He says farewell to Kumar and manages to catch the plane. The last shots of the film are of Guy mounting the stairs to the plane and Jill embracing him.

For critics and moviegoers accustomed to thinking in comparmentalized genre terms, *The Year of Living Dangerously* is something of a puzzle. Is it a political thriller, a love story, a film about journalists or a serious social problem movie? Perhaps it is all of those things, because it takes aspects of different genres and mixes them up effectively to produce a richly textured movie with different layers and strands. That is part of its fascination. Indeed, most Hollywood genre films have this intergeneric quality: musicals borrow from screwball comedy (Astaire-Rogers series), detective thrillers smack of film noir (*Maltese Falcon* [1941], *The Big Sleep* [1946]), westerns are melodramas (*The Searchers* [1956], *High Noon* [1952], sci-fi flicks resemble horror films (*The Creature from the Black Lagoon* [1954] *Forbidden Planet* [1956]). There are usually structures and elements within movies classed in one particular genre that crop up regularly in other genres. However, as I have already indicated, the intertexts that may be most usefully employed to make full sense of *Living Dangerously* are the recent movies about journalists. Beyond those, however, are a whole series of Hollywood journalism movies ranging from Howard Hawks' version of *The Front Page*, *His Girl Friday* (1940), to Billy Wilder's cynical *Ace in the Hole* (1951) *His Girl Friday*, although set in New York, could be seen as a comic treatment of the dilemma facing Guy Hamilton: how much do you sacrifice of your personal life for your journalistic career? In Hawks' comedy, Cary Grant is Rosalind Russell's ex-husband and ex-editor. He is desperate to win her back to journalism, but she is committed to becoming the wife of dull old Ralph Bellamy. In the end, of course, Russell surrenders to Grant's ruthless machinations and becomes a driven journalist again, with the bonus of falling in love and remarrying her ex-husband. The choice facing Guy Hamilton/Mel Gibson is similar but he makes the opposite decision, sacrificing journalistic opportunities for the sake of his relationship. In contrast to the comedy of *His Girl Friday*, the dark perspective of *Ace in the Hole* represents an obsessed newspaper man (Kirk Douglas) ruthlessly using the victim of a mining cave-in to boost his career but destroying himself in the process. In *The Year of Living Dangerously*, Hamilton/Gibson manages to bring himself back from the edge of self-destruction.

The film differs from C J Koch's original novel in some important aspects. For example, the voice-over we hear on the film's soundtrack is Billy Kwan's, so our view of Guy and Jill is shaped by the authoritative voice that all voice-over narrators have. In the novel, these events are being recalled years later in Australia by a journalist called Cook, one of the press corps in Jakarta. Billy Kwan emerges as a much darker figure from the pages of the novel: he has real hopes of marrying Jill and is bitter about being turned down; he has photographs in his files of women comprising 25 body types; he also has nude studies of Jill and it is implied that he watches Guy and Jill making love; he may also have shopped Wally O'Sullivan to the Indonesian police for his pederasty with Indonesian youths, leading to O'Sullivan's expulsion; it is probable that he intended shooting Sukarno rather than just making a protest with a banner. Guy Hamilton is represented as being half-English, rather than as having an American father as in the film. There is a character, Vera Chestukov, from the Russian Embassy who is dropped entirely from the film; her role is taken over by Kumar's wife; in the novel, it is Vera whom Hamilton dreams is drowning him in the swimming pool. In the novel Hamilton is much more Victorian in his outlook and full of outrage at what he finds in Billy's files.

The key casting decision made by the film-makers was using the American actress, Linda Hunt, in the role of Billy Kwan. It is made clear in the book that Billy is not a dwarf, but rather a very diminutive person. The casting of Hunt adds an androgynous element to the character, an extra layer of symbolic meaning. It is Kwan/Hunt who is obsessed by the crucial question posed by the film: 'What then must we do?', the question Tolstoy posed, which in itself echoes the question the people ask John the Baptist in Luke Chapter 3, Verse 10, 'What shall we do then?;' Faced with the immense problems of Indonesia, Billy comes down on the side of a kind of Christian love, a love that must be bestowed on whoever fate puts in our path: Ibu and her child in Billy's case. The Wayang, Indonesian shadow puppets, acquire a mystical meaning for Billy and through the concept of the puppet-master who creates balance, he attributes similar powers to the false idol, Sukarno. Billy's tragedy is that he invests too much faith in individual heroic figures. He is desperate to see qualities in Sukarno and Guy that are either not there or are unlikely to be fulfilled. Thus, when Ibu's child dies, that becomes symbolic of the fate of all the Indonesian people and of Sukarno's neglect, just as Guy's decision to use Jill's information about the arms shipment seems to Billy to prove him unworthy of his trust and of Jill. The idealistic Billy has no reserves to fall back on when the scales fall from his eyes. He descends into bitterness and malevolence. Just before he hangs the banner out of the window, he needlessly announces to a crowded bar that O'Sullivan is a pederast, thereby ensuring that in Jakarta's anti-Westerner environment the Australian journalist will have to leave the country. Undoubtedly, however, the figure of Kwan has been softened between novel and film and this may have something to do with the casting of Hunt. The androgynous quality she brings to the part makes Billy a more sympathetic character, gentler and much more positive about the burgeoning relationship between Guy and Jill, whom he had once asked to marry him. That is a not a criticism of the casting, because the role that Hunt enacts in the movie makes sense in that context, but it is worth noting the difference the casting of Hunt makes as it reflects the intention of Weir and his collaborators. Perhaps this softening effect evolved during the making of the film, as a result of casting Hunt and what happened during shooting.

It is another case, perhaps, of Weir using the actual shooting phase to explore the relationships and ideas of the script rather than just putting on to celluloid what is already there in the pages of the script, just as he had done during the making of *The Last Wave* when he followed his instincts and the promptings of the Aboriginal actors. Linda Hunt inhabits the role of Kwan so authoritatively that we are drawn into his vision of Hamilton/Gibson and Sukarno, so that the bitterness of the character when his idealized hero lets him down is entirely understandable. Using Billy's voice-over narration adds powerfully to this shaping of the audience's perspective. However, it might be asked, as with all voice-over narrations, where is this voice coming from? how much trust can we give it? does it have authorial status? The novel's narration is more conventionally realistic in that a fellow journalist is supposedly recalling these events years after. Further difficulty might be caused by the fact that three-quarters through the film Billy's voice-over narration dries up for the good reason that in the narrative Billy Kwan is killed. This adds to the problem of where the narrating voice has come from in the first place. From beyond the grave as in Billy Wilder's *Sunset Boulevard* (1950) in which a dead William Holden, lying face-down in Gloria Swanson's swimming pool, narrates the events leading up to the shooting? On a few occasions the film shows Billy typing up his notes on Guy for inclusion in his files; these notes are the basis for Billy's voice-over narration. We are inside Billy's head when we listen to the voice-over, they are his thoughts as he sits at his typewriter: 'Here on the page I am the master,' we hear him say, as he thinks himself master in the darkroom where he develops his photographs. In the throes of his final despair, we see him in his bungalow listening to one of Strauss's *Four Last Songs* and repeating bitterly the words, 'What then must we do?' as he types them on a page. He has discovered that he is no longer the master on the page or anywhere else; everything he has tried to create has fallen apart. He says to Guy about Jill: 'I gave her to you and now I'm taking her back. I gave you my trust . . . I created you . . . I thought you were a man of light. I made you see things.' Earlier in the film, Billy had offered to be Guy's eyes which has a double meaning: he will be Guy's official cameraman and he will open Guy's eyes for him, making him aware of the world around him and showing him what he must do.

The casting of Mel Gibson as Guy Hamilton perhaps is another important issue in judging the overall value of the movie. Weir had already used Gibson in *Gallipoli* as Frank Dunne, the townie from Perth, uncomplicatedly cynical, street-wise and a bit of a lad. Is it believable that Billy Kwan would invest so much faith in the character of Guy Hamilton as played by Gibson? First thoughts might suggest it would seem unlikely, because Gibson, despite his qualities as an actor, is not identified with hidden depths or endless spiritual potential. But that analysis changes if we, as the film encourages us to do, see Hamilton/Gibson through Billy's initial perspective. To Billy, the almost-dwarf, Hamilton is a handsome prince who can win the princess (Jill) in his place, just as the Prince of the shadow puppets can win the shadow Princess. Billy knows from the Wayang that the Prince can be selfish and fickle and that 'all is clouded by desire, as fire by smoke, as a mirror by dust . . . it blinds the soul', but he almost blindly invests in Hamilton so much of his own desires and beliefs that there is credibility in his claim that he has created him. In a very real sense, Hamilton is a Billy Kwan creation, forged from his idealistic and romantic imagination and intended to act in the world as Billy himself, because of his dwarf status, cannot. Billy sees in Hamilton what he wants to see, but we do not need to see the same potential. All Gibson the actor needs to achieve is to embody in himself the outward appearance that could give a character extravagant idealistic fantasies (Billy) with the form worthy of investing such faith in. Hamilton has to be handsome, as Billy is not; he must be attractive to Jill, as Billy is not; he must be able to exist in the real world, as Billy cannot. Thus, in that interpretation, the casting of Gibson makes perfect sense and works in the movie.

'All is clouded by desire, as fire by smoke, as a mirror by dust . . . it blinds the soul,' says Krishna to the Prince of the shadow puppets. Krishna's words are taken over by Billy and transmitted to Guy, but he is too clouded by the desire of his ambition to make it in the world of international journalism to heed the words. He says of his first foreign posting: 'Ten years I've waited for this. If I mess this up, they'll send me back to the newsroom in Sydney.' Hamilton has the driven quality of contemporary man, making, in Billy's words, 'a fetish of his career'. He starts off by making a hash of his first report back to Sydney ('This is travelogue . . . you could have written that in Sydney') and it is only with Billy's active help (the interview with the head of the Indonesian Communist Party) that he begins to make a success of his job. Pete Curtis, the correspondent for the *Washington Post*, played with reptilian authenticity by the impressive American actor, Michael Murphy, represents in the movie the opposite pole to Billy's idealism. Curtis is hugely ambitious (he's desperate to get a Saigon posting because he knows the Vietnam war is where the real action is going to be), deeply competitive (he picks a fight with Guy when his story about arming the peasants as a Third Force breaks), profoundly cynical and corrupt (he has no allegiances and he treats Jakarta as an extended brothel). When Guy is at his most estranged from Jill and Billy, he spends an evening with Curtis in which they get drunk, dancing with Indonesian bar girls to American imperialist rock'n'roll and being forced to leave by a uniformed Indonesian at gunpoint; they then go to the 'cemetery' where large numbers of prostitutes hang out. Curtis, a frequent visitor to this locale despite the prevalence of venereal disease among the women, stays to partake of the doubtful pleasures on offer while Guy leaves in disgust. It is not just sexual distaste that impels Guy to leave, but the sense of these Third World women being exploited by Westerners like Curtis. Another graphic instance of this is supplied earlier in the movie when Curtis, again, 'buys' a deformed dwarf to dance for Guy in a restaurant, a covert reference to Guy's relationship with Kwan, which Billy picks up on. Guy is angry with Curtis and the rest of the press circle are equally disgusted with Curtis. The American has gone too far, but his behaviour symbolizes the relationship of the journalists to Indonesia: they are distanced and unaligned, exploitative and cynical. Curtis represents how Guy Hamilton could have become if Billy Kwan had not created him. Indeed, when Guy betrays Jill, and thereby Billy, over the arms shipment story, it seems that he is moving towards the polarity represented by Curtis – 'all clouded by desire' – and towards losing his shadow, his soul.

Again a Peter Weir film is dealing with big questions. The Tolstoyan question, 'What then must we do?' taken over by Billy Kwan and incorporated as the central issue of the movie, not only refers to what we should do about all-pervading poverty and political corruption, indeed the misery of the world, but also what we must do with our lives to give them meaning and moral value. Billy's path of idealizing Sukarno and Guy Hamilton and of dispensing charity to one Indonesian family unit is shown to be illusory and self-defeating. When Ibu's child dies, Billy holds Sukarno responsible and his bitterness is that much more intense because of the naive faith he had invested in the dictator: 'He was a great man. That's why his betrayal is so hideous.' Sukarno was only 'a great man' in Billy's illusory world, just as Hamilton is 'a man of light' because Billy wills him to be. However, whereas Sukarno is irreclaimably corrupt, Billy's influence on Guy does have an effect. Billy's question (posed to Guy on his typewriter where he is master), 'Why can't you give yourself? Why can't you learn to love?' has a belated answer from Guy when he chooses to leave Jakarta and the career opportunities it presents to commit himself to Jill.

In Koch's novel, Jill is pregnant, which gives the Hamilton character an additional motive for opting for love. Wisely, in the film, they dispense with the pregnancy and represent the choice for Hamilton/ Gibson as being a straight alternative between his career and his relationship with the woman he loves. However, the movie may be a trifle fuzzy here: the fact that Hamilton could stay in Java and continue to write important stories could have been stressed more, so that his decision to go to the airport is more clear-cut. Additionally, in realistic terms, his leaving Jakarta does not mean he is giving up his journalistic career, but merely giving up an obsession that has been driving him: the need to make a success of his first foreign posting. That he is taking a risk of losing his eye by moving at all after the doctor's advice that he needed ten days' rest is also understressed, so that the movie can simplify the issue to the oppositional values: career vs love. The fact that the movie encourages the viewer to leave aside the complexities of the situation to focus on the love affair needs to be noted, but it does not rob the final scene of its power. This last sequence reverses the *Casablanca* closure, where Humphrey Bogart (Rick) sets aside his romantic involvement with Ingrid Bergman so that he can devote himself to fighting the Germans in Morocco and she can support her Resistance-leader husband. Bogart refuses to get on the plane, sending away his lover; Gibson keep his date with his lover and turns his back on a country in turmoil. In 1942, with the need to boost a wartime spirit of resistance, the makers of *Casablanca* felt unable to show Bogart walking away from a war for the sake of romantic involvement. In 1982, Weir and his co-writers could have Gibson choosing the personal over the public, love above duty. The imperatives of the times are different, but that cannot be the explanation for the differences between *Living Dangerously* and *Under Fire*, *The Killing Fields* and *Salvador*. In the latter films, as we have noted, the American journalist 'heroes' become radicalized by their experiences and involved in the country's problems. However, they are Americans reporting events in countries where the American government is heavily involved militarily and through its intelligence agencies. The journalists become increasingly aware of the dubious participation of their own government in Nicaragua, Cambodia and El Salvador. Their radicalization is dependent on their horror at the actions of their own government. Guy Hamilton has no such national stake in Indonesia. South-east Asia may have an important role to play in the Australian consciousness (the war against the Japanese and, later, Vietnam), but there is no suggestion that the Australian government played any covert role in Java, so Hamilton has no particular reason for being radicalized, except through Billy's example. Billy takes sides (albeit the wrong one), but Guy takes the classic journalist's stance: 'We can't afford to get involved.' Getting involved costs Billy his life; Guy's getting involved finally takes the form of emotional involvement with Jill. *Living Dangerously*, then, is a much less *engagé* (in the political sense) film than the three American movies; its engagement is concerned with the value of close human relationships. Guy's choice at the end of the movie is an existentialist one; he makes a decision in the light of the circumstances he finds himself in. He re-invents himself and chooses love.

Another recurring theme of Weir's movies that reappears in *Living Dangerously* is what it is to be an Australian. Billy Kwan is an Australian, yet he does not look Australian. He is half-Chinese and relates to the Third World more than to the West: 'In the West we want constants for everything, everything is right or wrong or good or bad, but in the Wayang no such final conclusions exist.' Part of his bonding with Guy has to do with Hamilton's dual nationality; in the movie Hamilton has an American father, while in the novel he is English. Neither of them quite belongs. Billy says, 'We're divided men. Your father an American, mine Chinese. We're not certain we're Australians . . . we're not quite at home in the world.' This lack of belonging is represented in their respective positions *vis-à-vis* the press corps. In Billy's final bitterness, he turns on his fellow press men and asks them why they never tell the truth. Hamilton is represented as never quite being at home with the juvenile antics and competitive ethos of his colleagues. Hamilton shows a sensitivity that the others lack: he allows Colonel Henderson, the British military attaché, to win a race against him in the pool because Henderson is a much older man and he can see that it means more to him. He gives Kumar, his assistant, money to give to his shopkeeper father who has to pay protection to the corrupt military. He writes a piece about the poor of Java that shows him to be a caring man. It is understated in the movie, but each of these actions can be interpreted as being the result of Billy's influence. Billy has to shape Guy to be worthy of his Jilly, the woman he loves but whom he is giving to Guy. Hamilton moves away from being the stereotypical macho Australian journalist and closer to what Billy wants him to be.

Sigourney Weaver plays the Englishwoman, Jill Bryant. Billy's dossier on her records 'she has a reverence for life. This is a spirit like a wavering flame which only needs care to burn high. If this does not happen, she could lapse into the bitterness and promiscuity of the failed romantic.' Weir seemingly worked on the character with Weaver to make her more substantial. Certainly, in the novel the Bryant character is something of a cipher, a problem not entirely excised in the movie. However, Weaver brings all her beauty and intelligence to the role and when she (Jill) commits herself to Hamilton/Gibson, the viewer can believe in her passionate commitment to the affair. Perhaps it is harder to accept that Bryant/Weaver could be so apprehensive about incurring the disapproval of her stuffy protector, Colonel Henderson, who is against her relationship with Hamilton/Gibson. Henderson acts as a kind of father figure to Jill, protecting her from predatory male figures like Curtis who makes a ridiculous play for her at Wally's bungalow party. He is the stern patriarch who reminds her of curfews, who plays the bagpipes to boost morale when the Indonesian mob are stoning the British Embassy and whom she has to placate when she leaves the Embassy reception with Hamilton and sleeps with him that night in Billy's bungalow. Jill also has to break away from ties and loyalties that impede the expression of her deepest feelings. By telling Guy about the arms shipment she is betraying top secret information, but she takes the risk out of a need to save him. Her loyalties, once she has entered into the affair with Hamilton, go deep, whereas Hamilton says to Billy when the latter upbraids him for using the arms shipment information, 'How far are my loyalties to Jill supposed to go?' Weir once again touches on gender issues here: Hamilton has to allow his feminine side to come through, the feeling, emotional side of him, before he can commit himself wholly to Jill. Jill only allows herself to fall in love with Guy once she realizes he is not just another predatory male like Curtis. She has had another relationship with Philippe, a French journalist, who has been posted to Saigon and she does not want to enter into a succession of brief relationships. Weir and Weaver do succeed in creating a more convincing Jill Bryant than Koch did in the original novel, but the weight of the film is still with the male characters, Hamilton and Billy. Apart from *Picnic*, this male domination is the pattern in Peter Weir's films, but this assertion has to be balanced with the reminder that this director is interested in exploring the feminine aspect of masculinity, whereby men can give up on macho attitudes and actions and express their gentler and intuitive selves.

Although the movie is further evidence of Weir moving away from the public to the private, from the exterior world to the interior, the representation of the political reality of Jakarta in 1965 is convincing. By that, I do not mean that the political issues at the heart of the movie are 'correctly' represented, as though there is a right line on this that the movie can be measured against. No, rather it is a matter of depicting the terror and irrationality of a country in the grip of internal turmoil with the opposing forces—the Communist left and the Muslim right—equally ruthless and terroristic in their methods. Oliver Stone in *Salvador* vividly communicates the sense of terror engendered in a facist state (El Salvador) when the military and death squads are given free licence by government thugs. Weir in *Living Dangerously* does not quite achieve the rawness of *Salvador*, but nevertheless the movie communicates an authentic vision of the breakdown of normal rules and behaviour, a picture of a society where the protection of diplomatic or journalistic status is as nothing compared to the force of a rifle butt or the authority of a soldier commanding a road-block.

In the last section of the movie when the Communist coup fails and the Muslim generals take over Sukarno, the audience recognizes that Hamilton's life hangs on a thin thread, a thread he seems determined to cut himself when he takes the decision to go to the palace and bluff his way past the guards. The randomness of the violence—the fury of the mob outside the American

Embassy, the blow Hamilton receives, the firing squads at the airport—constructs a picture of a world devoid of safety nets and the reassuring insulations of professional, national or financial status. This is the bare existentialist situation: to live or die, to choose life or death. The production had immense problems in Manila in the Philippines, where it was shot, because Muslim activists picketed the set and drove Weir back to Australia to complete the movie. The protesters were concerned that the movie was going to be unfair to the Muslim cause. Death threats were made that had to be taken seriously. In a strange way, Weir himself had to experience something of the dilemma of the main protagonist in the film: to continue to put himself in danger in the pursuit of his professional career or to choose the safety of his home country. Just as Hamilton chooses the safety of the womb (the plane, Jill), so Weir and his production team retreated to their native territory. Once again in a Weir movie, reality intruded on to the set and the filming process became an exploration and a working out of what was happening among the group of people involved in the enterprise.

Although the film could not be fairly stigmatized as anti-Muslim in any way, it is interesting that the representative Communist in the movie, Kumar, Hamilton's assistant, is portrayed sympathetically. His Communist views are certainly not endorsed but his basic decency as a character is underlined. He warns Hamilton about the death list the Party has him on and he takes a considerable risk in driving his former boss to the airport, considering he himself is now on the death list of the Muslim generals. The film seems to be saying that totalitarian creeds like Communism can attract men like Kumar who want to do something about the appalling nature of poverty and exploitation in their countries. Kumar's decency is then swallowed up by a ruthless Party machine that asks him to perform violent acts in the name of the people and the revolution. Kumar's wife, in Hamilton's dream and throughout the film, is represented as much more the Party apparatchik and indeed she is much higher in the Party hierarchy than Kumar himself. To describe *Living Dangerously* as apolitical is not quite accurate, because no film that deals with the representation of political turmoil and actual historical events, as this movie does, can ever be completely objective or unbiased. The film was made by

Westerners, white, male and middle-class, and all those factors, coupled with the fact that the production was financed by an American company and made for release on the international film market, are central to its point of view. That its point of view could be categorized as neutral in the strict political sense only reinforces a reading of the film as privileging the personal over the political, the collective and the public. Released in 1982, the film reflects the eighties' move away from political certainties to absorption with the self, where the political becomes the politics of relationships, revolving around questions of gender, sexuality, the importance of the interior life and the quest for individual fulfilment and happiness. Indeed, the movie reflects many of the concerns of New Ageism, a feature we have already noted about earlier Weir movies. It is also in the classic liberal tradition of the representation of a central figure struggling to make sense of his world, finding a solution to the problem by immersion in his personal life and thereby positing a solution of society's ills as well. *Living Dangerously* is unlikely to be high on the all-time-favourite lists of neo-Marxist and post-structuralist film critics with their dismissive attitudes to the importance of the personal or, indeed, the concept of the self itself.

So far, I have referred to *The Year of Living Dangerously* as a Weir film and I am conscious that this at best is a kind of critical shorthand. The movie can only be fully understood by reference to other films directed by Weir and other movies dealing with foreign correspondents entangled in moral questions about personal and professional responsibilities. It is important to keep this issue of intertextuality in mind, but additionally Weir had important collaborators in the making of the film whose claims to part-authorship cannot be ignored. C J Koch's original novel is clearly a significant source for the movie. Although some important changes were made in translating the novel into the film, in essence the thematic concerns of the book survive in the movie and, after all, Koch himself is one of the three credited screenwriters. If I make the value judgement that the film is better than the novel, then that may have to do with the fact that the cinema can represent large events such as political demonstrations, military coups and concrete reality in graphic terms, giving an extra physical dimension to the central love relationship and the moral choice facing the hero that the novel cannot manage. Additionally, the decision to put the narration into the hands of an anonymous Australian journalist, presumably some substitute for the voice of the author himself, unnecessarily distances us from the events and the characters without gaining very much in the process. The film-makers' decision (whosoever decided it) to have us see most of the events through Billy's eyes and narrative voice gives the spectator a way into the film, a way of viewing the events and characters, but one which we can resist or reject if we wish. When that narrative voice disappears and the point of view it has expounded is largely exploded by the narrative events, it leaves the viewer in no man's land. However, after the death of Billy, the rest of the narrative is largely seen through Guy's eyes (although not with the aid of a voice-over narration) and that signifies that some of Billy lives on in Hamilton. Voice-over, as has already been pointed out, presents a problem to the aware film spectator. Should we trust this disembodied voice on the soundtrack? What is it trying to sell? Is its version of events to be relied upon? Is there a tension between its explaining voice and the events we see on the screen? I think there is a tension between Billy's voice-over and the events he is narrating. Whether the film-makers were fully aware of this or not is almost beside the point. Viewers might find themselves bemused, for example, by the view of Hamilton/Gibson that Billy presents to us—this personable, uncomplicated Aussie journalist who seemingly has such vast spiritual potential—or Billy's perspective on Jill Bryant/Weaver as having a reverence for life when we see her merely as a beautiful but uncomplicated employee of the British Embassy. This voice-over narration, then, can only partly be trusted, because Billy's illusions are demonstrated to be illusions and, although Hamilton and Jill to a certain extent justify Billy's idealization of them, they remain all too fallible human beings, not much more heroic or noble than the rest of us. But that is part of the triumph of the film, that ordinary human beings can be seen to stumble towards some moral choices and to walk away from self-destructive patterns of behaviour related to notions of worldly success and professional duties. The decision to have Billy as the voice-over narrator, albeit it is given a realistic context (Billy typing up his notes for his dossiers), gives the movie an extra layer of complexity that adds significantly to a text that is already many-layered.

And it is this richness of texture that gives the movie its power. The choice that Guy Hamilton has to make is rendered the more significant by the skill with which Weir and his collaborators portray the attractions of worldly success and the desire to self-destruct. It is a peculiarly masculine drive, or, at least, one that is encouraged in men by the male conditioning process. Guy is attracted to the myth that you are never fully a man until you have put your life on the line to bring about your ambitions. According to this macho philosophy, popularized by Hemingway and other writers, a man only discovers who he really is when he has risked his life in dangerous circumstances. For Hemingway it was war or bull-fighting or deep-sea fishing or big-game hunting, and behind all that hairy-chested front there lurked a deep desperation and a search for oblivion. There is something of the Hemingway syndrome in Hamilton and he has to rescue himself, and be rescued, from it. But to make it triumphant and significant, the oppositional values have to be siren-like, to appear very attractive. We have to understand Guy's need for success and so Weir encourages us to share in his excitement when he gets the interview with the head of the Communist Party. The scene of the demonstration outside the American Embassy is also very effective in that it convincingly represents the hysteria and unleashed violence of political mobs and yet communicates the exhilaration that Guy and Billy both feel in the midst of that mayhem that they are shooting important footage and getting away with their lives in doing so. When Jill and Guy drive away from the British Embassy party and are out after the curfew time, we share in their devil-may-care exhilaration in driving through the road-block and surviving the gunfire. We have to understand why Guy, having seemingly blown his relationship with Jill, should be attracted to the self-destructiveness of Curtis' way of life and spend a drunken evening with the American that nearly ends in disaster. Despite the allure of Weaver in the part of Jill, we have to appreciate that Hamilton/Gibson could betray her and thereby endanger their love affair for the sake of his career. The movie is indeed half in love with the values it seems to despise. But that represents how most of us, according to Billy Kwan's philosophy, lose touch with our shadow sides and how everything becomes clouded with desire. If the choice were easy, then there would be little more to say. But, the sub-text of the movie seems to say, the allure of worldly success is real, the attraction deep, the drive to self-destruct hard to resist.

Weir is a romantic director and his romanticism pervades this movie. His men and women do not generally use sex to get to know one another; sex follows after initial attraction, misunderstandings, the sharing of fun and experiences. He rarely shows them in explicit love scenes; indeed, the love scenes between Gibson and Weaver are very restrained by contemporary standards. I do not think this arises out of a puritanism on Weir's part, but more out of a refusal to exploit sex for commercial reasons. It is not as though the sexual attraction between the two main protagonists is not communicated in the movie and, in Sigourney Weaver and Mel Gibson, Weir was employing two of the most personable stars of present-day cinema, but their mutual desire is conveyed through more subtle means than by merely showing them falling into bed with one another. It must also have been very tempting to end the film on a note of full-blown Hollywood romanticism of the *Casablanca* variety. What Weir does is a model of restraint, but yet the closing scene of the walk across the runway to the plane and the embrace of the lovers is one of the most romantic in all of cinema and it is all the more romantic because of its refusal to indulge the audience with clichéd underscoring and melodramatics. The tone is one of relief and peace. Hamilton has reached the place where he ought to be and Jarre's music emphasizes that. The final embrace of the lovers is recorded in long shot, as though the director is retreating discreetly from the scene.

The Year of Living Dangerously is overdue for reappraisal by the professional critics, who have never given it enough importance. In its own way, it is as effective a picture of a society in chaos and in the grip of fascist terror as Oliver Stone's *Salvador*. Stone's more realistic framework does not allow for the same complexity as Weir's more mystical and questioning approach. *Living Dangerously* handles the large question of 'What then must we do?'; Stone's film is largely content with recreating the terror while pointing an accusing finger at American foreign policy. *Living Dangerously* does not take sides, whatever Muslim critics of the film may say, because its primary focus is not political. There are real differences between the two films, but by placing Weir's film alongside *Salvador*, I am showering it with high praise indeed because for me *Salvador* was one of the very best movies of the eighties. *The Year of Living Dangerously* deserves a similar standing.

Witness

> And I must face a man who hates me
> Or lie a coward, a craven coward,
> Or lie a coward in my grave . . .

(Lyric of theme song from *High Noon*)

> *A big city cop who knows too much. His only witness – a small boy who's seen too much!*

(Publicity ad for *Witness*)

Witness was Peter Weir's first 'all-American' movie. It was financed by Paramount, one of the Hollywood majors, had a well-known American producer, Edward Feldman, American stars and an American setting. Feldman chose Weir to direct on the premise that a foreign director would be able to bring a fresh eye to the American scene that the film portrays: the contrast between the urban jungle of Philadelphia and the agrarian community of the Amish people, frozen in a kind of time warp in rural Pennsylvania. The film was the first opportunity for Weir to work with a major star of the American cinema, Harrison Ford, who had mostly played heroic parts in the *Star Wars* and *Indiana Jones* series up to that point in his career. How an independent-minded director like Weir fared working within the Hollywood machine for a major studio and a conventional American producer, and how he coped with the demands of a star persona and of a Hollywood genre, the police thriller, should clearly be at the heart of any analysis of *Witness* as seen in the context of Weir's overall career.

Kelly
McGillis,
Harrison
Ford,
Alexander
Godunov

The American film industry has always imported the talents of foreign directors; some have fared better than others in adapting themselves to the demands of the money men and studio executives. Among the European directors who, having made movies in their own native countries, escaped to the States in the thirties and forties were the Hollywood old-timers Billy Wilder, Douglas Sirk, Fritz Lang, Josef Von Sternberg, Robert Siodmak, Otto Preminger and Michael Curtiz. Directors such as Max Ophuls and Jean Renoir made some films in Hollywood before returning to continue their careers in Europe. Of those, Wilder, Siodmak, Preminger and Curtiz had long and successful Hollywood careers, Sirk and Von Sternberg achieved great success for a number of years and Ophuls and Renoir made only a handful of Hollywood movies. Wilder and Preminger seemed to have had more control than the others over the films they directed and that was almost certainly due to the fact that they formed production companies to make their films and did deals with the major studios for financing and distribution. When a Hollywood director was in essence his own producer, thereby having some degree of financial stake in the movies he directed, then his control over artistic decisions was increased and the interference from the backing studio and executive producers lessened. Where a director was employed merely as an employee director, then the question becomes whether he found the space within the movies he directed to impose some kind of personal vision on to the material, which very often would be generically determined. Douglas Sirk's fifties melodramas made for Universal are the focus of much debate. Are these films (*Written on the Wind* [1956] *All That Heaven Allows* [1955] *Magnificent Obsession* [1954] *The Tarnished Angels* [1957] *Imitation of Life* [1959], among others) pure Hollywood schlock or is Sirk, the one-time Marxist director in the German theatre, able to offer a critique of Eisenhower's America by using the conventions and clichés of the melodrama genre for his own purposes? The arguments put forward by critics who favour the latter interpretation sometimes seem to be rationalizations for the fact that they find those slushy 'women's pictures' very enjoyable. They have to explain their pleasure by over-intellectualizing and seeking respectable reasons for continuing to give these products of the Hollywood dream factory serious consideration. What this debate throws up is the question of the role of a director: is he or she the chief author of the movie or merely a craftsman employed to turn a screenplay into a film? Obviously, if a director is working on a screenplay of his or her own making, or at least a screenplay on which he or she has laboured with other writers, then his claims to authorship are enhanced. In a case where the director has had no part in initiating a project or in writing the screenplay, then the director may either be perceived as a craftsman whose primary job is to translate the script into celluloid form or as an artist who uses the given material and finds space within it to impose a personal vision.

These issues are especially pertinent to the Hollywood film industry, which is primarily a business enterprise. The Australian film industry is a business as well, but because of its comparatively small scale and the desire to establish a national cinema of some stature and artistic worth, in the heady days of the seventies there was almost certainly real space for directors such as Weir to carve out artistic freedom for themselves. Now, with *Witness*, Weir was taking on the Hollywood system with its New York money men, its studio system (albeit a very changed system from old Hollywood), its formulaic products and the power of star actors. Australian colleagues such as Bruce Beresford and Fred Schepisi had already made American films or were just about to, so the resurgence of the Australian film industry had had the inevitable effect of feeding new talent into the Hollywood system. Similarly, British directors such as John Boorman, Ridley Scott, Tony Scott, Adrian Lyne, Roland Joffe and Hugh Hudson had to work in America if they were to continue to direct major films, as the British film industry had more or less disappeared, and in the films they directed, they had brought, or were to bring, fresh eyes to the American scene (Boorman in *Point Blank* (1967), Ridley Scott in *Thelma and Louise* (1991) Hugh Hudson in *Revolution* (1986)). However, that analysis begs the question as to how much those movies were the product of the Hollywood system rather than the work of individual directors. For example, *Point Blank* was a mob flick starring Lee Marvin and both of those factors were major determinations of how the movie turned out. An argument could be made that Boorman's eye for the American city landscape was an essential element in whatever artistic success the movie achieved, but equally to ignore the institutionally and generically determined norms that shaped the movie artefact would be a mistake. For some, the Hollywood system will be perceived as inevitably harmful to the talents of any truly creative and innovative director. The American movies directed by Peter Weir have to be viewed diffferently from his Australian movies (and that includes *The Year of Living Dangerously*) because undoubtedly America provided Weir with a new context for his directing career and several new pressures on his integrity as an artist. Whether he survived as the Peter Weir who had become familiar to us through his pre-*Witness* films or whether he succumbed to a greater or lesser degree to the treadmill of Hollywood is a central question as we move to an analysis of the American films. Weir has never sought to disguise the fact that he wanted to become an international director and that to direct Hollywood films seemed to him to be a natural desire of any aspiring film director.

Synopsis: *The film opens with the funeral rites conducted by the Amish community over the death of the husband of Rachel Lapp (Kelly McGillis). The Amish community portrayed in the movie is supposedly based in Lancaster County, Pennsylvania. Rachel is to continue living on the farm which she now jointly operates with her father-in-law, Eli (Jan Rubes). Rachel has an eight-year-old son, Samuel (Lukas Haas), and together they set out by train for Baltimore, where Rachel's sister is expecting a baby. While waiting for the train at a Philadelphia terminus, Samuel witnesses the murder of an undercover detective in the men's room. John Book (Harrison Ford), the investigating officer, forces Rachel and her son to stay overnight in Philadelphia because Samuel is his only witness. At the police station, Samuel sees the photograph of one of the men who had carried out the murder. This turns out to be McFee (Danny Glover), an officer who has been decorated for his courageous work in the narcotics squad of the Philadelphia police force. Book informs his superior and mentor, Schaeffer (Josef Sommer) of this fact and Schaeffer tells Book that the information should go no further at this stage of the investigation. Later that day, McFee shoots at Book, wounding him, and Book realizes that Schaeffer himself must be part of the cover-up. It turns out that Schaeffer, McFee and other policemen have been involved in the theft and sale of a vast drugs haul and are now protecting themselves from disclosure. Book flees from the city with Rachel and Samuel, knowing that he is now a marked man and that* the cops will not hesitate to kill Samuel as well. They reach Rachel's farm and Book drives away only to collapse at the wheel because of the loss of blood he has suffered from the gunshot wound. The elders of the Amish community and Rachel tend his wound and agree to shelter him because of the danger to Samuel's life. Gradually, Book's wound heals. Samuel becomes fascinated wtih Book's gun and both Eli and Rachel express their disapproval of guns and violence in general. Rachel gives Book her dead husband's clothes to wear and clearly there is a growing attraction between the two of them. When Eli finds them dancing together to soul music, he warns Rachel that there has been gossip among the community about her relationship with Book and that she is in danger of being shunned by the elders. In a similar way, Schaeffer puts pressure on Carter, a colleague of Book's, to tell him where Book is hiding, saying the police force, like the Amish, is a cult, a club with its own rules, rules which Book has broken. Book is gradually drawn into the daily life of the Amish, rising before dawn to milk cows and helping to build a barn for a neighbour, a collective enterprise of the whole community. By this time, Daniel, Rachel's Amish suitor, has become aware of the tension between Book and Rachel and watches the 'English' with brooding suspicion and resentment. Book sees Rachel in a half-naked state and they stare at each other longingly, but he makes no move towards her, explaining the next day that if they had made love, he would have had to stay in the community or she would have had to leave. Book finds out that Schaeffer has had Carter killed. Some local town thugs torment and insult the Amish, including Daniel, on their way back from town. Book is unable to contain himself and beats them up, thereby blowing his cover because the incident is reported to a local cop. When it is clear that Book will be returning to the world he knows, Rachel goes to him and they make love. Schaeffer, McFee and another cop, Fergie, come to the farm heavily armed prepared to kill both Book and Samuel. Book shoots McFee and engineers the fall of a mountain of wheat on to Fergie. Schaeffer takes Rachel hostage, but Samuel rings the bell which brings the elders of the community running to the farm. Book, who has thrown away his gun, screams at Schaeffer, 'It's over. Enough.' Schaeffer realises he cannot shoot all of them and surrenders. The

*police come and the last shot of the film is of Book
driving away from the farm and passing Daniel walking
towards Rachel's house. Daniel, it is implied, is on his
way to claim Rachel, whilst Book and she have realized
that their love cannot bridge the chasm between the two
worlds they inhabit.*

Witness is both a cop thriller and a love story, but
whereas *The Year of Living Dangerously* successfully
merged elements from various genres, *Witness* does not
quite manage to cement its two narrative strands into a
seamless whole. This may be something to do with the
structure of the screenplay. After the flight back to the
Amish community, the film concentrates on the tensions
between the lovers and the community and the thriller
element is sidelined, although attempts are made to
keep that pot boiling with short scenes between
Schaeffer and Carter, Schaeffer and Elaine, Book's
sister, and telephone calls between Book and Carter
and between Book and Schaeffer. The final shoot-out
seems almost detached from what has gone on before
as the audience's attention is suddenly switched back to
the police corruption story and away from the love
affair between Book and Rachel. The extended
showdown between Book and the corrupt cops seems to
be generically determined—thrillers have to have violent
shoot-outs between the representatives of good and
evil. The only concession in *Witness* is that the chief
baddie surrenders when surrounded by the pacifist
Amish. Thus, the expectations of audiences are largely
met, Harrison Ford is able to act like a hero (although
he does win finally with words and not with a gun) and
an action-packed ending is supplied. The brief coda of
Ford leaving Rachel and the encounter with Daniel
rounds the film off on a more downbeat note.
  The Amish community seemingly did not take too
kindly to the film-makers' intrusion into their community
(the film was partly shot in Lancaster County) and
resented the exploitation of their way of life as an
element in a product for mass entertainment. Almost
inevitably, the movie topples over into glossiness in its
representation of the Amish. Although some attempt has
been made at authenticity, everything about the Amish
looks just too clean, pretty and cute. Clearly, Weir and
his collaborators wanted to create a stark contrast
between the supposedly backward community of the

Amish and the symbol of present-day America in the movie, the urban decay of Philadelphia. But there is a sense of imbalance, of tipping the scales, of glossing over difficult issues or ugliness so as to throw into relief the barbarity of modern society as symbolized by the inner city of Philadelphia. The film opens with shots of the Amish walking through the high cornfields. John Seale's photography emphasizes golds and browns, gentle reassuring colours, and Maurice Jarre's music is soothing and melodic. The Amish seem like relics from a vanished agrarian past, a vision of America as it might have been 300 years ago. The Amish talk to each other quietly, they pray together, they eat together and a sense of community is communicated. The wind ripples through the cornfields, the Amish are seen walking against the sunset and the underscoring is resonant.

However, when Rachel and Samuel leave the community on their trip to Baltimore, the film contrasts images of contemporary American life with the simplicity and peace of the Amish community. The horse-and-buggy in which Daniel, Rachel's suitor, drives them to the station, causes a tailback comprising a huge container lorry and a string of cars. Eli, Rachel's father-in-law, warns her to be careful 'among the English'. Rachel and Samuel are excited by their train journey, but Daniel drives the horse-and-buggy parallel to the speeding train in an image that symbolizes the contrast between a simpler past and the technological present. In the railway station in Philadelphia where they have to wait three hours for a connection to Baltimore, Samuel wanders around peering at this strange new world, walking up to an Orthodox Jew because he mistakes him for an Amish. In the city nothing is what it appears to be. Everyone and everything is anonymous. The image of the city as jungle finds its correlative in the brutal murder of the undercover cop in the men's room, the act that makes Samuel the witness of the title. The killing is carried out with ruthless efficiency by McFee/ Glover. He is in no panic and even finds time to calmly wash the blood off his hands. The boy's instinctive terror is brilliantly conveyed by the young actor, Lukas Haas, and by Weir in his staging of the scene. The station is then taken over by the police authorities and there is a telling image of Rachel and Samuel huddled together on the bench while all around them the professionals go about their daily business of cleaning up after another murderous act in this city which seems to breed only alienation and destruction. Book/Ford arrives to take over the investigation and strikes up some kind of relationship with the boy: 'So he was a big guy like me:' 'Big guy,' Samuel replies smilingly. The fatherless boy sees a substitute father figure in the big guy Book and we learn later that Book tries to be a father to his sister Elaine's children and takes a rather judgemental line on her lifestyle.

Book then leads Rachel and Samuel into the lower depths of Philadelphia, as he tries to get leads on the killing. He deals violently with a suspect and Rachel complains that she doesn't want her son 'spending time with a man who carries a gun and goes around whacking people.' 'Whacking' becomes Rachel and Book's word for what he does in the police force and Philadelphia. Elaine, Book's sister, reluctantly agrees to harbour the Amish for the night. Divorced and cynical, Elaine represents an urban contrast to Rachel's rural simplicity and purity. When Rachel prays before eating in a hot dog restaurant, Book is embarrassed and he is irritated when Rachel tells him that Elaine believes he likes policing because he thinks he's right about everything. At the police station, various police officers make clumsy overtures of friendship towards Samuel. A handcuffed criminal scares the boy and then he discovers that cops can be criminals as well, as he picks out McFee's picture and tells Book that he is the killer. Book informs Schaeffer of what the police chief already knows, that McFee had stolen forty-two million dollars' worth of speed (550 gallons of P2P) and that this corruption on the force had led to the killing of the undercover cop. Book may think he knows everything, but he doesn't, because here he is telling the very man who is at the head of the corruption he is trying to expose. And so McFee shoots at Book in an underground car park, a symbol itself of urban alienation, and escapes leaving Book badly wounded. When Book announces that they have to get Samuel out of the city, Rachel says that Book had claimed they'd be safe in Philadelphia. Book has to admit, 'Well, I was wrong.' Book, the policeman who tries to make the city safe for its citizens, finds it is a deadly place for him as well.

These scenes set in Philadelphia, sandwiched between the short opening section of the funeral and the departure from the city by Rachel and Samuel, are among the most urgent of the movie. They represent the most recognizably thriller elements and portray a familiar urban landscape of modern America: people living in fear amidst a sea of corruption, brutality and alienation. The film's use of urban locations is striking: the vast anonymous railway station that helps to emphasize the isolation of the vulnerable Amish mother-and-son, the unlovely men's room as a fitting setting for a sleazy murder, the vulgar and brassy bars where Book goes to establish leads, the busy police station where men and women, cop and criminal, are caught up in a crazy game called law enforcement, Elaine's untidy and cramped apartment and the cheap hot dog café where Book, Rachel and Samuel grab something to eat. The overall impression is one of tawdriness, darkness, desperation and loneliness. If producer Feldman wanted a foreign director to bring a fresh eye to the American scene, then Weir seems to have justified his faith in his representation of the city in these Philadelphia scenes. British directors such as John Boorman in *Point Blank* (1967) and Ridley Scott in *Blade Runner* (1982) had achieved similar effects, so it is by no means an unique achievement and these scenes owe a debt to many a police thriller as well. Weir was working within a tradition of the Hollywood urban and cop thriller where the city is portrayed a a brutal and alienating environment and where those entrusted with protection of the citizens are themselves up to their necks in chicanery and murder, but there is no doubt that the movie works off those traditions of the genre very effectively.

The film now changes direction and location. Book is cared for in the peaceful and rural surroundings of the Amish community. Here, in contrast to the bustling and noisy city, there is peace and safety. The elders talk to one another in gentle tones and they apply healing herbs to Book's gunshot wound. Book gets well under their care and there is a strong sense that his improving physical health symbolizes a healing of his soul as well. In his fever, he clings on to Rachel's hand and their mutual attraction becomes obvious when he is back on his feet, although she still disapproves of his 'whacking' and he makes fun of her puritanical ways, for example, the clothes he is given to wear have no buttons because they are, according to Amish beliefs, unnecessary adornment. The colours of the interior shots are warming and primary and when the action moves outdoors, there is sunlight, the gold of the corn and the space of a rural community, whereas Philadelphia had offered garishness, sombre tones and crampedness.

Thus, Weir is once again dealing with the theme of the clash of cultures, just as he had done in *Last Wave* and *The Year of Living Dangerously*. Although the Amish community is portrayed as narrow and suffocating in its moral proprieties (the threat of shunning that Eli warns Rachel about) and the point is made that it constitutes a closed society demanding loyalty of its members just as the Philadelphia police force does, there is little doubt that the Amish come out of the movie better than the cops. Eli is Rachel's mentor, the guardian of the ordnung, just as Schaeffer is Book's mentor and the guardian of the bonds and unwritten rules that are meant to tie cops to one another, but Eli is a much more sympathetic figure than Schaeffer. Schaeffer is willing to kill repeatedly to protect the gains he has made from his corruption and to be able to continue his respectable way of life. Book, in hiding from Schaeffer, phones him at home and his genteel wife answers the phone and speaks to Book as though this were an ordinary conversation between friends. Schaeffer has a comfortable suburban existence; he is clothed in official respectability and has the outward appearance of the just man who is employed to protect society from crime, yet the reality is that he is living a lie, using his position to pump back into society the poison that he is paid to keep off the streets. So far down the path of evil has he gone that he is willing to have an eight-year-old child killed so that his hypocritical facade might continue to hide the depth of his depravity.

Eli, on the other hand, tends Book's wound, shelters him, shares jokes with him and is what he is. He is not hypocritical like Schaeffer; he accepts the rules of the ordnung and lives by them, thus he is concerned when Rachel seems to be transgressing by her attraction to Book. When Eli lectures Samuel about guns, he puts into words sentiments that are basically sympathetic: 'We believe it is wrong to take human life. That is only for God.' In this scene of Samuel being fascinated by Book's gun, the movie enters into the territory once more of westerns, where the boy is fascinated with the

gun of the professional gunfighter and the mother/
pacifist figure argues that using guns is wrong (the
classic example of this motif is represented in *Shane*
where Alan Ladd as Shane teaches Brandon de Wilde
as Joey to shoot and Jean Arthur as Marion, Joey's
mother, expresses her hatred of guns). Of course, the
Freudian implications of Samuel's fascination with
Book's gun is obvious and it is fairly explicit in Eli's
statement, 'Touch not the unclean thing.' But although
the shunning is threatened and it is clear that Rachel
will not be able to break away from the rigid bonds of
the community, the reality of that kind of repressive
belief system is not explored in depth. The elders are all
too lovably quaint and the Amish are portrayed in
general in such a picturesque manner that no sense of
the oppression, intrinsic in that kind of extreme
puritanism, is conveyed. The Amish community is largely
used as a positive contrast to the horrors of modern
America and any real harshness is glossed over. This
ideological intent on the part of the movie is mainly
signified by the way the scenes in the Amish community
are shot: the soft focus, the use of warm colours, the
creative things the members of the community are
shown doing. John Seale, the director of photography,
uses lighting effects to represent the peace and safety
that the Amish community symbolizes.

Witness strays into western territory repeatedly,
especially in the barn-raising scene. This could be an
episode straight out of a movie about the frontier; the
male members of the community pool their skills to erect
a barn for one of their neighbours, while the women
cook and serve the meals. Maurice Jarre's underscoring
for this sequence has more than an echo of Aaron
Copland's western music (*Rodeo*, *Billy the Kid*,
Appalachian Spring) and the scenes evoke America's
past when the new frontier had to be tamed, when the
pioneers survived because they lived in close-knit
communities and men and women built things for
themselves rather than handing the job over to
professionals. John Book rediscovers his talents as a
carpenter (an interesting sidelight on this sequence is
that Harrison Ford, while he was a struggling actor,
made his living through carpentry). *Witness* also has
resemblances to the 1952 western *High Noon*: in that
movie Gary Cooper plays a retiring sheriff with a
Quaker wife who disapproves of violence; he too

becomes isolated because he resists the bad guys who come gunning for him; he wins through with the active help of his pacifist wife, just as Book triumphs over the forces of evil with the aid of the pacifist Amish community. Present-day America requires 'whacking' of John Book; old America, as symbolized by the Amish community, allows him to build and share in the communal spirit of a closed society that supports and shares. Whereas his old 'club' is out to kill him, his new club is nurturing and welcoming, despite the suspicions about his relationship with Rachel. Daniel and he continually eye each other as rivals for Rachel. At the end of the day, against the golden sunset, the Amish go home singing after the effort of the barn-raising. The contrast with Philadelphia could not be more stark. In the city people compete with one another, they are harsh, unforgiving and frequently psychopathic. Book himself has been shown to be brutal in his dealings with suspects, because that is how his urban surroundings and the police force which employs him have taught him to survive. In the idyllic rural environment of Lancaster County, he can allow himself to show his caring side and co-operate with people rather than harass and judge them.

So, again in a Peter Weir film we have a representation of the effect of an older culture on the main character, just as David Burton in *Last Wave* and Guy Hamilton in *Living Dangerously* had been affected by the Aboriginal and Indonesian cultures respectively or as the young women and Michael had been in *Picnic*. Perhaps Weir had been chosen as director for *Witness* because it had been recognized that he had handled this type of clash of culture theme in his earlier movies. Certainly, it must be one of the reasons Weir felt he could take on this project, remembering that he is a director who only seems to work on movies that mean something personal to him. However, just as the Aborigines had made protests about *Last Wave* and the Muslims about *Living Dangerously*, in making this movie Weir found himself the target of criticism from the Amish community.

It is almost as though the film-makers were over-conscious of the possible intrusion into the closed Amish society and were therefore too intent in representing the Amish in an idealized manner. Their way of life is shown in rather too picturesque a style. It is almost a tourist's view of the Amish, almost like Hollywood representing Scotland in the musical *Brigadoon* (1954) or in many a movie about Ireland. In their desire not to offend, the film-makers stray into sentimentality and prettiness. The puritanical strictures and oppressive *ordnung* of the community are mentioned but are never seen being carried out, whereas the oppression of the cop and city culture are explicitly represented. The layer of gloss on the portrayal of the Amish has to be seen as being in the tradition of Hollywood movies about religious minorities, such as the Quakers in *Friendly Persuasion* (1956) or in many a film about Jewish or Catholic communities. Hollywood's desire is still to avoid offending and *Witness* testifies to that enduring strand in generic products of the American film industry. In seeking not to offend, however, they still manage to offend in one way or another. In this process, it is clearly difficult to define Weir's part, but the tendency towards prettiness that *Picnic* and sections of his other films reflect seems to have been actively encouraged in *Witness* with the results we have already commented on. Thus, a certain weakness of the director may have coalesced with the inclinations of the producer and the studio to produce the glossiness that many people have detected in the Amish sequences in *Witness*. It might be unfair on Hollywood to blame it all on the commercial demands of the business, when there is evidence that Peter Weir himself has been accused of prettification in other films of his.

These commercial exigencies may explain how one crucial scene in the movie is shot, the sequence where Book sees Rachel in a half-naked state and they gaze at each other in thwarted passion. This scene has an eroticism that is missing from Weir's other movies. If the scenes of the girls dressing in *Picnic* can be termed mildly voyeuristic and the love scenes in *Living Dangerously* are almost chaste by contemporary film-making standards, the Ford-McGillis scene has an erotic charge that appears in no other Weir film. Earlier in the movie, there is a charming scene where Ford inveigles McGillis into dancing with him to the record of *What a Wonderful World*. It is a courting scene and if *Witness* resembles a western at times, here in this sequence, it takes on the generic characteristic of a musical where the hero seduces the heroine through dance. In their thirties musicals Fred Astaire always breaks through Ginger Rogers' resistance by getting her to dance with him, just as Gene Kelly would woo and win Cyd Charisse, Vera-Ellen or Leslie Caron in the MGM musicals of the forties and fifties. Here in *Witness* Ford recaptures some of the joy and spontaneity of his youth by dancing to Sam Cooke's soul classic and introducing the puritanical Rachel to the exhilaration of courtship dancing. Eli, in terms of the Amish morality, is right to see the danger of this episode, because the dance is a symbolic love-making between Book and Rachel. Their move towards fulfilling their mutual passion seems thwarted in this scene with biblical echoes when Book/Ford gazes at Rachel's nakedness and she stands there not attempting to cover herself up. But it forces Book the next day to speak about their situation and explain why he did not move towards her. Once it has been established that he will leave the farm, it is only a matter of time before their passion is expressed in love-making. The brief scene of half-nudity denoting frustrated passion undoubtedly would have been a calculated element in the minds of the Hollywood film-makers. Contemporary Hollywood movies almost invariably feature a degree of female, and male, nudity leading to explicit love-making. This scene and subsequent love-making scenes are not very explicit by Hollywood standards, but are more erotic than is usual in movies directed by Weir, so it could be argued that commercial pressures are once again apparent in the style in which these sequences are shot.

Another argument that could be used to bolster the view that *Witness* is a Peter Weir film, despite all the generic and industrial determinations that came to bear on the making of the movie, is the fact that once again we have a hero who goes through a process that could be described as feminization. In his milieu of urban Philadelphia, John Book is macho; he is abrupt in his manner, cynical and brutal in his methods. He is also patriarchal in his attitudes, disapproving of his sister's way of life and trying to take the place of the absent father in his relationship with her children whilst being scared of tying himself down to that kind of commitment in his own emotional life. Badly wounded, he is forced to be vulnerable in the surroundings of the Amish. He looks ridiculous in the clothes of Rachel's dead husband until she alters them for him. His tough-cop city ways are useless when faced with milking cows at four o'clock in the morning and his facility with guns and whacking are redundant in the pacifist community. Although Daniel and he are very wary of each other, there is no question of resolving their rivalry in time-honoured Hollywood fashion by slugging it out, because Daniel shares the Amish's attitude to violence. It is not only Book's sexual nature that becomes involved with Rachel but his emotional side. To show his desire and to give himself in an outpouring of emotional and sexual need is a step forward for John Book. By dancing and singing with Rachel, he recaptures something youthful in himself. By caring for Samuel, Rachel's son, by putting his safety above everything, he is committing himself to caring values that are swamped in Philadelphia where the macho bonds of the cop club are meant to override every other tie. Rachel's values have weakened the hold that machismo has over Book, just as Jill's loving influence over Hamilton/Gibson draws him away from his male, ambition-driven path towards self-destruction in *Living Dangerously*. However, in *Witness*, the feminization can only be seen as partial, because, after all, Harrison Ford is the star and he has to be heroic at some stage, and also the logic of the narrative is that there is an unbridgeable chasm between the worlds of the Amish (Rachel) and of the city (Book). The scene where Book/Ford beats up the local yobs who are taking advantage of the Amish's pacificism encapsulates this split in the hero. The movie invites the audience to side with Ford's intervention when he expertly slugs the yobs who have been humiliating the very masculine Daniel, who is straining at the leash of his pacifist beliefs before Ford takes over. These yobs deserve their bloody noses, the movie implicitly says, and we are invited to feel a sense of relief that at last someone has done something and Harrison Ford has behaved like the Harrison Ford we have grown to recognize in movies such as *Raiders of the Lost Ark* (1981). Thus, Ford is allowed to become feminized to a certain extent, but is yet condoned in exercising his macho skills of whacking. The movie has it both ways because the hero figure can reveal his gentler side and still behave like a hero should, acting tough on behalf of people who can't defend themselves against the bullying actions of unsympathetic types. The irony is that his returning to the whacking ways of his home town blows his cover and his pursuers are able to hunt him down on Rachel's farm.

At this point, the movie seems to remember its generic roots and resort to structures properly belonging to the thriller, or perhaps even the western, as three gunmen, the renegade cops, ride into town. Indeed, the style in which Weir constructs the build-up to the shoot-out, with the men walking three abreast down the hill towards the farm, shotguns clutched in their hands, pays scant attention to realism and makes implicit homage to the ending of *High Noon*, when the three henchmen meet Frank Miller off the train and walk four abreast down the main street of the town where Gary Cooper is sheriff. The resemblances of *Witness* to familiar elements of the western genre are difficult to ignore: the good guy forced to hide out in an isolated community, the relationship with the boy, the simple community celebrations, the hunting down of the fugitive by the bad guys and the extended shoot-out. But then, as has been pointed out already, most Hollywood genres share common characteristics with other genres. It could be argued that *Witness* takes a staple western plot and adapts it to the urban cop thriller. The shoot-out resembles many western gunfights, especially in the barn scene where the bad guys stalk the good guy who is hiding in the loft. Weir is not an action director; after all, he made a war film, *Gallipoli*, which has very few scenes of actual warfare. The shoot-out at the end of *Witness* is quite effectively done, but it is there, one senses, because of audience expectations, or what the producers perceive as audience expectations. The western-style shoot-out could be justified on other grounds if you are prepared to read the representation of the Amish community as symbolic of America's rural and frontier past. In that context, it makes artistic sense to film the final showdown in the style of a western shoot-out because all along the film has seemed to make those implicit connections. The context also allows the chief bad guy, Schaeffer, to surrender to the pacifism of the Amish and the plea of the reborn Book whose 'Enough! Enough!' seems to be not only a plea about the futility of his boss's further resistance but also a more generalized *cri de coeur* about violence in his own professional life. Thus, the film has its cake and eats it. It shows the violence in the time-honoured style of thrillers and westerns and then it shakes its head in disapproval and says enough is enough. In this violent climax, the movie does seem to have been wrested out of Weir's hands and shaped by generic and institutional determinations. The producers and the studio required that kind of conventional action climax and audience expectations of a cop thriller would have been a powerful argument in favour of the kind of sequence that represents the hero victorious over the bad guys. It is very unlikely that Weir, having accepted the assignment in the first place, could have bucked the system enough to dispense with this familiar element of the genre.

However, the downbeat ending of the movie in the form of the brief coda after the shoot-out resembles other closures, or lack of closures, in earlier Weir films. Not even Hollywood could engineer a wholly happy ending out of this love story. For Rachel to leave with Book or Book to stay with Rachel would have strained credulity beyond bursting-point, given the culture chasm between their two worlds. In addition, the movie has implicitly condoned their love-making only when it has become clear that Book is going to leave. For either to change their minds would have been to break that promise. There is a kind of inverse puritanism at work here. If the film had portrayed Rachel leaving her community, then that might have seemed like a comment on the narrowness and oppressive nature of the Amish cult, so Rachel stays and Book returns to Philadelphia. Hollywood money-men reputedly always have one question ready for film-makers when they present a project for backing 'Do they go to bed?' Well, in *Witness* they do, but their love-making is not so disruptive that the woman is forced to run out on the community to which she owes her final loyalties. In a sense, it is another example of the movie having its cake and eating it. Weir's handling of the final scene is sensitive and assured. In long shot, we see Book driving away from the farm, up the incline which the three gunmen had strode on their way to the shoot-out. Daniel is striding down the road, the car slows down, it is not clear whether any words or gestures are exchanged and Daniel continues walking towards his goal, his claiming of Rachel. The music, the upright demeanour of the actor playing Daniel (Alexander Gudonov), the contrast between the purposeful striding figure of the Amish man and the less impressive outline of Book enclosed in the car, all point to the movie's underlining the rightness of this. Daniel represents the frontiersman, the pioneer, the farmer, surrounded by open fields and scorning the machine. Book, the city man, is enclosed in that symbol of the modern age, the car, and he is leaving to go back to the urban jungle. It is clear that the movie sees him as the loser of the two. To a certain extent, this ending goes against audience expectations of action pictures in which the hero has to be seen to be triumphant and to win the girl.

Harrison Ford was a major star by the time he made *Witness* and identified in the public's mind with heroic parts. Both these factors affect the way *Witness* was fashioned. Most Hollywood stars, even in the present day, have to be likeable, not to say lovable, and even when they are represented as enacting less than admirable actions, their essential likeability must come through. That is not to say that basically likeable stars cannot take on parts where they are meant to be disliked by the audience. For example, Michael Douglas played Gordon Gecko, the ruthless bonds dealer, in Oliver Stone's *Wall Street* (1987). There was nothing intrinsically likeable about that character, but the fact that a good guy actor such as Douglas played the role perhaps altered how audiences read the part. Robert De Niro is one of the few major stars who can regularly take on detestable parts (*Taxi Driver* [1976], *Raging Bull* [1980], *Cape Fear* [1991]) and survive at the top. However, it is difficult to imagine Harrison Ford in a psychopathic role. He may send up his screen persona in some of his movies, but essentially he plays the all-round good guy who struggles to be decent in a world that tends to corrupt and dehumanize (*Presumed Innocent* [1990], *Regarding Henry* [1990]). In *Witness* the camera privileges Ford by focusing on him and giving him centrality in the frame, that is, within the screen space. Not only does the camera consistently look at him, he becomes the cynosure of all eyes among the Amish, which is justifiable within the narrative as he is the outsider in the community, but also has the effect of reinforcing the centrality of the star persona. In the exchange of looks between Book/Ford and Rachel/McGillis, it could be argued that there is something like parity between the man and woman in the sense that the woman gazes at the man as much he looks at her. However, in the scene where McGillis is seen washing herself, it is the female star who is naked and, thus, it could also be argued that the movie reinforces stereotypical roles for male and female stars: the woman as a sexual object to be gazed at by the male hero and, through identification, by the male audience. But the movie ensures that Ford is likeable. He strikes up an instant rapport with Samuel, Rachel's son, which the other cops fail to do; he is willing to appear ridiculous in his Amish clothes; he takes control when the town bullies take advantage of the Amish's pacifism and does the job of all Hollywood heroes by standing up for the little guy. He is even seen singing and dancing to a soul classic. In fact, the star is portrayed as an all-round guy whose very faults – abruptness, anger, brutality – not only fade away in his new surroundings but can be recycled to aid the right side when the forces of evil menace Rachel and Samuel. The Hollywood business machine would have perceived *Witness* as a 'Harrison Ford movie'. The necessity to shape the movie around the star persona of Ford is one element that Peter Weir would have had to contend with. In Hollywood wisdom, Ford was where the money was, not only in terms of the huge fee he would have been paid as a star, but also in terms of his marquee value. Marquee value is the amount of extra tickets it is calculated a star name above the title can sell. Ford has immense marquee value and, therefore, according to Hollywood lore, it makes sense to build the movie around him and to make him look good in it.

In directing *Witness* then, was Weir merely an employee director more or less delivering the formulaic product expected by his employers, or was he able to adapt the elements and conventions of the cop thriller to the communication of his own obsessions and vision? There is a kind of Weir signature to the film that identifies it, by comparison with his other movies, as part of his canon. However, it is undeniable that the movie was heavily determined by generic and institutional demands. Had Weir been his own screenwriter or producer, then it is probable that the manner in which Ford is used in the film or how the action sequences are shot would have been different. Commercial considerations probably dictated how the growing passion between the Book and Rachel figures was represented (the use of the Sam Cooke soul classic, the semi-nudity). The generally soft-gloved treatment the

Amish community receives might have been less apparent and some of that Hollywood gloss might have been shed. But then if Weir had written or co-written the screenplay, we would be discussing a different film. The screenwriters fashioned the screenplay within the tradition of the Hollywood thriller, merging that genre with a love story set against the quaint background of the Amish. Impressive and pacy as the Philadelphia sequences are, there is a sense that those qualities are intrinsic in the generic material, which has been crafted by Hollywood professionals, and that, given a certain level of competence in the director, producer, cameraman and actors, those scenes direct themselves and have an in-built generic dynamic which it would take a heavy-handed director to ruin. In this American context, Weir can no more than tinker with the elements and ensure that a level of excellence is achieved; he becomes the foreman of the expert team who have been producing movies like this all their professional lives.

However, when the movie moves away from the urban thriller context, Weir is back in familiar territory and he can put more of a personal stamp on the film. The opening sequences (the funeral, the departure for Baltimore) are recognizably directed by Weir. They may remind us of sequences from *Picnic*, *Gallipoli* or even *Living Dangerously*. However, Hollywood cuteness soon intrudes and production values take over. The Amish have to look picturesque and quaint. Ironically, there is a scene in the picture where tourists surround the Amish when they come to town and we hear these representatives of middle America talk about the Amish as quaint and cute. The movie aims to represent these Americans as patronizing and crass, but unfortunately the movie itself is open to the charges of quaintness and cuteness. In *Last Wave* and *Living Dangerously*, Weir avoided over-sentimentalizing or glamorizing Aboriginal and Indonesian cultures. He had no such control over *Witness* and the representation of Amish life it encompasses.

With all its faults, *Witness* is one of the best thrillers that Hollywood produced during the eighties. It is entertainment and Weir has always claimed to want to entertain his audience more than anything else. But while entertaining them in his earlier films, he had managed to give them something substantial to chew over as well. *Witness* pretends to substance but falls short by a considerable distance. Yet Weir must take some of the credit for the effectiveness of the movie as a thriller and as a love story.

The Mosquito Coast

Witness was released in 1985 and in the following year Weir completed his second American film, *The Mosquito Coast*, which again starred Harrison Ford, had John Seale as its director of photography and Maurice Jarre writing the score. The screenwriter was Paul Schrader, one of the most interesting of the Hollywood writers who had emerged in the seventies. Schrader's screenplay, however, was adapted from a novel by Paul Theroux. The source material for any movie is not always an insignificant factor, as some critics argue. It is true that the film text itself is the sole producer of meaning for us, the spectating subjects, and the original novel from which the movie screenplay was fashioned is a quite distinct artefact, but a comparison between source material and the finished film can surely tell us something about the intentions of the film-makers and, perhaps, the special demands placed on them by the need to create a film for the mass entertainment medium that is the cinema. The film-makers' intentions, it needs to be added, do not dictate the meaning of the film, however. No movie, or any work of art, has one given meaning which it is the job of the critic to winkle out and expound on. How movies are read will depend on the specific subjectivity of the viewer and will be affected by many different factors such as historical

Helen
Mirren,
Harrison
Ford

143

perspective, gender, race, class, belief systems *et alia*. A reading of the movie might well dispense with any notion of intentionality on the part of the makers and concentrate on what the text (the movie itself) actually says, and not what notionally it was intended to say. Nevertheless, the source material can be used to throw light on the intentions of the film-makers and those intentions, as they are interpreted by a close reading of the text, can be employed to show what the film actually says as distinct from what the makers' intentions were.

Synopsis: *According to his son Charlie Fox (River Phoenix) who narrates the movie in voice-over, Allie Fox (Harrison Ford) is an inventor of genius. Employed by a farmer in Georgia to invent a cooling system for asparagus, Allie concentrates on creating an ice-making machine run on kerosene. He builds it as a scale model and calls it Fat Boy. When he presents it to his employer, Polski, he is impressed by its ingenuity but complains that it is not what he had employed Fox to do. This, for Allie, symbolizes America's loss of direction; he complains continually that the country has become a toilet, that it wastes its resources through planned obsolescence, is crime-ridden and addicted to junk of all kinds. This rampant consumerism is made worse for Allie by the fact that much of this junk is Japanese-made. America is also headed for an inevitable nuclear holocaust. Mixing with migrant workers from Central America, who have left the jungle to share the consumer culture that Allie so deplores, gives him the idea of uprooting and taking Fat Boy to the jungle – 'Ice is civilization!' he proclaims. He makes the spontaneous decision to take his family, which consists of Mother (Helen Mirren), Charlie, Jerry (Jadrien Steele) and two eight-year-old girl twins, to Mosquitia in Central America. On the boat trip they meet the Reverend Spellgood and his family, an evangelist from Baltimore with his particular brand of Christianity called 'Jedoof' that he is selling to the indigenous population. There is an instant rivalry between the two men. Allie, although he can outquote Spellgood on the Bible, puts forward his faith in scientific ingenuity and adapting the resources of the world to improve existence, whilst Spellgood peddles a simplistic God-fearing religiosity. Emily, Spellgood's precocious daughter, disturbs Allie's eldest son, Charlie,* by her frank allusions to sex and her general worldliness. Once in Mosquitia, Allie buys a township called Jeronimo. They are ferried down the river by Mr Haddy, who is quickly won over by Allie to his endeavour. Jeronomo turns out to be not much more than a clearing in the jungle with a few dilapidated shacks and poverty-stricken inhabitants. Allie soon galvanizes everyone to work, stating that he is there to be told what to do by the inhabitants; in fact, he delegates and cajoles the natives into planting crops, starting a fish farm, building houses and constructing Fat Boy, the huge ice-making machine. Soon the natives are calling him Fadder and indeed Allie behaves in an extremely patriarchal manner to them and to his own family. At this stage, Charlie, the narrator, is still impressed by his father's genius and power. However, he creates an alternative community, a secret place called the Acre where the children go to do their own thing. Spellgood pays a visit and Allie angrily expels him from the community, although some of the natives are clearly worried by this confrontation with the representative of the Christian religion. Fat Boy successfully produces ice, but soon the inhabitants are taking the ice for granted, so Allie decides to carry a block of ice to a tribe in the jungle. On the journey there, he begins to act autocratically towards his sons and the first crack in their relationship begins to emerge. The tribe are hostile, especially as the ice has melted on the way. There are three white men there, whom Allie wrongly supposes to be prisoners of the tribe. He surreptitiously tells them how to find Jeronimo. The men turn out to be vicious mercenaries, who arrive at Jeronimo and intimidate Allie and his family. Allie decides they must be eliminated; he locks them up in a space at the bottom of Fat Boy, enlisting Charlie's aid in trapping them in the contraption and then lighting the apparatus that will ensure the men will freeze to death. In their panic, they fire their rifles, causing Fat Boy to explode and destroy the whole settlement. The river is polluted with chemicals so it is impossible to stay there. Along with Mr Haddy, the family float on an improvised barge up river to the ocean. On a stretch of beach, Allie announces he is finished with chemicals and that they will build a new natural civilization where they are. However, Mother and the children want to return to America; Allie tells them that America has been destroyed in a nuclear war, the apocalyptic event that he has consistently forecast. Charlie knows that this is a lie and the knowledge that his father has lied makes him lonelier than he has ever felt before in his life. Allie breaks with Mr Haddy, who warns him that if he builds on the beach, the sea will flood them out once the rains come. Allie is extremely unpleasant to Mr Haddy and increasingly autocratic and paranoid in his dealings with his family. The family are washed out to sea on their house, which Allie has constructed to float. Mother and the children want to float downstream to Mr Haddy's, but Allie forces them to go upstream. Jerry, especially, wishes his father dead, a wish that voices Charlie's repressed desire as well. They come across Reverend Spellgood's church and so incensed is Allie with his successful and exploitative brainwashing of the natives that he sets fire to the church. Spellgood shoots him; paralysed from the neck down, Allie is transported by his family towards the open sea. Allie dies and Charlie, in voice-over, tells of his sense of release and his feeling that the world now seems limitless to him.

Paul Theroux, the author of the original novel, *The Mosquito Coast*, has often been likened to Graham Greene as a writer. *Mosquito Coast* has some passing resemblances to Greene's *The Quiet American*. In Greene's novel, Pyle, a naive and blundering young American, tries to shape the politics of Vietnam in the last years of French rule there. Greene portrays Pyle as insensitive and shallow, creating havoc through his blundering initiatives while maintaining the pious air of someone carrying out good works. Something of the same is true of Theroux's charismatic central character, Allie Fox, who comes to Mosquitia to do good and ends up causing the very destruction and pollution that he himself is running away from in America. Fox represents quintessential American virtues: a get-up-and-go energy and initiative, ingenuity, a pioneering spirit allied to a puritan work ethic, but he also represents American arrogance and imperialism when he tries to recreate the American frontier in a Central American jungle with predictably disastrous results. In the novel, Fox is represented as being just as exploitative of the Mosquitians as the deplorable Spellgood with his bogus Jedoof. The novel is also a rite-of-passage story with Charlie, Allie's son, making his way towards adulthood and discovering that he has to 'kill' his father in order to begin to live.

Paul Schrader had written and directed several movies about obsessives before he came to write the screenplay for *Mosquito Coast*. He had created the character of Travis Bickle for Scorsese's *Taxi Driver*– the vigilante Nam veteran who becomes obsessed with the human filth polluting New York. There was also the puritan father played by George C Scott in *Hardcore* (1978) whose daughter disappears into the nightmare world of snuff movies. *Raging Bull* had been a raw account of the life of the boxer Jake LaMotta and *Mishima* (1985) a portrait of the Japanese writer Mishima, who committed hara-kari after the failure of a military *putsch* that he had instigated. It is understandable, then, that Schrader was attracted by Theroux's novel, because in the figure of Allie Fox, there is another obsessive, who symbolizes aspects of the American character, both in its strengths and weaknesses. Allie is a softer obsessive, especially as played by Harrison Ford, than Travis Bickle or Jake LaMotta. In the original novel, Theroux builds a less sympathetic picture of Fox than the movie does. His racism and diatribes about America are less appealing on the page than when they are voiced by Ford. In the novel Allie, the patriarch, is harder on Charlie, challenging him to prove himself in dangerous feats like sitting on a rock as the tide rolls in or climbing the mast shrouds. As in *Witness*, we have the central role of one of Weir's movies fashioned to suit Ford's screen persona. That is not to say that this part does not represent something of a departure from Ford's usual screen persona. Ford is unkempt and angry for most of the movie; he turns his family against him and acts arrogantly and cruelly to almost everyone. However, because Ford is playing him and the camera once more privileges Ford, the spectator is encouraged to view Allie as an amiable eccentric who perhaps goes a mite far in attempting to bring about his vision, rather than as a blundering autocrat who walks over people to get his own way. In terms of the character Theroux portrayed in the novel, Ford represents an error in casting, but we must look at the film as it exists and note how Ford's persona and the performance he is allowed to give by Weir, the director, have the effect of sentimentalizing the character and, to a great extent, letting him off the hook. Good guy stars, however outrageously they are depicted as behaving, finally have to be lovable.

However there is still an ambiguity at the heart of the representation of Allie Fox in the movie that is similar to the ambivalent feelings that Travis Bickle or Yoshima or even LaMotta arouse in earlier Schrader movies. When Travis Bickle wipes out the exploiters of the child prostitute at the end of *Taxi Driver*, the movie stirs up ambivalent emotions in most spectators. You cannot approve of De Niro's actions because he has been portrayed as a repressed psychopath, a social time bomb just waiting to explode, but, simultaneously, the pimps, especially the character played by Harvey Keitel, have been portrayed as so loathsome that the brutal blood bath in which they are killed by Bickle/De Niro seems almost justified. After all, the avenging angel has exterminated these people in order to save the twelve-year-old Iris from a life of exploitation and degradation. The ironic coda to the movie depicts Bickle/De Niro as having been feted as a folk hero for protecting the girl and having her restored to her despairing parents. The sophisticated young woman whom Bickle had courted and who had rejected him makes it clear that she is now interested in him. The movie's ambivalence about these violent actions is communicated to the spectator. In the same way, but in a less extreme manner, Allie Fox is allowed to voice the disillusionment and prejudices of many Americans in his diatribes about what America has become. It is represented in a half-comic style, but perhaps, the sub-text states, there is more than a little truth to it, despite the racism that runs through some of his diatribes and the extreme isolation and alienation that the character seems to stand for.

Charlie's voice-over tells us that he believed that the world belonged to his father and that everything he said was true, so we are meant to perceive Fox's attacks on the ills of present-day America through the boy's eyes. At the same time, the film-makers must have been aware that much of what Fox says would have struck a chord with many Americans. 'Look around you, Charlie, this place is a toilet. How did America get this way?' says Allie. He makes a direct comparison with the ideals with which America had been built in the first place: 'Land of promise, land of opportunity . . . give us the wretched refuse of your teeming shores.' Now Allie claims it is a case of, 'Have a coke, watch TV. Go on Welfare. Get free money. Turn to crime. Crime pays in this country.' Allie, in other words, is voicing many of the sentiments that most of middle America would agree with: 'This country is going to the dogs. Nobody cares. I just work here, that's the attitude. Buy junk, sell junk, eat junk.' When he goes in to a DIY store to buy a strip of rubber seal, he is offered some that has been made in Japan: 'Who are you working for? The Japanese? I don't want my hard-earned dollars converted into yen.' The notion that the Japanese are taking over American business has hardened since this movie was made. Hollywood itself has fallen victim to the predatoriness of huge Japanese electronic firms. Allie's diatribe about the wasteful, junk culture of modern America might strike a bell even with those of a liberal persuasion except that it is linked with racist attitudes. He refers to the migrant workers as savages and says that they are part of the problem that America is facing. His views also are to be seen in the context of a philosophy of extreme individualism, where significant change can only be brought about by the actions of those who strike out on a lone path and who are natural leaders. Allie says that no one ever thinks of leaving America except himself and that he is 'the last man'. When he does make the decision to leave America for Mosquitia, the references that are brought to mind are those of the hardy pioneers who left the shores of Europe to found a new civilization across the Atlantic and also the families who went west on wagon trains to civilize the west. The irony is that Allie is seen as eccentric in modern America and has to leave the country in order to find his frontier to tame. All the frontiers have been used up in modern America and the pioneering spirit is hopelessly outdated as everyone indulges in over-consumption. The toilet that is America is also headed for a nuclear holocaust. So Allie has more than a passing resemblance to Schrader's Travis Bickle who wanted to wash away all the scum and the refuse off the New York streets, or to George C Scott's avenging father as he tracks down the monsters who had used his daughter in snuff movies. Allie Fox is another of Schrader's puritans imbued with the work ethic and with Manichean notions of right and wrong, good and evil. Schrader's speciality is in looking at the contradictions and ambiguities at the core of American puritanism and

Fox is another figure through which he explores this obsession.

The repellent Reverend Spellgood is another debased representative of the puritan ethic, who uses evangelical Christianity to enslave the superstitious natives of Mosquitia. Allie instantly recognizes Spellgood as an enemy. After all, Allie plays God himself; his creation, Fat Boy, almost looks human and he talks about its entrails and kidneys as though it were a person. Fox has taken too literally the notion of himself as a creator; he sets himself up as a rival to God because He had left the world incomplete. True invention was a matter of 'things being revealed'; it was man's job to understand how the world worked, to tinker with it and to finish it. Charlie's voice-over tells us why Allie hated missionaries like Spellgood so much: 'They taught people to put up with their earthly burdens. For Father, there were no burdens that could not be fitted with a set of wheels or runners.' Spellgood, excellently played by André Gregory, is indeed nauseating with his denim-clothed, Blue Jeans Bibles, his false *bonhomie* and the overweening arrogance that he is right. Allie hates Spellgood partly because he sees too much of himself in the evangelist. In a sense these characters represent two forms of American imperialism which are opposed to one another, one representing American technological know-how, albeit of a rather eccentric kind, and the other, evangelical imperialism with its desire to profit from, and enslave, the unsophisticated natives of Mosquitia. In the end, for all Allie's good intentions, his influence is even more destructive than Spellgood's and just as exploitative. Like Pyle in *The Quiet American*, he blunders into an alien culture and tries to import Yankee notions of accomplishing things, thereby bringing mayhem to the very people he is trying to help.

The clash of cultures, represented by the intrusion of American technological know-how via Allie Fox and fundamentalist evangelism via Spellgood into the jungle of Mosquitia, is a theme that Weir had handled in previous films, so he must have found the overt subject-matter of *Mosquito Coast* palatable. Although most of the action takes place in Mosquitia (actually shot in Belize in Central America), the film encapsulates a view of America in the eighties, not only through the early scenes set in Rome, Georgia, but also through the words and actions of Allie Fox who has escaped from the States because he feels himself an outsider in his own country. Weir once more brings an outsider's perspective to the American scene, albeit a perspective largely created for him by Schrader's screenplay, which in its turn leant heavily on Theroux's original novel. One of the difficulties of the film is the question of how much it endorses Allie's views. Is he to be seen as an obsessive crank or as someone who has something relevant to say about modern-day America? After all, it is Harrison Ford who is saying it and everybody likes Harrison Ford. In one scene, Allie/Ford tells how he had not been able to watch his own mother dying and how people had criticized him for being callous. 'I loved her too much to watch her die,' he says and then he makes a direct comparison between this incident in his life and his attitude to America: 'No one loves America more than I do, you know. That's why we left because we couldn't bear to watch.' For Allie, America is dying and he can no longer bear the pain of watching while it sinks under a pile of consumerist junk and Japanese yen imperialism. But it is made clear that his bitterness is born of deep love of his country. He is not indifferent and oppositional just for the sake of opposition as some 'commie wimps' might be. It is because this country he loves has lost contact with its ideals, its new world opportunities, that he has to leave. When he sees Jeronimo for the first time, after his initial disappointment he describes it as perfect because they can build it up from scratch, just as the Pilgrim Fathers had to do way back in the seventeenth century. In Allie's mind, America is already a ruined country and what they are doing in the jungle is rebuilding a civilization from a smoking ruin. Allie is so single-minded in his mission to bring American know-how to the inhabitants, that he is blind to the reality of what is happening. He is as much a missionary as Spellgood, and is just as exploitative. He says to the natives that he is there for them to tell him what they want, then he proceeds to tell them what they should do.

Under the guise of equal partnership, he practises at best a benevolent paternalism, which soon turns to dictatorship, certainly in relation to his own family. He brings the puritan work ethic to bear on the people of the jungle: 'Work and more work', never questioning whether this is the right thing for them. If Spellgood enslaves the natives through superstition, Allie smothers them with paternalism and a pioneering philosophy imbued with the conviction that things can only get better through the application of scientific thought and sheer hard work. When Spellgood comes to visit Jeronimo, the pioneering motif is reinforced by the style in which Weir shoots the scene. The confrontation between Allie and Spellgood is filmed like a shoot-out between hero and villain in a western. A low-angle shot picks out Allie's hand fingering his axe hanging at his side, just as a gunman would have felt for his holster. Charlie feels the need to break away from this pioneering settlement ('just the way America might have been') and have his own private place, the Acre, which he tells the others not to tell Allie about. Charlie's rites of passage necessarily require him to break with the Law of the Father and the Acre is a step on that path for him. The family come together, however, for Thanksgiving ('Our first Thanksgiving in the New World') and this further reinforces the idea of starting over and creating a new civilization.

The gigantic ice-making machine, Fat Boy, is the crucial element in bringing American civilization to the jungle. Allie as God creates Fat Boy just as Frankenstein created the Creature. It becomes a temple of science, just as Spellgood's church has become a temple of religion. However, when Fat Boy successfully produces ice, Allie proclaims, 'This is no miracle, this is thermo-dynamics!' The indigenous population start taking his ice for granted and Allie's decision to take some ice to a remote Indian tribe is prompted by his need to encounter 'pure people who would see his ice and be amazed'. Already then, disillusionment is setting in; the inhabitants of Mosquitia are becoming like Americans, taking things for granted and wasting resources. If the scene where the people have fun pushing ice blocks down the chute echoes a scene in Kazan's *East of Eden* (1955) when Raymond Massey and his sons celebrate his seemingly successful experiment in refrigeration, so may the sequence in which Allie and his sons trek through the jungle only to find that the ice has melted by the time they get to the tribe. In *East of Eden*, Massey's early refrigeration business is ruined when a fall on the railroad track holds up the train with the frozen vegetables on board, causing the ice to melt. Similarly, in *Mosquito Coast* the ice has melted by the time they reach the tribe. Allie finds that some of the tribe speak

English and that they have seen white men before. His quest for a pure people is doomed to failure. His obsessive attempt to create an unspoilt civilization is also doomed as is implied when the mercenaries invade Jeronimo and begin to menace this new world.

Already Allie's new civilization is losing adherents to his mortal enemy, Spellgood. When he returns from the interior, he finds that several members of the tribe have deserted and gone over to the other side. Ironically, Allie has realized that the tribe had taken him for a missionary. Allie is continually confusing in his mind illusion and reality. He thought the mercenaries were prisoners of the Indians; this misunderstanding on his part arises from his delusion that what he is doing in the jungle is creating a new America, much as the early settlers in the States had done. When it is obvious that the men are criminals and determined to exploit Jeronimo in various ways, including the possible rape of his wife, Allie tells Charlie, 'No one who has the slightest spark has to endure a moment's oppression in this world!' His solution is to employ the methods of the mythical wild west and eliminate the bad guys. Charlie, though he is clearly disturbed by his father's decision and his own part in carrying it out, helps to trap the men in Fat Boy. Allie explains his actions by likening the murder of the men to killing insects: he kills an insect and says, 'That's not his blood. That's my blood.' So to protect what he has created, Allie murders. His actions can be fairly described as fascistic: the powerful must eliminate their enemies and the ends justify the means. However, because the mercenaries are represented as being such unredeemed wretches (there are racist overtones in the 'bandido' manner in which these roles are played) and because it is Harrison Ford carrying out their extermination, the audience are implicitly encouraged to think this action is acceptable. There is a tension between the actions of the Allie Fox figure in the narrative and the star persona of Ford and indeed the style in which the actor plays the part. Ford is never quite able to suggest the darker side of Fox, a side that the original novel brings out quite explicitly and which is there in the Schrader screenplay. Therefore, the impact of his extremism and the implications of his obsessive individualism and paternalism are never fully represented. Yes, he does go *too* far, the film seems to say, and he is *too* obsessive, but basically he is a good guy, because after all, this is Harrison Ford.

When Fat Boy explodes, destroying Jeronimo and polluting the river, Allie has brought about in miniature what he had forecast America would suffer: a nuclear holocaust. In his mind America has been destroyed, because Jeronimo symbolizes America as he would like it to be. He tells his family that they cannot go back to the States because there has been a blinding flash, a cataclysm that has brought about the ending of that world. Millions of Americans had been burnt to a crisp. 'No, that was Jeronimo,' says Mother holding on to reality. Charlie also clings on to reality: 'I knew Father had lied to me about America being blown up. That lie made me feel lonelier than I'd ever felt before.' Charlie has broken free of the Law of the Father. He sees that his father is imperfect and that he has to strike out for his own personal freedom, but such is the depth of his love that the road to freedom will be a hard one, filled with guilt and a sense of betrayal. Allie's defeat over Jeronimo only makes him more inflexible. He refuses to consider returning home: 'In the end Robinson Crusoe went back home but we were staying.' His decision to build a natural settlement on the sea shore, he sees as a pioneering effort. He wants to return to the past completely and give up all chemicals. He treats Mr Haddy with contempt and refers to him as a savage, giving him his Omega watch as compensation for losing his boat in the explosion. 'Anyone without vision has no place here,' Allie pronounces in a manner that tells his family, and us, the audience, that he is now totally paranoid and isolated in his thinking.

'Dead things go downstream, Mother. Life is upstream,' says Allie in his God-like way, his way of explaining his decision to head their floating home away from the safety offered by Haddy to share his home with them. When Allie has to dive into the river to unfix the anchor and does not reappear for several minutes, the boys think he has been drowned and instantly shout, 'Let's go to Mr Haddy's.' Even Mother betrays Allie, as he recognizes when he surfaces and shouts 'Traitors!' His paranoia is now rampant, the ultimate symptom of the obsessive visionary and the isolate. But his paranoia, as many persecution complexes have, has a basis in fact. His sons are thinking dark things about him. Charlie's voice-over tells us this: 'I imagined what it would be like to stick a knife in him.' Jerry, the younger son, voices what Charlie only allows himself to think. Allie justifies his actions in the manner of all selfish nuts by explaining he's doing all this for us. When they sail round the bend of the river and see Spellgood's evangelist settlement, Allie calls it a 'Christian concentration camp'. The awfulness of contemporary American evangelism is represented by Spellgood on a video recording telling the passive population, including Mrs Keniwick (Butterfly McQueen) who had fled from Jeronimo to the dubious safety of Jedoof, that prayer was as simple as making a telephone call. Spellgood's success is the ultimate insult to Allie; he has brought Mosquitia American civilization in the form of pioneering get-up-and-go know-how and he has failed; Spellgood has brought a Blue Jeans Bible and a packaged product called Jedoof and the people seem to want what the evangelist is selling rather than the prospect of building a new world from a smoking ruin. Emily, Spellgood's precocious and cynical teenage daughter, tells the family that America is intact, which confirms their father's lie for Charlie and Jerry. When Allie sets fire to Spellgood's church, the family, even the loyal wife and mother, decide to abandon him to his paranoiac delusions, but the evangelist, raving about communists, shoots Allie. The last sequence of the movie shows Allie, mortally wounded, being cared for by Mother and his children. Allie has achieved a kind of peace and speaks of the 'faulty world' he has tried to improve on. 'The human body is a bad design. Nature is crooked. I wanted right angles, straight lines.' But his attempt to improve on God's creation has failed. His spirit is indomitable, however. 'We're still going up river, Mother,' he says just before dying. Charlie's voice-over explains his mixture of sadness and hope: 'Once I had believed in Father and the world had seemed small and old. Now he was gone and I wasn't afraid to love him any more. and the world seemed limitless.' The last shot of the film is an overhead long shot of the 'boat' heading towards the open sea, the limitless world that Charlie has talked about.

Once more, then, Weir, in directing *Mosquito Coast*, is handling large themes. However, the film is very much an adventure story, an adult version of *Swiss Family Robinson* or *Robinson Crusoe*. Like *Witness*, its cinematic reference is often the western; the Fox family travel by boat to Mosquitia to open up the frontier just as in western movies the family travel west in a covered wagon to find their Eden in the wilderness. Where in the western the endeavour is to convert the desert into garden, wilderness into civilization, in *Mosquito Coast* their goal is to transform the jungle into a pioneer settlement, a version of the America that could have been and which will never be possible given the degradation (in Allie's eyes) that the country has fallen into. Thus, the film is hooking into some central American myths about the pioneering spirit and how early Americans risked all to tame the wilderness with their ingenuity and indomitable spirit. *Mosquito Coast* implicitly challenges these myths by representing Allie Fox's pioneering venture as an allegory for what really happened in the past when the American frontier was there to be opened. Just as the early settlers and pioneers moving west had exploited the native Americans, so Allie and Spellgood come to Mosquitia to exploit the native Mosquitians.

If we are encouraged to look with more favour on Allie's well-meaning endeavours, there is no denying that he brings chaos into their lives. Despite his protestations that he is doing it for them, it is clear that he is working out some obsession of his own: he wants power over nature and people. As America encroached on native American territory, the official apologists of the government, the army and big business, as represented, say, by the railroad companies, claimed that the Indian would benefit from the march of progress. That hypocrisy is similar to Spellgood's stance as he profits from the Mosquitians' superstition and builds himself a business in the jungle. Allie's goal is not monetary gain, but, in some ways, it is more sinister: sway over the lives of the people and god-like powers of creation. Despite Fox's humour and despite Ford's likeable quality as an actor, Allie is close to being a fascist who believes in the right of the superman to take control and boss lesser creatures around. When his control is threatened, he resorts to violence and terror, by exterminating the mercenaries and by terrorizing his family.

The film offers not only a discourse on America's imperialist past, but also on its imperialist present. It was made in the mid-eighties when an American invasion of Nicaragua was being contemplated by the

Reagan administration, which also supported the fascist dictatorship in El Salvador and actually did invade Grenada. The movie, of course, never directly confronts issues like those, but by implication it says something about American excursions into what it considers its own backyard. *Mosquito Coast*, representing Americans invading a fictional Central American republic as it does, must be interpreted in the context of the historical circumstances in which it was made. There is a critique implicit in the movie of that type of American arrogance that assumes that it has a superior civilization it can export to neighbouring countries, which are, according to this analysis, crying out for the benefits of a free enterprise, consumer culture.

Imperialism and the effects of it had been a thematic concern in at least three earlier Weir films: *Picnic at Hanging Rock*, *The Last Wave* and *Gallipoli*. In *Picnic* the imperialism consists of the cultural imperialism of Britain, in *Last Wave* it is the imperialism of the white Australian towards the native Aborigines and in *Gallipoli* it is the military imperialism of the mother country, willing to sacrifice Australian youth to defend the British Empire. So yet again, Weir found himself representing a form of cultural and economic imperialism in a movie he directed. This theme is, in a sense, handed to him by Theroux via Schrader, but it can hardly be an accident that Weir found himself directing a movie that dealt with, however obliquely, a central concern of his other movies.

The movie is also a rites-of-passage tale just as, in a certain light, *Picnic* and *Gallipoli* had been. Charlie Fox is the figure through whose eyes and words we are told the story of Allie and his *Swiss Family Robinson* adventures in Mosquitia. Charlie has to grow up in the course of this adventure and shed the blinkers he wears because of his father's domination. He has to learn what all sons have to learn, that his father is a flawed human being, that he does not know everything and that only when he frees himself from his father's Law will he be able to grow and see the world as his oyster. He is an adolescent who is unsure of his manliness and that is why he reacts so strongly to this father's taunts: 'Pull yourself together. Be a man.' In Freudian terms, Charlie is going through an Oedipal conflict and that conflict is all the more disturbing because he has hitherto loved his father and seen him as almost a God. When the image is smashed, his father's fall from grace is all the more dramatic and earth-shaking, hence Charlie's loneliness that he feels when he knows Allie is lying about America being destroyed by a nuclear holocaust. Charlie's wish, the death of his father, leaves him feeling forlorn and guilty but alive to the new possibilities of a world that is not defined by his father's word. Thus, in representing on film Charlie's journey towards adulthood, Weir is touching on thematic territory that he had already dealt with in *Picnic* (the Appleyard College girls and Michael) and in *Gallipoli* (Archy and Frank's explorations and adventures as they strike out on their own in the world).

Gender issues are raised in *Mosquito Coast*, as they had been in previous Weir films. Involved in the rites-of-passage theme is, of course, the question of what it is to be a man. Allie seems to be in no doubt. Being a man involves being a totally independent individual. A man is free, he can control his own life and make decisions to change his destiny. Thus, he makes an almost instant decision to turn his back on America and go to Mosquitia. He takes the decision for the family as the patriarch and there seems no attempt on his part to consult Mother or the children. Indeed, he tells Mother to leave everything behind her, including the unwashed dishes, which to her smacks of liberation. But in Allie's world, the gender roles are fixed. He makes the decisions and has the world-view. He invents things and makes the money on which the family live. He views any questioning or resistance as betrayal. We see him building and repairing machines, constructing the home and ordering the work force, including his own family, around. Mother is seen cooking, sewing and tending to the sick, the traditional female roles. We never learn the character's name; she is called by the generic Mother, which in itself defines her role under this patriarchy. Allie constantly tells his sons to be men, not to give into softness or whining. He is amiable to the children, mostly jocular, but he is not a father to whom they can turn if they have to shed tears and show weakness. Allie represents aspects of a patriarchy and a model of masculinity that are repressive and harsh. As Allie feels more cornered, his patriarchal, male side becomes more dictatorial and his feminine side, which expresses itself in his sense of fun, is lost. He cannot see that what he is doing is leading his children into destruction. Mother can see it and finally has to make the crucial decision to save her children by abandoning Allie. Only Allie's being shot by Spellgood prevents their escape from the prison of patriarchal domination. The male characteristics of isolation and shutting down on emotion, of obsessive work and emphasis on achieving, have led Allie into a kind of madness where he is blind to the effects on himself and those closest to him of his increasingly arbitrary decisions. Helen Mirren as Mother does not have many opportunities in the movie. Mother is represented as passive and accepting, until she finally decides to make the break. Even then, she has to revert to being a nurse to the dying Allie. Although there is an implicit critique of an extreme masculinity in the movie, the feminine values of caring and sharing are not represented strongly enough, partly because the figure of Mother is such an under-emphasized role in the narrative. This almost certainly has to do with the need to create a star role for Ford. Helen Mirren is a distinguished actress, but she hasn't carved out a significant film career, and, in Hollywood movies, the star status of the leading players does affect how the narrative privileges the characters. Once again, as in *Witness*, the film foregrounds the Ford character played by the major star of the movie, at the expense of all the other characters.

Finally, is *Mosquito Coast* a Hollywood product, skilfully put together by an expert team of creative personnel and directed by a craftsman, journeyman director, Peter Weir, or does it bear the recognizable signature of Weir to such an extent that we can talk about it as being 'his' movie? Undoubtedly, Weir had to contend with certain limitations imposed by the nature of the project: he was employed as a director to work on someone else's script. The script was written by one of Hollywood's most talented writers, Paul Schrader, who himself was adapting the work of a prestigious novelist, Paul Theroux. In a sense, then, Weir was coming to the material at two steps removed from the initial creative act: Theroux to Schrader to Weir. But I think *Mosquito Coast is* recognizably a Peter Weir film, although it would be a nonsense to claim that it is *only* that. Some of the weaknesses of the film, for example, are part of a pattern that has emerged in his work in general: the tendency to prettify and to the picturesque. There is very little sense in the movie of the steaminess and discomfort that life in a Central American jungle would entail. There is a certain inevitable touch of gloss in how the Fox family adapt to their jungle surroundings. It is all rather too beautiful and clean. Their unkemptness has a chicness and cuteness that belie their primitive surroundings. This is jungle à la Hollywood; going native means stars can look chicly dishevelled, almost as though Ford were at home in Beverly Hills on his day off and he had decided to paint the kitchen. At times, the film does indeed come close to being an adult version of *Swiss Family Robinson*, when what was needed was the representation of the effort it would have taken to transform a jungle clearing into the kind of civilization that Allie envisioned. The portrayal of the Mosquitians also tends to the patronizing. They are seen dancing and singing with Spellgood and the Foxes when they arrive in Mosquitia; generally, they come over as rather simple and easy-going, prey for the manipulations of both Allie and Spellgood. Another weakness has already been mentioned: the casting of Ford and the consequent, almost inevitable, softening of the main protagonist. If someone with a harder edge had been cast, say, De Niro, George C Scott or Anthony Hopkins, then the reality of Fox's selfish obsessions would have been communicated with more force. The need to make Ford the central figure in the narrative also unbalances the movie, so that Charlie's journey towards adulthood is overshadowed and the woman's perspective is almost entirely ignored.

However, *Mosquito Coast*, with all its faults, is still an unusual Hollywood film. It tries to balance the generic demands of telling a family adventure story with an attempt to address the big questions that I have tried to analyse in this chapter. At times Weir achieves a lyrical quality in scenes like the boat travelling up the river to the accompaniment of an evocative Jarre score. There is also a scene where two Mosquitians in a small boat pass by the huge, newly-constructed Fat Boy in the darkness of night and as they gaze up at it in awe, we share their view of the construction as some kind of mysterious, religious symbol. Allie, for all his anti-religious aggressiveness, erects temples which the natives see as symbols of the unknown rather than of things being revealed. Weir is on familiar territory here: Fat Boy is the equivalent of Hanging Rock, the underground caves in *Last Wave* or the Pyramids in

Gallipoli. Weir also elicits powerful performances from the young people in his cast, particularly River Phoenix as Charlie and Jadrien Steele as Jerry. The movie moves, so that the pace of the narrative is maintained, the restlessness of the *mise-en-scène* seeming to be a metaphor for Allie's ceaseless energies. However, once again Weir creates an elegiac, downbeat ending, with Allie's death and Charlie's words of closure on the soundtrack. The death of the father heralds a new beginning for Charlie and his family, so the audience can leave the cinema in a hopeful frame of mind, despite having witnessed the death of the star. In the original novel, Allie's end is considerably more horrific; he crawls on to a beach and is killed by scavenging vultures. In the movie, they opted for the final showdown between Spellgood and Allie, as in a western, with the bad guy winning the shoot-out and losing the sympathy stakes. Allie is allowed to become human again in his death scene, returning to the kindly patriarch figure that he has been intermittently through the course of the movie.

Thus, Weir emerges with credit from his second bout with the Hollywood machine. He had helped to create a work of entertainment which, despite its glossiness, had managed to engage with several large thematic concerns and say something of political significance in the context of its time. His next American movie would once again present him with a charismatic central character, a story set in an almost exclusively male milieu and with another major Hollywood star in the leading role.

Dead Poets Society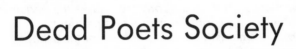

'My girls are the crème de la crème . . .'
(Maggie Smith as Jean Brodie in the movie *The Prime of Miss Jean Brodie*)

Put the light where the money is.
    (Hollywood studio instruction to lighting cameramen)

With *Dead Poets Society*, Weir was returning to a setting similar to that featured in his first big success, *Picnic at Hanging Rock* – an oppressive educational establishment, this time an all-boys' academy in Vermont, New England (although the film was actually shot at the St Andrew's School in Middleton, Delaware). Just as Appleyard College in *Picnic* had been represented as an arm of British cultural imperialism, so Welton Academy seems to ape British public schools, although the particular cultural influence is represented as being specifically Scottish and Calvinist. Weir was once again working on someone else's original script (by Tom Schulman), but the themes and plot of *Dead Poets Society* are so reminiscent of *Picnic* that Weir must have been the first director the producers, Touchstone Pictures in association with Silver Screen Partners IV, would have thought of to make the movie. For Weir, the material gave him the chance to rework recurring thematic concerns and the only question for him in accepting the assignment must have been whether it was too close to subject-matter that he had already mined in *Picnic*. A bonus would have been that he would be working with another major star of the contemporary American cinema, Robin Williams.

Sean Leonard, Robin Williams

Synopsis: *The time, 1959. The setting, the beginning of the school year at Welton Academy in New England.*

163

Welton Academy is an expensive private boys' school which sees its main task as preparing its pupils for Ivy League colleges. It is a very traditional school believing in the four pillars of Religion, Honour, Discipline, Excellence. At the ceremony that marks the beginning of a new school year, the academy's headmaster, Mr Nolan, reminds pupils and parents of the school's excellent 100-year record. He also introduces a new master, John Keating (Robin Williams), who was himself an honours graduate of the academy and has been teaching for six years at a private school in London. New boy Todd Anderson is a shy, introverted young man, whose brother had been a Merit Scholar at the academy. Nolan and Todd's father remind Todd of his obligation to live up to that standard. Todd is sharing a room with Neil Perry, whose stern father also has high expectations of him. He forces Neil to give up his deputy-editorship of the Annual, the college magazine, so that he can concentrate on getting the qualifications he needs for medical school. Todd meets Neil's friends—Charlie Dalton, also known as Slick, Knox Overstreet, Richard Cameron and Steven Meek. He takes some ribbing from them about being the brother of a valedictorian, but he finds it difficult to accept their offers of friendship, mainly channelled through Neil. We see the very traditional teaching methods of the college being put into practice by Hager, a severe trigonometry teacher, and McAllister, a cynical Classics master. Then Keating takes his new students to the hallway where photographs of old pupils are displayed and he asks them to consider the fact that these former Welton students are all dead now; had any of them regretted that they had not 'seized the day'? 'Carpe diem' becomes Keating's watchword and his unconventional teaching methods capture the boys' imagination, although Cameron, the most conservative of the group, worries whether Keating will give them a test on what he has said. Knox is invited to dinner at the Danburys, (friends of his lawyer father); there he meets Chris, who is the girlfriend of the football-playing son of the family. Knox falls in love with Chris and his attempt to woo her becomes the goal of his application of Keating's 'carpe diem' philosophy. For Neil, seizing the day means pursuing his interest in acting against his father's wishes. He gets the part of Puck in a local production of A Midsummer Night's Dream. Keating also teaches the *class poetry in an unconventional manner. Checking up on Keating's record as a pupil, the boys discover he was a founder member of the* Dead Poets Society; *they ask him about it and he tells them that it was a society that used to meet at the old Indian cave; it was dedicated to sucking 'the marrow out of life' and to reading the great poets. Neil makes the suggestion that the group resurrect the Dead Poets Society and meet at the old Indian cave. There, late at night, they enjoy reading poetry and releasing some of the inhibitions that Welton forces on them. Keating continues to teach unorthodoxly, quoting from Walt Whitman liberally. Each of Neil's group seems to be influenced by the* carpe diem *philosophy: Todd finds his voice in one of Keating's classes, Knox asks Chris out, Charlie expresses himself through playing the sax, calling himself Niwanda and proving his prowess with local girls, two of whom he invites to a meeting of the society. Meek and Pitts make a radio that can receive Radio Free America with its rock 'n' music (radios are banned at Welton). Charlie takes his rebellion a step further by having an article printed in the* Annual *demanding that girls be admitted to Welton and then, when Nolan is telling the school what a disgrace the article is, having a phone ring and announcing that it is God calling and that he supports admitting girls. Charlie is beaten by Nolan. Neil's father finds out about his part in the play and forbids him to go any further with it. Neil defies him and is a major success in the play, watched by Keating and his friends; Neil's father arrives halfway through and is furious; afterwards he orders Keating to stay away from his son. He takes Neil home and tells him he is leaving Welton to go to military academy and that he must forget about acting. That night, dressed in his Puck costume, Neil shoots himself with his father's gun. An enquiry is held at the school and soon it becomes clear that Nolan wants to make Keating a scapegoat. He is accused of both encouraging Neil to pursue acting against his father's explicit wishes and the boys to set up the Dead Poets Society. One by one, the boys are brought into Nolan's office where the combined pressures of the headmaster, their parents and the threat of expulsion force them to sign a statement that blames Keating for what has occurred. Keating is dismissed. In the final scene, Nolan takes over Keating's class and is in the middle of teaching poetry in the* traditional Welton manner when Keating comes to collect his personal things. As he is about to leave, Todd calls him 'O captain, my captain', which Keating had encouraged them to do when he first started teaching them. Todd explains that they had all been forced to sign the document. Nolan tries to silence him, but Todd climbs on his desk, another symbol of Keating's influence, because he had once asked the boys to climb up on their desks in class to get a new perspective on things. One by one the rest of the boys climb on their desks as a gesture of support to Keating and as a symbol that his encouragement of them to find their own way has borne fruit. Only Cameron of the 'Neil group' holds out. Keating's last words as he leaves the school forever are 'Thank you, boys.'

The historical context of the narrative of *Dead Poets Society* is important to an understanding of the movie. The action takes place at the end of 1959, a decade during which America had gone through an era of repressive conformity. Anti-communist hysteria had led to the McCarthyite witchhunts, which had legitimized the persecution of thousands of liberals and radicals in government, academic and artistic circles. The House Un-American Activities Committee (HUAC) had investigated so-called communist infiltration into Hollywood movies, leading to the blacklisting of many Hollywood artists. Government employees and teachers had had to prove their loyalty to 'Americanism' if they were to keep their jobs. Although the McCarthyite threat waned by the mid-fifties, Eisenhower's Presidency continued till 1960, symbolizing the dullness, materialism, philistinism and puritanism of corporate America. However, during the late fifties, the cauldron of protest was beginning to bubble with the civil rights movement, feminism and the dissatisfaction of youth coming to the fore. Rock'n'roll symbolized a new strain of rebellion in popular music and Hollywood found rebellious young stars such as James Dean and Paul Newman to typify the new mood of restlessness. Then Kennedy was elected and talk of a now frontier was in the air. The rebellions of the sixties were underway.

The group of students that initiate the resurrection of the Dead Poets Society in the movie are poised by the end of the movie to be the student rebels of the sixties. Their catalyst is John Keating/Robin Williams, who, if not actively encouraging them to rebel, certainly enjoins them to find their own voice and not to march in step with the masses. His voice is a plea for non-conformity, for spontaneity, for the poetic and the spiritual. His first lesson emphasizes his belief in seizing the pleasures life has to offer and in going for what you want. Each individual has to follow his dreams. When the cynical McAllister questions whether you can make artists out of the boys, Keating corrects him and says, 'We're not talking artists, George, we're talking free thinkers.' Keating is continually quoting Walt Whitman, the oracular American poet, and in the same conversation with McAllister he throws in a quote that sounds like it might be from Whitman, but which turns out to be his own:

'Only in their dreams can men be truly free. It is always thus and always thus it will be.' Unlike David Burton in *Last Wave*, the adults in *Picnic*, or Guy in *Living Dangerously*, Keating, it is implied, has not lost touch with his dreams and what drives him to teach is his desire to put his students in touch with their own alternative reality. Thus, when Neil Perry dreams of being an actor, Keating actively encourages him to explore that side of himself, whilst advising him to clear it with his father first. Todd, the inarticulate youngster living in the shadow of his illustrious brother, has to be encouraged to find his own voice. Keating helps him in various ways, but particularly in the scene where he has Todd out in front of the class after he (Keating) has written a line from Whitman on the blackboard: 'I sound my barbaric YAWP over the rooftops of the world.' He has Todd sounding his YAWP and the blocked words pour out of him. 'There's a barbarian in you, after all,' says Keating to Todd. Weir's revolving camera captures the heady exhilaration that Todd feels when, with Keating's encouragement, the words that were stuck flow out of him. The movie then cuts to Keating on the touchlines shouting encouragement to the boys playing soccer, to the accompaniment of Beethoven's *Ode to Joy* from the final movement of the Ninth Symphony. Keating's credo, then, is to release the joy, the imagination, the poetry, the sensuality and spirituality of the students.

In opposition to this are the ambience and traditions of Welton Academy itself. These are very effectively represented in the opening sequences of the movie. The movie starts with the camera focusing on an idealized painting of Welton past students, then pans into a shot of a young boy having his tie straightened; a photo is taken of two brothers in school uniform. A candle is lit and one of the older teachers instructs an old retainer of the school about what he must do during the ensuing candle ceremony in the assembly hall. These instructions are communicated in half-whispers which add to the solemnity of the occasion. We see older students carrying banners in the procession that is about to enter the hall: Knox is carrying the banner with the word 'Discipline' on it and Cameron the 'Tradition' banner, which, in the light of his function in the narrative, is quite significant. A piper leads the procession into the hall; the tune is *Scotland the Brave*.

Nolan, the headmaster, announces, 'Ladies and gentlemen, the light of knowledge' and the flunkey lights one candle, passes it to a boy, who then lights the candle of the boy next to him, thereby signifying how knowledge is passed on. Nolan speaks of the four pillars that make Welton 'the best preparatory school in the United States: Religion, Honour, Discipline, Excellence'. When Neil and his group congregate in Neil's room later, they, with characteristic adolescent cynicism, designate the four pillars as 'Travesty, Horror, Decadence, Excrement.' However, such shows of rebellion have to be contained within their tight little group because they are thoroughly dominated by the culture of the academy, as enforced by Nolan, Hager, McAllister and the rest of the masters, with the active support of their fathers. Both Neil Perry and Todd Anderson, in particular, are represented as suffering under the Law of the Father. Neil, especially, has to do what he is told and when he mildly questions his father's decision that he should give up his deputy editorship of the *Annual*, his father takes him outside and tells him never to dispute with him in public again. He then screws him down with some emotional blackmail about how much it means to his wife and him that Neil gets to Harvard and how much they are sacrificing to send him to such an expensive school. Welton Academy represents patriarchal order and power; the fathers are intent on making sure that their sons imbibe its macho, competitive lessons and come out as men fit to take their place in the Ivy League colleges, which will then in turn train them to be highly-qualified, highly-paid and highly-competitive professionals of one kind or another, America's upper-middle-class elite workers. The struggle of Neil, Todd, Knox, Charlie, Meek and Pitts involves them in recognizing that there is more to being a man than discipline and obeying a code of honour. *Dead Poets Society* thus deals with recurring Weir themes of what it is to be a man, and the harmful effects of society's institutions.

By this stage in his career, Robin Williams had established a screen persona of caring non-conformity in movies such as *The World According to Garp* (1982) and *Good Morning Vietnam* (1987). After the latter movie, he had become a major star and undoubtedly his taking on of the role of Keating affects how we read the movie. Williams as a performer would find it almost impossible to risk being disliked by an audience. His trademark is a lovable eccentricity and John Keating must have appeared a natural role for him to play. It is a part that the audience ostensibly cannot fail to sympathize with and the movie works hard to erase any reasons for audiences withholding their approval of the character. Williams, the star, is allowed to do his imitations of Marlon Brando, John Wayne, effete English Shakespearian actors and sundry other funny voices in a performance guaranteed to emphasize his talents. The script also provides safety nets for the character in case the audience might have some lingering doubts about his motives. For example, it is stressed how heterosexual Keating is. After all, here he is teaching in a boys' school and provoking deep loyalties and love from his young charges, so any charge of latent homosexuality must be dealt with by stressing his interest in women. Thus, Keating makes frequent references to the joys of wooing women and in one scene when Neil comes to visit him in his room, Keating is shown gazing at the photo of his girlfriend in London whilst writing her a letter. When Neil asks how he can stand being away from her and teaching at Welton, Keating replies that he is there because he loves teaching. To make it seem that Keating is not recklessly encouraging his boys to risk their futures, when Charlie Dalton deliberately lands himself in trouble with 'the telephone call from God' escapade, Keating is shown telling him that he must be cautious because a wise man knows when to take risks and when not to.

But despite the film's endeavours to whitewash the

character of Keating, the name of another fictional teacher, Jean Brodie, keeps coming to mind. In many ways, Keating is a more benevolent, male version of Miss Jean Brodie, the heroine of Muriel Spark's novel and the film starring Maggie Smith as Brodie. Brodie was a character who represented the kind of teacher who, timid in her own life, lived vicariously through her pupils by encouraging them to live exciting, dangerous lives, acting out Brodie's own fantasies, with disastrous results for several of them, including the death of one girl who foolishly tries to join her brother in the Spanish Civil War. Keating is continually telling his boys to 'suck the marrow out of life' and to 'gather ye rosebuds while ye may'. He quotes Whitman's lines 'that the powerful play goes on and you may contribute a verse' and asks the boys, 'What will your verse be?' Keating's own version of 'carpe diem', his adding his own verse to the powerful play, has hardly smacked of daring and adventure. Having been an honours student at Welton, he has returned to his old school to teach, after teaching in London for a number of years. Hardly the stuff of Whitmanesque grandeur or dreams. As Keating is represented in the movie, he seems to have taken a soft option by choosing to return to his old school to teach away his life.

In every movie he stars in Robin Williams gives a variation of his standard performance—ingratiating, child-like antics that tells us he has to be loved—and as Keating, Williams gives us a man who constantly behaves theatrically, a man who acts from the first moment he appears in the classroom to the last shot of him leaving the school. Keating is the star of his own drama that he presents to the boys every day, in and out of the classroom. To compensate for the dullness of his life a a schoolmaster at an expensive prep school, he sets himself up as an oracle, but a second hand oracle because his quotes about living life to the full come from Thoreau and Whitman. As represented in the movie, Keating is a self-conscious, theatrical young man who is desperate to make an impression on his charges and to make them love him. He does indeed manipulate their emotions and tries to shape the boys like putty. Something is represented in the movie that is, indeed, very close to Robin Williams working an audience either in a theatre, on television or in a film. This side of Keating is what gives the movie some depth. If you accept the Keating figure as he is presented transparently in the narrative – the inspirational, unconventional and passionate teacher who shows the boys the 'less travell'd by' path – the movie becomes a representation of a straight battle between the goodies and the baddies, the forces of spontaneity and imagination against the forces of regimentation and patriarchal power. However, if you read the character of Keating in a less approving way, then ambiguities open up and the movie gains a layer of complexity that it at first does not seem to have. An irony is then implicit: Keating can be a phony and a manipulator, a man who has shut himself away from life but who enjoins his pupils to act out their dreams as compensation for his limited existence, a male Jean Brodie, and yet also he can be seen as a benevolent influence on them. Indeed, if the figure of Keating presages the rebellions and the indulgences of the sixties, then he also encapsulates much of the phoniness and pretentiousness of that decade as well as some of the genuinely progressive and liberating aspects of the time. In the sixties, one can imagine Keating cheering from the sidelines as youth rebelled, supporting sexual freedom while now chastely married to his girlfriend and quietly working his way towards that headmastership or academic post he is destined to fill, while students battered at the doors of the Democratic Convention in 1968.

Let us trace how the movie sets out to represent Keating as this charismatic figure who is to transform the lives of the group of boys who set up the Dead Poets Society. Before we see Keating in his classroom, we are presented with a montage of classroom scenes each signifying that the teaching methods at Welton are tedious and based on rote learning: we hear the chemistry master droning on, the trig teacher talking about penalties for late prep and the Classics man (McAllister) having the boys decline in unison the Latin word *agricola*. Then, by contrast, we have Keating entering the classroom from his preparation room; he is humming the *1812 Overture* and walks right through, disappears out of the room for a second, then pops his head back in and says, 'Well, come on' to the amazed boys. This is a man who knows the value of an unexpected entrance and exit, a teacher who has calculated the effect of his every gesture and word. In

171

other words, Keating is a theatrical fellow and the theatricality continues in the hallway of the school when he announces they can get his attention by addressing him 'O captain, my captain', which comes from a Whitman poem about Abraham Lincoln. The boys, then, it seems, are to see Keating as a Lincoln-type figure. However, to offset any sense of false grandeur, he tells them of his youth when he was an intellectual lightweight and copies of Byron were kicked in his face. He asks one of them to read Shakespeare's sonnet 'Gather ye rosebuds while ye may' and launches into an explanation of his 'carpe diem' philosophy. 'We are food for worms . . . peruse some faces from the past . . . not much different from you, are they? These boys are now fertilizing daffodils . . . you hear them whispering Carpe diem, carpe diem.' And Keating lowers his voice to a stage whisper as the boys stare at the photographs of past students and are enthralled by the performance of this strange master. 'Make your lives extraordinary,' exhorts Keating. The movie fails to draw attention to the obvious fact that Keating has not taken his own advice because there he is, a schoolmaster in this very traditional boarding school in New England, living a quite unextraordinary life. The only occasion when this issue is raised is during the scene when Neil visits Keating in his room and says, 'You can go anywhere, do anything, how can you stand being here?' and Keating gives his, 'I love teaching' explanation. Teaching is very often (but, of course, not always) the bolt-hole for people who are scared of the world and who feel themselves incapable of doing anything else other than teaching; the enclosed world of private boarding schools is even more of a safe escape from reality than state day schools are. Keating has made it even safer for himself by returning to the very prep school that had prepared him for college education. But the movie is ostensibly not interested in drawing attention to such contradictions. It is too intent on setting up Keating as a life force.

The next scenes show Knox falling in love with Chris at the Danburys. Mr Danbury, the friend of Knox's father, says, 'I know where you're headed. Like father, like son,' meaning Knox is destined to become a banker like his father. But Knox is filled with feelings of romantic love and later he acts out his love à la Keating when he tracks down Chris at her school and, in front of her classmates, reads out a love poem that he has written about her. Poetry is the next lesson we see Keating teaching. He asks one boy to read from the standard poetry textbook by Mr Evans-Pritchard, but then stops him, calling Evans-Pritchard and his approach 'excrement'. He tells the boys to rip out the pages, which they joyfully do, although Cameron takes a ruler and carefully detaches his pages and only because he has been ordered to do it by a teacher. Keating is against armies of academics measuring poetry. The boys, he says, will learn to think for themselves, or, at least, as John Keating thinks, an against-the-grain interpretation might suggest. 'We read and write poetry because we're members of the human race and the human race is full of passion,' he says ringingly. 'Poetry, beauty, romance, love—these are what we stay alive for.' But poetry and literature in general are not passion, nor romance nor love; it is the representation of these and Keating seems to fall into the old trap of living through words, and other people's words at that; love and passion seem to be ideas that are transmitted through great writers but are not lived by Keating himself. If Evans-Pritchard's critical approach is to measure literature on a graph, Keating's seems to present literature as a substitute for living. No wonder he says, 'Words and ideas can change the world'; that is the consolation of many an academic and teacher who watch life from the sidelines.

When the boys decide to resurrect the Dead Poets Society, Keating leaves a copy of verse in Neil's desk. On the title page there is this inscription: 'I went to the woods because I wished to live deliberately. I wanted to live deep and suck the marrow out of life. To put to rout all that was not life. And not, when I came to die, discover that I had not lived!' Indeed, this is the Keating credo put into words by Walt Whitman. And so the boys go to the old Indian cave and conduct meetings of the Society. Once more, then, in a Weir film, white males find inspiration and solace in the surroundings of a past civilization. There, in the Indian cave, the boys revert to a variety of primitivism. Weir shows his skill in representing mystery and other-worldliness in the sequence in which he shoots the boys escaping to the cave on that first night: in the mist, these figures clothed in black duffle coats and carrying torches that pierce the darkness, run towards the horizon, with Jarre's score underlining the almost mystical nature of their quest. This scene is reminiscent of the style used in filming the girls at Hanging Rock and something of the same air of mystery is produced. The scenes in the cave itself where the boys read poetry aloud and tell horror stories are less convincing, indeed they seem rather straining for effect. When they dance round in a circle to drumbeats whilst intoning a jazz poem, the film seems to be heavy-handedly pointing to the effect the Indian cave is having on them. Similarly, when Charlie demands that he be called Niwanda and paints an Indian fertility symbol on his chest whilst applying warpaint to his face, the movie seems to be in danger of overstating its case.

The movie's cultural references consistently underline the Keating world view. When he takes the boys for soccer coaching, he has each of them read a line of poetry before practising kicking the ball. Beethoven's Ninth underscores the boys winning a game and, of course, Neil's path to freedom is represented as taking the part of Puck in Shakespeare's *A Midsummer Night's Dream*. If Keating acts out his life in front of his audience of pupils, his main protégé also chooses acting as the way he will find himself. Keating imitates life and passion; his is a show of seizing life by the throat and gathering rosebuds. Williams' performance as Keating exactly catches the putting on of a show that is at the heart of what the character stands for: not so much living life, but the imitation of life through poetry, drama and literature. The life experience at second hand, love and passion through the eyes of poets. The passion in Keating's life is safely thousands of miles away. And so when the movie identifies its definitive victim figure, that is, a victim of patriarchal attitudes and the forces of reaction, it alights on the boy who seeks his freedom through imitating life in drama and who acts out his dreams not in reality but in a make-believe world created by one of the greatest dramatists the world has ever seen. The rebellion is once again realized in terms of art and artifice, just as the Dead Poets Society represents rebellion through poetry and a romanticization of primitive cultures. Charlie Dalton plays the sax, wears a beret and is clearly going through his existentialist phase; Neil Perry wears the garland of Puck and hopes to lose himself in the world of theatre, pretending he is someone else. If the rebels of the sixties could be divided into those with a strong political orientation and those that favoured change through altering consciousness via drugs, art and therapy, then the boys of the Dead Poets Society would certainly be destined to belong to the latter. The issues at stake are thoroughly depoliticized; the class, race and gender issues that might have been addressed in the movie are largely ignored. These are white, privileged, upper-middle-class males rebelling against the rule of the patriarch. Young WASPS who, with the encouragement of an unconventional teacher (by Welton's standards), kick over the traces to a degree. The girls who are represented in the narrative are shown to be the passive object of male fantasy (Chris) or rather dumb creatures who do not understand the higher things in life (the two girls who visit them in the cave). Certainly, in terms of gender issues, the movie can be interpreted as rather regressive. It is the silence, the things left unsaid, the issues not addressed, that give the film finally a rather hollow ring.

However, having said that, *Dead Poets Society* undoubtedly manipulates emotion in an expert and seductive way. The final scene, when Keating returns to his classroom, now taken over by the movie's ogre, Nolan, and the boys rebel against the patriarchal order by showing their love for Keating, is very difficult to watch without feeling strong emotions. Weir's *mise-en-scène* effectively works up to this stirring, tearful climax. At the beginning of the sequence, the victory of Nolan seems complete. The boys are cowed and when Nolan asks Todd what page they have reached in the Evans-Pritchard textbook, Todd cannot even stammer out a reply. He has lost the voice he had seemed to find under Keating's tutelage. It is Cameron, the traitor, who tells Nolan pages have been ripped out and that they seemed to have skipped the 'realists.' Cameron is the first member of the Dead Poets Society to sign the document incriminating Keating; it is Cameron who advises the rest to save their skins. Keating seems as impotent as his former charges when he timidly asks Nolan whether he can collect his things. Only when he is about to leave the room does Todd find the courage and the voice to blurt out that they had been frightened into sending him down the river. He then stands on his desk and acknowledges Keating's leadership in the words, 'O captain, my captain.' The music swells to an almost militaristic triumphalism (there are bagpipes in there somewhere) and, one by one, the boys of the Dead Poets Society climb on their desks while Nolan threatens them impotently. Even the sickly mother's boy who has been shown to be ill and timid throughout the movie finds enough temerity to climb on his desk. Hawkins, a macho young man who had presented 'the cat sat on the mat' as his poetic creation when Keating asked them to write a poem, joins in the rebellion. And Keating beams back at them approvingly. At this point, it is clear that Keating is no longer a mere teacher, but a guru, the status that, consciously or unconsciously, the movie has been endeavouring to grant to the character from the start. Only the fink Cameron stays seated, but he has been represented as much less likeable than any of the other main schoolboy characters. The movie is suggesting that Keating may have lost this particular battle, but he has won the long-term war for the souls of these boys. As they grow into manhood, they will follow the path trodden by Keating rather than Nolan. How they can do that and still be the bankers, lawyers, doctors and engineers they are clearly destined to be is an issue the movie does not address.

Dead Poets Society has the most defined closure of any Weir film. It is the most triumphal in tone, the least ambivalent. It is deliberately and consciously manipulative of the audience's emotions and, thus, it is pure Hollywood. How the spectator reacts to it depends entirely on how willing you are to have your emotions manipulated. It depends partly on how much you have been stitched into the narrative and, through a process of identification, empathize with the characters. In traditional Hollywood style, the movie endeavours to sweep you along with the emotion it so consciously manufactures. Whatever my reservations about the essential shallowness of the movie, I have to admit to finding the final sequence hard to resist.

One of the more interesting aspects of the movie is how it finds a parallel to the McCarthyite persecutions of the fifties in what happens to the boys near the end. When Neil Perry shoots himself, Nolan and Mr Perry want a scapegoat. Implicitly, the movie suggests they cannot face up to their part in Neil's suicide—their repressive, patriarchal attitudes that forced Neil to abandon his dreams and his poetic, spiritual side. Thus, Keating has to be blamed and to pin it on Keating, they need to pressurize and terrify the boys. The ultimate threat is expulsion and all that that means for their futures. Nolan enlists the help of their parents and, one by one, pressure is exerted on them to sign the document that accuses Keating of the blatant misuse of his position as teacher. This is exactly what happened to the unfriendly witnesses who appeared in front of HUAC in 1947 and the early fifties. Charged with communist sympathies in their pasts, the witnesses could buy themselves immunity and save their professional lives by naming names: telling the Committee the names of people whom they had known during their communist acitivities. If witnesses proved reluctant, they were threatened with being charged with contempt of Congress, prison sentences or loss of career. Many succumbed to this pressure, especially in Hollywood itself. The movie is honest enough not to show the boys being able to resist the pressure of Nolan and their parents. Charlie Dalton refuses and he is expelled, but he is from a rich family and has been trying to get himself expelled anyway. Dalton makes his expulsion certain when he hits Cameron after the latter returns from the inquisition and almost exults in the fact that he has co-operated with Nolan. 'There's something called an honour code in this school,' he explains. 'When a master asks you a question, you're supposed to tell the truth.' Honour, in McCarthy's time, was patriotism and Americanism and anyone who did not co-operate with the Committee was automatically assumed to be un-American and plotting the overthrow of the American Constitution. 'If you guys are smart, you'll do exactly what I did and co-operate,' Cameron advises. 'Let Keating fry. Why ruin our lives? You can't save Keating, but you can save yourselves.' This was exactly the argument put to people squirming in front of the McCarthyite persecutors. Todd, over whose soul the main battle of the movie had been fought, resists for a few minutes, then the movie cuts away from the scene as though it cannot bear to represent the capitulation of the boy whom Keating has helped to find himself. Weir orchestrates these scenes of inquisition and betrayal very effectively and the movie acquires more status as a relevant social document from the representation of the McCarthyite goings-on than from all the windy rhetoric of Keating with his self-conscious quotations from Thoreau and Whitman.

Weir's *mise-en-scène* also creates some telling

images. The bells chime in the tower and the birds clustering at dusk over the open fields break and scatter; there is a cut to a revolving shot taken at the foot of the stair well in the academy showing the boys pushing their way up and down the stairs. The juxtaposition of shots makes the point: the birds in the open countryside, the boys cooped up in the prison of the school. When Knox makes his decision to woo Chris, he has a joyful bike ride over the fields surrounding the academy. He is howling like a savage in sheer exhilaration and excitement. There is a long shot of a lone piper in Highland dress playing by the lake that is still enshrouded in mist. Mr Perry has been portrayed as an unfeeling autocrat throughout the movie, but when he discovers his son's body, Weir films him in slow, slow motion and with a distorted howl of anguish issuing from him as he lunges towards the body. Then we see the distraught parents cradling the dead body of their son in their arms. Weir creates powerful images of loss in this sequence and it is all the more effective because the character represented as experiencing the anguish is a figure in the narrative that we as spectators have been encouraged to dislike.

Keating, the main protagonist in *Dead Poets Society*, offers his charges a vision of an alternative reality. He has a vision of an alternative reality himself, but seems content to preach it rather than live it. But because he has his dreams and an alternative vision, this connects him with other Weir protagonists. Of all the movies directed by Weir, *Dead Poets Society* features the most charismatic and supposedly unambivalent central character. John Book and Allie Fox had their faults, but John Keating as played by Robin Williams approaches saintly status. In the scene where Neil Perry kills himself, he dons the hat made out of long twigs that he has worn as Puck in *A Midsummer Night's Dream*, but it has clear associations with Christ's crown of thorns. Neil Perry is crucified in Keating's place. Keating performs the function in the narrative of being the life force in opposition to the deadening power of the patriarchal system represented by Nolan, Mr Perry and the other hardline fathers and masters. That he is represented in such a saintly way has undoubtedly something to do with Robin Williams' penchant for playing wise fools, endearing clowns and visionaries with a key to wisdom that escapes lesser mortals. Weir almost certainly had to work within the limitations set by this imperative to present the star in this charismatic and almost holy light. None of his other heroes have had that kind of uncomplicated goodness. In making this Hollywood movie, Weir probably had to contend once more with star egotism and persona. Williams was where the money was and the star had to be made to look good at all costs. Williams, in his movies, has to be made to look good and be lovable in different ways from Harrison Ford. The pressure to create this star role for Williams does weaken the movie. If Weir had had more control over the project, he might well have made Keating less cute and self-consciously charming. Williams gives an indulgent performance, one that draws attention to itself constantly. But despite this, Weir sustains interest and sympathy, once more managing to elicit powerful performances from the younger members of his cast. The pacing of the film is skilful, as Weir allows his camera to dwell on the beauty of the Delaware countryside or records the daily routine of Welton Academy. Colours that stay with you after seeing the movie are the warm browns of autumn and the crisp snowy whites of winter. He stages the dramatic climaxes of the movie expertly (Neil's suicide, the inquisitions by Nolan and the final classroom scene), but there is a certain lack of conviction about some of the scenes in the Indian cave and in Knox's wooing of Chris that edges the movie perilously close to a standard Hollywood picture of adolescent life. When it sentimentalizes the young people, the movie is at its most Hollywood.

Dead Poets Society certainly handles large themes: individual freedom versus conformity, the need for spontaneity in life, the relevance of our dreams to the reality we create for ourselves. But it suffers from a Hollywood pretentiousness, a self-conscious seriousness, that has been a flaw in other Weir films. Yet it is an entertaining and moving film that does at least make you think about important issues. Too often Hollywood movies of the eighties were empty; they were about nothing except sensation and spectacle. *Dead Poets Society* goes straight to the audience's tear-ducts. It is quite blatant in its attempted manipulation of the sympathies of the spectator. It is the kind of movie that almost affects you against your will because you are aware of the manipulative process that you are being subjected to, but it is done so effectively that you give in to the emotions; later you begin to analyse what the movie has been selling. *Dead Poets Society* is a well-crafted exercise in Hollywood emotionalism. How you react to it finally depends on your resistance to a film-making style that seeks to immerse you in the emotions of the figures in the narrative. If you resist totally, then the movie may well seem a rather superficial exercise in creating a portrait of a so-called charismatic central character. If you succumb to its blandishments, then the movie provides a powerful emotional experience.

Green Card

For them, Green Card *was a very risky project, even though its budget of $12 million was carefully kept down . . . getting a green card work permit is not relevant to most American lives.*

(Peter Weir)[1]

'All your ideas are from the same place.'

(Georges in *Green Card*)

If John Keating represented a life force in *Dead Poets Society*, then certainly the same can be said about Georges Fauré (Gérard Depardieu) in Weir's next film, *Green Card*. Indeed, *Mosquito Coast, Dead Poets Society* and *Green Card* all have a charismatic male figure at the core of the narrative, a force representing non-conformity and spontaneity, imagination and vision. Each of them acts upon the other people in the story and changes their lives dramatically with, in *Mosquito* and *Dead Poets*, ostensibly disastrous results, although it is implied that the long-term consequences will be beneficial. In all the films Weir has directed, some figure or event intrudes into the main characters' lives and forces them to re-examine in a fundamental way their beliefs and way of life. It is not accidental that three out of the first four Hollywood films Weir directed has a strong central male role. It is a function of the star system in the American film industry that such roles be found for leading male stars. In *Witness*, the focus is certainly on John Book/Harrison Ford, but, although he intrudes into the Amish community and disrupts it, he does not change their lives; it is his life and attitudes that may have been changed by the end of the movie. In *Green Card*, we have Weir once again dealing with the themes of clash of cultures, spontaneity in opposition to

Gérard
Depardieu,
Andie
MacDowell

control and order, civilization versus primitivism.

In *Green Card*, Weir was directing his own original screenplay. In addition, he was his own producer in an Australia-France co-production for Touchstone Pictures. On this movie Weir was no journeyman director working on some other writer's script or toiling for some dominating producer. Having set up the project himself and having found the financial backing for it, he had more control over this movie than on any of the other three American films he had made. In essence, then, he was in a perfect position for a director: working on his own script, acting as his own producer and having put together the whole project with international finance for a Hollywood independent. If Weir is ever to be considered as an *auteur*, then *Green Card* would have to be used in evidence.

Synopsis: *Bronte Parrish (Andie MacDowell) works for the New York City Parks Department as a horticulturist. She desperately wants to rent a particular smart apartment because of the splendid greenhouse attached to it. Georges Fauré (Gérard Depardieu) is a Frenchman who wants to acquire a green card in order to gain residency. This he can do by marrying an American citizen. Anton, a mutual friend, brings Georges and Bronte together for the purpose of a show marriage, which will give both of them what they want: Georges, a green card, and Bronte, the apartment with the greenhouse, because the trustees of the apartment block will only rent to couples. They meet for the first time on the day of the wedding, marry and then part, apparently forever, with the idea that a formal divorce will be sought later. Some time after, Bronte encounters Georges in a restaurant, where she has gone with her friend, Phil, and another colleague from the Green Guerrillas, a volunteer group which reclaims derelict sites of the city for gardens for the poor. Bronte gets a call from Mr Borsky of the Immigration Department informing her that he and a colleague would like to call in and check the validity of their marriage. Bronte returns to the restaurant to find Georges, but he has been sacked by the owner who refers to him as trouble. However, she manages to get a message to him and they meet the officials together. They concoct a story that Georges has been in Africa 'shooting' elephants with a camera and that he is a composer for the ballet.*

He raises doubts in Borsky's mind, however, when he does not know where the bathroom is in the apartment. They have to face another interview at the Immigration Department's office on the next Monday; Bronte decides that Georges will have to move in for the weekend so that they can learn enough about one another to convince the officials that they are genuinely married. They immediately begin to come into conflict: he smokes, she hates it; he is a meat-eater, she is a vegetarian; she believes in doing good, he believes nothing ever changes in the city whatever is done to ameliorate it. They meet Bronte's smart friend, Lauren (Bebe Neuwirth), in the supermarket; Georges invites her back for lunch, which he cooks. Lauren invites both of them that evening to her parents for a dinner party. Bronte decides to go because Lauren's mother has some rare plants and trees in her conservatory that she hopes will be passed on to the Green Guerrillas when they (Lauren's parents) sell the apartment. Lauren turns up late at the party with Georges. After dinner, the artistic guests listen to music, and Georges, who has announced he is a composer, is asked to play the piano. He attacks the piano in a thundering modernistic style, which convinces some of the guests he is a composer. Then he plays the piano gently and creates a spontaneous poem about trees which seems to persuade Lauren's mother to give the Guerrillas the legacy. Georges and Bronte begin to open up to each other after the dinner: he tells of his criminal youth and she talks of her genteel; literary background. They are obviously attracted to one another, but they sleep separately. They have fun taking polaroid snaps of their supposed life together and then Bronte's parents unexpectedly pay a visit. Georges pretends he is a visiting handyman, though Bronte's father realizes he is not. Bronte goes out with Phil in the evening; when he is forcing his attentions on Bronte, Georges rises from his bed and orders the vegetarian out of the apartment, announcing that he is Bronte's husband. Bronte is furious and throws Georges out of the flat. He sleeps in the hallway and is allowed back in the next morning. They have to go to the Immigration Department for their interview. They both manage well and as they talk about one another in separate rooms, it is obvious there is real love there. Georges makes a slip, however, that tells the officials that the marriage is a put-up job. They separate after the hearing. Georges sends her the manuscript of a piece of music with a note saying he would like to say a last goodbye. They arrange to meet at the café where they had first been introduced to one another, but when Bronte sees Georges, he is with two immigration officials. Georges has to leave the country immediately and if he does, Bronte will not be able to keep the apartment. Bronte says she doesn't care about the greenhouse. They kiss, Bronte puts back on the wedding ring she had had for the ceremony and Georges promises he will write every day and each letter will say, 'When are you going to come?'

Green Card is from the generic stable of Hollywood romantic comedy. Structurally, romantic comedies usually have a man and a woman meeting cute, getting to know one another, subsequently falling out through misunderstandings caused by gender issues and differences of personality, and then finally coming together in marriage or the promise of marriage. The Tracy-Hepburn comedies of the forties and fifties often pitted husband against wife, but basically the structure was the same, whilst the Doris Day-Rock Hudson comedies of the late fifties and early sixties usually had Hudson chasing Day with lascivious intent. However, the movie that is specifically brought to mind by *Green Card* is *The Clock*, directed by Vincente Minnelli in 1944. The action of both movies takes place over a few days and is set in New York. Indeed, in both movies New York itself becomes a character in the narrative. In *The Clock*, Robert Walker plays a GI on a weekend's leave in New York; he meets Judy Garland in Pennsylvania Station and gradually they fall in love and decide to get married. All sorts of impediments are put in their way before they can achieve their goal and then they have to part when the soldier's leave ends. In *The Clock* Garland and Walker conquer New York and discover it to be a helpful and friendly place; in *Green Card*, New York separates the pair of lovers and the promise is that Bronte will join Georges in France. Weir's New York is a much less benevolent city than the New York of *The Clock*, where City Hall officials, cops, milkmen, strangers on buses and in restaurants all help to bring the lovers together. No such generosity affects the immigration officials in *Green Card*, indeed no one wishes them well throughout the whole movie. The stranger in town, Georges, is variously sacked, suspected and then ejected.

The first sequence of *Green Card* shows (in an overhead shot) drumsticks beating a drum. It is a street scene with an African-American youth busking. We see Bronte looking over at the noise of the drums. She is hearing something she as yet does not understand. She also passes a food stall where a black man with dreadlocks is moving sinuously to reggae music on the radio. This African motif is continued when she enters the Afrika café to meet her friend Anton, who has arranged that she meet Georges there before they go through their marriage ceremony. In the midst of this sophisticated modern city, the movie seems to be saying, there are primitive urges and people in touch with the rhythms of sensuality. Georges arrives at the café and, in a scene that parallels a scene at the end of the movie, he stares at Bronte through the window. Then Weir cuts straight to a shot of a newly-married pair outside City Hall kissing and being showered with confetti by their friends. The camera pans to take in Bronte and Georges who watch the happy pair enviously. They say goodbye awkwardly, two people who are married but who know nothing about one another. 'I'll never forget Afrika,' Georges says, meaning the café. The whole of this first sequence has a fine economy to it. Many of the themes of the movie are introduced: the city, the contrast between the shambling Georges and the neat, college-educated Bronte, the spontaneity and sensual rhythms that the cavernous city cannot stifle, the African motif.

We then see Bronte being interviewed by the trustees of the apartment block. To explain her husband's absence, she makes up the fact that Georges is now in Africa and that he is a composer of African music, though, she is careful to say, he himself is not African. A tiny, aggressive and inquisitive woman, Mrs Bird, is one of the trustees and she will reappear constantly throughout the movie poking her nose into their affairs because she suspects something is not quite right about their story. She is particularly worried that Georges will play his drums in the apartment. Drums are a constant motif and are played on the soundtrack to signify the upset that Georges causes in Bronte's ordered and controlled existence and to denote a kind of primitivism

187

that he too represents. We see her in her apartment greenhouse admiring her exotic plants and trees. A greenhouse is an imitation jungle, an ersatz version of nature. Bronte knows a great deal about horticulture but it is academic knowledge; she is shut off from her own real nature and seeks to control it, just as she seeks to control nature in her greenhouse and to bring the countryside to the Lower East Side in her do-gooding activities with the Green Guerrillas. And it is just those horticultural skills she possesses that impress the interviewing board and win her the apartment and the greenhouse.

Weir cuts from the scene with her in her new greenhouse to the bare branches of a solitary tree in the city. We hear the hideous noises of the urban jungle: police car sirens, angry traffic and pneumatic drills. Bronte tries to construct safety and beauty in her living quarters, because the world outside is so discordant and ugly, just as she and her friends in the Green Guerrillas try to save stretches of the city for greenery and beauty.

Gradually, Weir builds up a picture of contemporary New York. After scenes at a Green Guerrilla site, Bronte, Phil and another male friend go to the trendy All-Nations restaurant, where she finds Georges serving tables. When Phil, Bronte's sometime boyfriend, announces that he does not eat meat, Georges responds with the question, 'Why not?' The reason is, as Bronte tells Georges later in the film, that Phil is 'careful about what he puts into his body'. Phil is careful about life, careful in the sense of being a nice New York community activist, whereas Georges is perceived to 'eat' life — it is vegetarianism versus meat-eating, intellect versus instinct, the politically correct opposed to the spontaneous and the pleasurable, the trendy opposed to the unreconstructed. Georges takes their order and does not allude directly to the fact that he and Bronte are married. After this scene of Bronte and Georges meeting in the restaurant, Weir cuts to a shot of two birds being affectionate to one another in a cage in Bronte's apartment and the greenhouse being liberally sprinkled with water. Georges symbolizes love and growth. Phil, the nice, right-on environmentalist, symbolizes dullness and a kind of urban, middle-class self-righteousness.

When Bronte has to find Georges again, she learns

he has been sacked from the restaurant because he has been rude to a customer. 'He's trouble,' says the owner. When Georges arrives at the apartment block, Oscar, the doorman, tells him, 'When I first saw you, I said to myself this guy just stepped out of the jungle.' Oscar recognizes the primitive quality in Georges, although he means he knows that Georges has just come back from Africa. When Mrs Sheehan and Mr Borsky from the Immigration Department arrive at the apartment, Georges calms Bronte down and takes control of the situation, but he is not adept at it. He calls Bronte Betty by mistake. His description of how they met is long and confused; it involves a tale of their both being laden with parcels at Christmas and how they had bumped into each other, picking up each other's parcels by mistake. It sounds like a scene from a movie; indeed, it is exactly what happens in *Falling in Love*, the 1985 Robert De Niro–Meryl Streep film about two married people getting involved after just such an incident in a New York book store. Georges almost gives the game away when he fails to direct Borsky to the bathroom, opening two doors in the corridor before picking the right one.

Georges' habit of smoking appals Bronte, whilst her decaffeinated coffee tastes horribly to him. At the supermarket, he tells her to return the birdseed (muesli) to the shelf; he wants white bread, she wholemeal. When they meet the worldly Lauren ('Everything in my life has been French lately'), Georges tells ther that he and Bronte are old friends so he 'doesn't fuck her'. Georges cooks a gorgeous meal for the three of them, but Bronte complains that it's not healthy because of all that butter. Lauren thinks Georges is gorgeous and tells Bronte that she had not liked Phil because he was so earnest. Lauren, in her own smart New York way, is on the side of spontaneity and sensuality and it is she who brings Georges to her parents' dinner party, hoping that Georges will inject some naturalness into the proceedings. The dinner table talk is about art and the environment. Lauren tells Bronte that she is 'going to wind up as some grand old Kate Hepburn surrounded by lots of beautiful plants'. This is just one of the numerous self-referential elements in *Green Card*. Andie MacDowell has something of a young Hepburn about her and Weir clearly included this reference deliberately to draw attention to this and to the genre of

romantic comedy he was working in with *Green Card*.
Later in the movie, Georges/Depardieu talks about his
youth when he was involved in stealing cars, violent
escapades and general 'wild man' stuff, which sounds
very much like the version of Depardieu's early years
that we have learned through the media. Weir merges
the star with his part and uses details from the actor's
real life story to give credibility to his character. It has
the effect, as does the Hepburn reference, of distancing
the audience from the movie and reminding them that
they are watching fiction.

The fact that Georges/Depardieu is a Frenchman is
not irrelevant. He stands for a kind of unreconstructed
European sensuality, a type of gentle machismo, as
opposed to the puritanism and right-on attitudes of the
American Bronte and her friends. These white, middle-
class New York people are cultivated like the plants in
her greenhouse. After the tasteful recital by one of the
other guests at the dinner party, Georges' spontaneous
and totally spurious musical composition injects a force
and power into the evening that has been lacking
amidst the genteel conversation and arid music-making.
'It's not Mozart,' says Lauren's mother. He makes up an
impromptu poem to the accompaniment of seductive
piano music:

> Let the little children come under the trees
> But there are no trees for the poor lost children.
> Decay is their toy, despair is their game.
> They have only chaos to climb.

This instinctive expression goes straight for the
emotional jugular and wins over Lauren's mother in a
way that Bronte's reasoned arguments have failed to
do. Not that Georges cares much about bringing
gardens to the poor. 'Nothing will change down there,'
he says. 'Go to the country if you want trees.' Back in
the apartment, Bronte tells Georges that her father, a
writer, named each of the children after a famous
author: Austen, Colette, Eliot, Bronte. Bronte complains
that all Georges' ideas are so right-wing and he
responds by saying that all her ideas are from the same
place, meaning the literary and artistic background she
comes from, the world of concerned environmentalists
and niceness. 'You're nice and you look for the same
thing in men. Two nices. Phil, he's nice,' Georges tells
her. 'He's different. He's a gardener,' Bronte says
defensively. Since *Michael*, Weir has always been rather

hard on concerned people: the professionals who look after the Aborigines in *Last Wave*, the geologist in *The Plumber*, the missionary in *Mosquito Coast*. Community activists, social workers and trendies in general seem to attract Weir's dislike almost as much as academics and pedagogues.

In some scenes of the movie, some of the humour and situations become contrived and clichéd. For example, it seems inevitable that Bronte's parents will have to pay an unexpected visit and that Georges will somehow have to disguise the fact that he is living in the apartment. Once it is decided he is to be handyman, then the line, 'I need a screw', is not long in making its appearance. This is clichéd writing and the whole sequence is one where the director Weir is being rather tolerant of the Weir who wrote the screenplay. *Green Card* continually flirts with Hollywood cliché and does not avoid sinking into it from time to time. Some of the dialogue is also heavy-handed and almost sentimental. When they are in the park supposedly rehearsing the reasons why they fell in love, Georges says, 'Because I began to hear music again', which refers to the African drums and music that has featured on the film's soundtrack. Weir uses this African music to effect when the couple are undressing separately after the dinner party and thinking about each other in the other room. The drums underscore the images of their mutual mounting passion. But the device could hardly be called subtle. On the morning after Georges has thrown the vegetarian Phil out of the flat, Weir shows us the goldfish which he had previously bought for Bronte swimming in the pond in the greenhouse, the two birds in their cage and his and her underwear hanging side by side on the clothes line. A creative use of cliché or just cliché? The whole plot of the film is predicated on an improbability, as many previous Hollywood romantic comedies have been. It does not seem very likely that such a controlled, rational and independent woman as Bronte would venture into a contrived marriage in order to gain an apartment with a greenhouse, an apartment which, it seems, she has to compete for with other applicants despite the fact she has got herself married. However, if her action is read as her unconscious desire to break up the order of her life and to gamble on what the dice throw up, then it makes more sense. She is hearing a distant beat of drums that symbolizes her need for passion in her life. Georges brings that feeling and passion into her life but she takes some time before she can recognize her own needs. The long exchange of looks that Weir has them act out on their first meeting represents their unconscious recognition of what they might mean to each other. However, they have first to surmount the differences between them in the classic tradition of Hollywood romantic comedy.

Are the gender issues as represented in *Green Card* realized in a progressive or regressive context? Certainly, it could be argued that the Kate Hepburn tag that Bronte carries in the narrative can be read in two ways. Hepburn was usually strong-minded and independent in her movies, but in the marital comedies in which she starred with Spencer Tracy, she inevitably had to succumb to his manly charm and toe a certain line which allowed her still to be independent-minded, but only within the constraints of patriarchy. In short, Hepburn's independence stopped far short of rejecting marriage and men. In the same way, Bronte/MacDowell is portrayed as independent, active and intelligent, the characteristics of the screen persona of Katherine Hepburn. However, she too is changed by the influence of Georges/Depardieu and finally she falls in love with him. The closure of the movie bears the promise of the lovers reuniting and 'marrying' for real. Georges has acted upon Bronte, rather than the other way round: he does not seem to have been changed by her. Within the structure of the movie whereby he is meant to represent a life force (feelings, spontaneity, sensuality) that comes into her life and shakes it up, that is unexceptionable, except that the gender issue cannot really be avoided. Her need for the greenhouse, her living alone as a woman in a large apartment, her asexual existence, are seen as symptoms of her problem. Bronte is shown to be incomplete in her niceness and her unsatisfactory relationship with the unattractive and bloodless Phil. Only someone like Georges can make her life complete. He woos her, he has to bring her over to his side of the fence by burrowing under her defences and pointing out how dried up she is. At one point, he states the indefensible, 'You need a good fuck', which is a classic male chauvinist rejoinder to any independent woman living without a man.

Thus, *Green Card* is open to the charge of sexism, albeit a mild form of it, it should be stressed, but then the attitudes to gender have not always been politically correct in previous Weir films. It is almost as though Weir is deliberatly cocking a snook at politically correct attitudes. And after all, he does allow his hero to be feminine to the degree that it is Georges who cooks the glorious meals, who has poetry in his soul, who is the more overtly romantic and sensual. Weir continues to explore notions of masculinity in the figure of Georges, who is a curious mixture of unreconstructed chauvinism and the new man. He is allowed to be masculine, even macho (the tattoos on his arms and his talk of revenge), but at the same time he is shown to be sensitive and feeling. She tells the immigration official that, 'He says he's not sensitive, but he's a very sensitive man.' Bronte has seen beyond the surface machismo to the sensitive soul inside him. He tells Borsky that Bronte has peace and he doesn't. She trusts people and he doesn't. He has passion which she lacks; he, as Bronte says, 'eats life', while she nibbles at it. To play these figures of, on the one hand, the life force (all spontaneity, instinct and soul) and on the other, the New York trendy (all social concern, environmentalist and rationality), Weir could hardly have cast more appropriately than Gérard Depardieu and Andie MacDowell. Depardieu had built up his 'wild man' reputation in movies such as *Les Valseuses* (1974) and *The Moon in the Gutter* (1983), whilst revealing his more sensitive side in *Jean de Florette* (1986) and *Cyrano de Bergerac* (1990). MacDowell had played the New York sophisticate in *sex, lies and videotape* (1989) and *Object of Desire* (1991). Weir, the writer, used aspects of Depardieu's own life, as, at least, it has been transmitted through newspapers and magazines, to create the character of Georges. For Bronte, Weir probably used aspects of the actress's usual screen persona, filling the portrait with observations he had made of young, middle-class New Yorkers. No doubt part of the movie's commercial rationale was to exploit Depardieu's success with *Florette* and *Cyrano* on the North American continent by starring him in an American film. He plays the outsider who comments on, and disrupts, the New York scene; he is the polarized opposite of the New York Phil, who is all Greenwich Village right on. It is very clear where Weir's sympathies as a writer and director are; he, the foreign director, sees America and New York through Georges' eyes and, indeed, he could be accused of throwing the picture Depardieu's way. It is Depardieu who is allowed to be boyish, charming, clownish and capering, while MacDowell has to be disapproving and resistant. Unfortunately, the targets Weir chooses for his social satire seem too easy and too familiar: vegetarians, pretentious artistic types, concerned environmentalists, the health-conscious. Thus, we are implicitly asked to take the side of meat-eaters versus muesli-eaters, smokers versus non-smokers, individualists against community activists, unreconstructed males rather than new men. There is a staleness about Weir's approach, as though he had allowed himself to choose easily recognizable targets rather than go for greater depth. Much of the disapproval Weir expresses in his portrait of trendy New Yorkers would find enthusiastic support in middle America and that is an uncomfortable position for any liberal film-maker to be in. A sharper edge to Weir's scalpel would certainly have given the movie more substance.

All major directors have marked time at some stage during their careers. They make minor films in between their major works, perhaps as a chore to make money and sometimes because their inclinations lead them to make a movie that is less challenging and therefore less demanding on them. Hitchcock could make the lightweight *To Catch a Thief* (1955) and *The Trouble with Harry* (1955) in the midst of his most creative period when he directed *Rear Window* (1954), *Vertigo* (1958) *North by Northwest* (1959) and *Psycho* (1960). Ford made stinkers such as *Mogambo* (1953) and *The Wings of Eagles* (1957). Howard Hawks could make a monstrosity such as *Land of the Pharaohs* (1957). So perhaps Peter Weir is entitled to make *Green Card* as a sort of interlude in his career, a movie that has all the marks of a carefully-crafted commercial product that hopes to do well at the box office. 'This year's *Pretty Woman*' trumpeted the publicity for *Green Card*. Hugely successful as that picture was, it is hardly the type of glossy product a maverick director such as Peter Weir would like to have his films associated with. *Pretty Woman* (1990) is pure Hollywood schlock, a fantasy of shopping, sex and transformation, all parcelled up in glossy wrappings that include Richard Gere and Julia Roberts. *Green Card* is much more acerbic and grounded in reality, but it has a certain element of wish fulfilment in it as well, including the falling in love of the man and woman and the promise of a happy ending. It is a superior version of Hollywood romantic comedy, but probably has to be seen as disappointing from a director who has always handled large themes in his movies and has chosen unusual, challenging subjects. The only really unusual subject in *Green Card* is the concept of the arranged marriage that is to bring Georges his work permit. However, that kind of bureaucratic barrier between lovers has been exploited before in romantic comedies from Hollywood, notably in Howard Hawks' *I was a Male War Bride* (1947). Weir, then, in writing and directing *Green Card*, was handling staple comedy situations and the evidence is that he found it difficult to find genuinely original inspiration because of this. With *Green Card*, there is a sense of an imaginative and original director marking time.

However, there are interesting aspects to the movie. Depardieu, when he is not being encouraged to be over-cute, is very watchable in the role of Georges. Weir also creates interesting character parts for Danny Dennis as Oscar the doorman and Jessie Keosian as Mrs Bird, the interfering and suspicious co-tenant and member of the trustees board. It is revealing about the film's ideological intent that Oscar is clearly meant to be a sympathetic character and yet he makes disparaging remarks about women's lib. Weir uses Jessie Keosian's tiny stature to good effect in comparison with Depardieu's girth, particularly in one scene in the elevator when she peers up at him accusingly. Bebe Neuwirth as Lauren is excellent as a New York kook and Ethan Phillips as Borsky and Mary Louise Wilson as Mrs Sheehan, the immigration officials, benefit from the restraint in Weir's writing. It would have been easy to portray them as bureaucratic ogres who come between the lovers and force them to separate. They are seen as fairly benevolent people doing an unpleasant job. Phil is the one completely unsympathetic character in the film and he performs the function of making Depardieu look that much more attractive by comparison and of symbolizing Bronte's self-defeating attraction to bloodlessness and emotional frigidity.

Nevertheless, clichés abound. In Hollywood comedy of this ilk, there is almost always a scene where the woman locks the man out of the apartment and he is discovered the next morning by the interfering neighbour. The scene where Georges arrives unexpectedly at the dinner party is straight out of many a domestic comedy and even his bravura performance on the piano has a familiarity about it that lessens our pleasure in the scene. The more serious charge that Weir once more romanticizes primitive cultures (Africa, in this case) and associates instinct and sensuality with black people in his attempt to satirize middle-class, rational whites, has to be acknowledged. The African motif that runs through the movie consistently refuses to integrate with the rest. It seems tacked on, as though Weir was desperately looking for an opposing value to put up against the rationality and civilized values of Bronte and her associates. But to tag Georges with this African label seems spurious and at times it descends into a cuteness that is excruciating. For example, when Georges writes a note to Bronte asking to see her one last time, he makes a direct reference to his supposed African connections; 'For Bronte: Africa, Tuesday. The elephants have been restless, so restless I just can't sleep. I'd like to say a last goodbye before the next safari.' On her way back from parting from Georges after the immigration interview, a man offers Bronte some African jewellery in the street, 'Bijoux Africain', which she refuses. However, when the lovers finally express their love together and promise to reunite, the soundtrack has the African-American group, the Emmaus Group Singers, singing:

Last night I had a dream
Keep your eyes on the prize
You must believe
Everything is going to be alright.

Bronte, it is implied, in admitting to herself that she loves Georges, is no longer refusing African jewellery or only half-hearing the beat of African drums, she is embracing sensuality and instinct, feelings and soul, and rejecting the cold rationality and civilized concern of Phil and her New York friends. Aboriginal culture in *Picnic* and *Last Wave*, Indonesian culture in *Living Dangerously*, the Amish in *Witness*, native Americans in *Dead Poets* and now Africanism in *Green Card*. The colonization and romanticizing of primitive cultures are a definite feature of Weir's films. Perhaps there is an inherently patronizing and stereotyping tendency in

Weir's exploitation of these motifs. My particular reservation about *Green Card* is that the Africanism is welded rather unconvincingly on to this story about white middle-class New Yorkers. There are no Africo-American characters in the narrative other than when they are being used as symbols of sensuality and spontaneity and when their music is being used to signal the characters' inner needs.

So does *Green Card* signify Weir's final selling-out to the Hollywood machine? *Green Card* is not a bad film, it's just not particularly good. For most other writer-directors, to have made *Green Card* would have been something of an achievement, but because we have certain expectations of a Peter Weir film, it must be perceived as a fall from his own high standards. As the writer-producer-director of *Green Card*, he has to take most of the praise or criticism for the movie. Ironically, this is the film over which ostensibly he seemed to have had most control. Yet how much freedom does a director ever have when producing a formulaic product for the world film market? Parameters are in place immediately you are seeking the backing of major studios or independents and when you are operating within generic boundaries, such as the romantic comedy genre, then audience and film executive expectations come strongly into force.

That is not to say that originality is impossible because of those limitations: expectations about gangster films did not prevent Coppola from triumphing with the Godfather movies (1972, 1974, 1990), or Scorsese with *GoodFellas* (1990). The Coen brothers can make a movie about Hollywood, *Barton Fink* (1991), that is highly original despite the weight of tradition of the movie-about-movies sub-genre. Thus, formulaic and even clichéd structures and plots need not mean that formulaic and clichéd films are finally made. A talented director and writer can make creative use of cliché and formula and turn out something fresh and innovative.

Green Card is not an example of that, because, despite its numerous qualities as a movie, the weight of the clichés and the basic formula of romantic comedy tip it over into being an almost routine Hollywood product. It is not so much that *Green Card* shows Weir as having sold out to Hollywood conventions; it is more a case of his having taken on conventional structures and elements and of having failed to make anything particularly original out of them. But it is an honourable failure and this lapse in his record cannot be interpreted as Weir having lost his way as a director or as a writer. Every major director has made lesser films as part of his canon and *Green Card* can be seen as a lightweight addition to the list of films this imaginative director has chalked up during his career.

Conclusion

It's summoning up the ideas that's the hard thing — the inspiration, the passion

(Peter Weir)[1]

Visions of alternative realities. Visions that are flawed, dangerous, fanciful, liberating, transcendent, perhaps even with a touch of occasional phoniness to them. That is the stuff of a Peter Weir film.

Peter Weir again and again has expressed his distaste for the categorization of his films and the academization of film in general, so perhaps I should follow his lead and not try to capture, in the butterfly net of criticism, the exact nature of these visions Weir has communicated in his movies. Each of the film texts discussed in this book will mean many different things to many different people at many different times. There are no closed readings, no given meanings. When I review the films myself in years to come, no doubt I will read them in quite a different way. What I have tried to do in my analysis is to put the movies in a total context and to study Weir's contribution to them within his total position. No creative artist is an island and I can agree with Roland Barthes that texts, and that includes films, are multi-dimensional spaces with many 'authors' contributing to the writing, which have many more meanings than the one given meaning constructed by an author-God. Yet it would seem perverse to deny that Peter Weir, the human being and not a critical construction, is a very important contributor to whatever meaning it is possible to extract from the films he directs and that in recognizing that personal contribution we are adding to our own pleasure in viewing the films.

Too many books about film directors merely become a lionization of the chosen genius. Thus he, and it is almost invariably a male because of the sexist nature of the film industry, can usually do no wrong and everything he directs is perceived as having some intrinsic worth. I have not pretended that everything that Peter Weir has directed is of equal value or that any of his films is a masterpiece of the cinema, whatever that may be. All in all, I think Hollywood's influence on Weir has led to his directing less interesting films than he did in the first half of his career. That is not to say that I do not value *Witness*, *The Mosquito Coast*, *Dead Poets Society* and even *Green Card*. In the Hollywood context, they are still considerable achievements and show Weir trying to impose his personal vision on material that, in one way or another, is shaped by institutional and generic determinations. However, in my opinion, *Picnic at Hanging Rock* (for all its flaws), *The Last Wave*, *Gallipoli* and *The Year of Living Dangerously* make up a quartet of major achievement, which his Hollywood experience has not been able to emulate. The non-American films have a resonance and an immediacy that the glossier and more linear narrative fictions of the Hollywood quartet lack. However, that is not in any way to criticize Weir for going Hollywood. The opportunity to direct big-budget American movies is the dream of most directors. Current news is that Weir is due to make a film for Hollywood producer Paula Weinstein so it seems that he has now become a semi-permanent American director. This must be partly due to the fact that the Australian film industry has run out of steam and the heady days of the early seventies are long gone.

There has been some discussion of his directing a film about Napoleon starring Gérard Depardieu. However, I cannot help but think that Weir would benefit from returning to his roots and making a film closer to home about an Australian theme. It is not accidental that his four best films (again in my opinion) are all, in one way or another, about specifically Australian themes, although, of course, they have much wider significance as well. Perhaps the Australian film industry will revive enough to raise the budget for a major Weir movie, because certainly the film industry there could benefit from a successful Australian film directed by one of their directors whose talents Hollywood has exploited in the last decade.

Is Weir then an *auteur*? I have tried to demonstrate that individual films contain many discourses that stem from various sources: genre, dominant ideology, institutional determinations and the contributions of key individuals. No film, at least no commercial film made for the mass market, is ever the product of the personal expression of one person. However, it seems perverse not to acknowledge that some individuals, whether they be directors, writers, producers or actors, do manage to ascribe their personal signature to the films they make. Weir is one of those directors who, because of his determination to pursue the themes that interest him and to invest the films he makes with a recognizable style, *has* a personal signature, but that does not mean he is the sole author of the movies he directs. He has to share claims to authorship with various screenwriters and the writers of the original material from which the raw material of the shooting script has been culled. Every film that Weir has directed has had strong family resemblances to many other film texts. Weir has been working within generic traditions and the mode of production which the film industries of Australia and America, in their different ways, have incorporated. He has adapted those traditions and conventions to his own artistic needs, but the American films reflect that he almost certainly had to rein in his personal style to the demands of the Hollywood machine. If Weir is not an *auteur*, he is certainly a director round which a cluster of themes and stylistic motifs congregate. A Peter Weir film summons up expectations that thematic concerns such as the influence of dreams and the psychic, the feminization of men, the quest for meaning and significance in life and the questioning of established institutions, will be at the heart of the movie. In a sense, that has become Peter Weir's commodity value in the film market place: the handling of large, resonant themes in works of entertainment that use star names and unusual settings.

If Weir is to continue to work largely in the American film industry, then that is a welcome sign of health in a Hollywood that has become increasingly unadventurous and sequel-orientated. When its leading directors, such as Scorsese and Spielberg, are reduced to directing remakes of old Hollywood movies (Scorsese's *Cape Fear* [1991] and Spielberg's *Always* [1989], a remake of the forties movie *A Guy Named Joe* [1944]), or to making sequels to their past hits (Coppola with *Godfather III* [1990]), then it can safely be asserted that taking risks is certainly not the name of the game in Los

Angeles. In that dire context, Peter Weir shines out like a beacon as a director who is willing to hold out against the blandishments of outright commercialism. It is unlikely that a press release will announce that Weir is due to direct Schwarzenegger in *Terminator 15* or Mel Gibson in *Lethal Weapon 27*. Weir *is* a commercial director; he wants to reach the widest possible audience with his films. Hence, for example, his appearances on chat shows with Depardieu to publicize *Green Card*. No international film director, as Weir has now become, can afford to live in an ivory tower and have a high disdain for the market place. But his record in the past, comprising the evidence of the films he *has* directed and also the type of projects he's turned down, marks him out as a director who cares about the kind of film he directs. The hope is that the credit, 'A Peter Weir film', continues to hold out the promise that you are about so see something unusual and original in the cinema and that he does not become submerged by the business machine that the American film industry inevitably is. My instinct is that there are many more fine and idiosyncratic films to come from Peter Weir.

Notes

Introduction

1 Brian McFarlane and Tom Ryan, 'Peter Weir: Towards the Centre' from *Cinema Papers* no 34, Sept-Oct 1981, pp. 322-329

Starting Out

1 David Stratton in 'Mystery and Imagination: Peter Weir' from *The Last New Wave: The Australian Film Revival* (Angus and Robertson, 1980), p. 59.
2 Sue Mathews, *35mm Dreams: Conversations with Five Directors about the Australian Film Revival* (Penguin Books, 1984), p. 87.

The Cars That Ate Paris

1 Mathews, p. 91.
2 Brian McFarlane, 'The Films of Peter Weir' from *Cinema Papers* no 26, April-May 1980, p. 8.

Picnic at Hanging Rock

1 Robert Winer in 'Witnessing and Bearing Witness: The Ontogeny of Encounter in the Films of Peter Weir' from *Images in Our Souls: Cavell, Psychoanalysis and Cinema,* eds Smith and Kerrigan (Johns Hopkins University Press, 1987), p. 83.
2 Stratton, p. 78.
3 Winer, *ibid.*
4 Mathews, p. 95.

The Last Wave

1 Mathews, p. 97.
2 Stratton, p. 75.
3 Ibid. p. 77.
4 Ibid.
5 Mathews, p. 97.
6 Quoted in *The Last New Wave,* p. 78.
7 Mathews, p. 97.
8 Ibid. p. 98.
9 Winer, p. 90.

Gallipoli

1 Winer, p. 93.
2 Mathews, p. 87.

The Year of Living Dangerously

1 C J Koch, *The Year of Living Dangerously* (Michael Joseph, 1978), p. 38.

The Mosquito Coast

1 Paul Theroux, *The Mosquito Coast* (Hamish Hamilton, 1981), p. 82.
2 Pam Cook ed, *The Cinema Book* (British Film Institute, 1985), p. 50.

Green Card

1 Lynne Truss from 'Directing off the Feminine Side' *Independent on Sunday*, 17 February 1991, p. 21.

Filmography

Short films

Count Vim's Last Exercise (1967): *The Life and Flight of the Rev. Buck Shotte* (1968); *Three to Go* (Michael episode); *Stirring the Pool* (1970); *Homesdale* (1971); *Three Directions in Australian Pop Music* (1972); *Incredible Floridas* (1972); *What Ever Happened to Green Valley?* (1973).

Feature Films

The Cars That Ate Paris (1974)

Producers: Hal and Jim McElroy
Screenplay: Keith Gow, Piers Davies and Peter Weir, based on a story by Peter Weir
Director of Photography: John McLean
Editor: Wayne Le Clos
Production Designer: David Copping
Music: Bruce Smeaton
Cast: Terry Camilleri (Arthur), John Meillon (Mayor), Melissa Jaffa (Beth), Kevin Miles (Dr Midland), Max Gillies (Metcalfe), Peter Armstrong (Gorman), Edward Howell (Tringham), Bruce Spence (Charlie)

Picnic at Hanging Rock (1975)

Producers: Hal and Jim McElroy
Executive Producer: Patricia Lovell
Screenplay: Cliff Green based on the novel by Joan Lindsay
Director of Photography: Russell Boyd
Editor: Max Lemon

Composer and Arranger: Bruce Smeaton
Artistic Adviser to Peter Weir: Martin Sharp
Art Director: David Copping
Costume Designer: Judy Dorsman
Cast: Rachel Roberts (Mrs Appleyard), Dominic Guard
(Michael Fitzherbert), Helen Morse (Diane de Portiers),
Vivean Gray (Miss McCraw), Jacki Weaver (Minnie),
Kirsty Child (Miss Lumley), Anthony Llewellyn-Jones
(Tom), Frank Gunnell (Mr Whitehead), Anne Lambert
(Miranda), Karen Robson (Irma), Jane Vallis (Marion),
Christine Schuller (Edith), Margaret Nelson (Sara),
Ingrid Mason (Rosamund) Jenny Lovell (Blanche), Janet
Murray (Juliana), Peter Collingwood (Colonel
Fitzherbert), John Jarrett (Albert)

The Last Wave (1977)

Producers: Hal and Jim McElroy
Screenplay: Peter Weir, Tony Morphett, Petru Popescu,
based on an idea by Peter Weir
Director of Photography: Russell Boyd
Editor: Max Lemon
Music: Charles Wain
Production Designer: Goran Warff
Cast: Richard Chamberlain (David Burton), Olivia
Hamnett (Annie Burton), Gulpilil (Chris Lee), Frederick
Parslow (Reverend Burton), Vivean Gray (Dr Whitburn),
Nandjiwara (Charlie), Walter Amagula (Gerry Lee), Roy
Bara (Larry), Cedric Lalara (Lindsey), Morris Lalara
(Jacko), Peter Caroll (Michael Zeadler), Athol Compton
(Billy Corman)

The Plumber (1979)

Producer: Matt Carroll
Screenplay: Peter Weir
Director of Photography: David Sanderson
Editor: G Turney-Smith
Production Designer: Wendy Weir
Cast: Judy Morris (Jill), Ivar Kants (Max), Robert Coleby
(Brian), Candy Raymond (Meg), Henri Szeps
(Department Head)

Gallipoli (1981)

A Robert Stigwood – Rupert Murdoch production

Screenplay: David Williamson from a story by Peter Weir
Director of Photography: Russell Boyd
Musical Score: Jean-Michel Jarre
Design Co-ordinator: Wendy Weir
Military Adviser: Bill Gammage
Cast: Mel Gibson (Frank Dunne), Mark Lee (Archy Hamilton), Bill Kerr (Uncle Jack), Bill Hunter (Major Barton), Frank Dunne (General Gardener)

The Year of Living Dangerously (1982)

Producers: Hal and Jim McElroy
Screenplay: David Williamson, Peter Weir and C J Koch
Musical Score: Maurice Jarre
Design Co-ordinator: Wendy Weir
Director of Photography: Russell Boyd
Cast: Mel Gibson (Guy Hamilton), Sigourney Weaver (Jill Bryant), Linda Hunt (Billy Kwan), Michael Murphy (Curtis), Bill Kerr (Colonel Henderson), Noel Ferrer (Wally), Bembal Roco (Kumar), Domingo Landicho (Hortana), Paul Sonkila (Kevin Condon)

Witness (1985)

Producer: Edward Feldman
Associate Producer: Wendy Weir
Screenplay: Earl Wallace and William Kelley from a story by William Kelley, Pamela and Earl Wallace
Director of Photography: John Seale
Musical Score: Maurice Jarre
Cast: Harrison Ford (John Book), Kelly McGillis (Rachel Lapp), Josef Sommer (Schaeffer), Lukas Haas (Samuel), Jan Rubes (Eli), Alexander Gudonov (Daniel), Danny Glover (McFee), Brent Jennings (Carter)

The Mosquito Coast (1986)

Producer: Jerome Hellmann
Screenplay: Paul Schrader
Production Designer: John Stoddart
Musical Score: Maurice Jarre
Director of Photography: John Seale
Cast: Harrison Ford (Allie Fox), Helen Mirren (Mother),
River Phoenix (Charlie), Jadrien Steele (Gerry), André
Gregory (Rev Spellgood), Conrad Roberts (Mr Haddy),
Martha Plimpton (Emily Spellgood)

Dead Poets Society (1989)

Producers: Steven Haft, Paul Junger Witt, Tony Thomas
Screenplay: Tom Schulman
Musical Score: Maurice Jarre
Director of Photography: John Seale
Cast: Robin Williams (John Keating), Robert Sean
Leonard (Neil Perry), Ethan Hawke (Todd Anderson),
Josh Charles (Knox Overstreet), Gale Hansen (Charlie
Dalton), Dylan Kussman (Richard Cameron), Norman
Lloyd (Mr Nolan) Kurtwood Smith (Mr Perry), Alexandra
Powers (Chris)

Green Card (1991)

Producer: Peter Weir
Screenplay: Peter Weir
Musical Score: Hans Zimmer
Director of Photography: Geoffrey Simpson
Cast: Gérard Depardieu (Georges), Andie MacDowell
(Bronte), Bebe Neuwirth (Lauren), Gregg Edelman (Phil),
Danny Dennis (Oscar), Jessie Keosian (Mrs Bird)

Bibliography

Books

Berryman, Ken: *The Australian Film Industry and Key Films of the 1970s*. Carlton: Australian Film Institute, 1981.

Mathews, Sue: *35mm Dreams: Conversations with Five Directors about the Australian Film Revival*. Australia: Penguin Books, 1984.

McFarlane, Peter: *The Projected Muse*. Adelaide: Rigby, 1977.

Murray, Scott ed.: *The New Australian Cinema*. Melbourne: Nelson, 1980.

Pike, Andrew and Cooper, Ross: *Australian Film 1900-1977*. Melbourne: Oxford University Press, 1981.

Smith, Joseph and Kerrigan, William eds: *Images in Our Souls: Cavell, Psychoanalysis and Cinema*. Baltimore and London: Johns Hopkins University Press, 1987.

Stratton, David: *The Last New Wave: The Australian Film Revival*. Sydney: Angus & Robertson, 1980.

Articles

Dempsey, M.: 'Inexplicable Feelings: an Interview with Peter Weir', *Film Quarterly* 33 (4), Summer 1980, pp. 2-11.

Ginane, A.I. and Murray, Scott: 'Producing *Picnic*: Pat Lovell', *Cinema Papers* 5, March-April 1976, pp. 298-301.

McFarlane, Brian: 'The Films of Peter Weir', *Cinema Papers* 26, April-May 1980, pp. 4-22.

McFarlane, Brian and Ryan, Tom: 'Peter Weir: Towards the Centre', *Cinema Papers* 34, Sept-Oct 1981, pp. 322-29.

Index

Ace in the Hole, 103
Adventures of Barry Mackenzie, The, 28
Advise and Consent, 2
Age of Consent, 27
All That Heaven Allows, 60, 122
All the President's Men, 100
Alvin Purple, 28
Always, 201
Antonioni, Michelangelo, 44
Appalachian Spring, 131
Archer, Anne, 49
Armstrong, Gillian, 54
Astaire, Fred, 133
Australasian Films, 18
Australian Film Development Corporation, 19, 28, 31, 38
Australian Film Institute, 26

Barthes, Roland, 199
Barton Fink, 197
Beau Geste, 71
Beresford, Bruce, 123
Bergman, Ingmar, 3
Big Sleep, The, 103
Billy the Kid, 131
Birthday Party, The, 26
Blade Runner, 129
Boetticher, Budd, 2
Bogart, Humphrey, 109
Boorman, John, 123, 129
Boyd, Russell, 53
Brando, Marlon, 169
Brealey, Gill, 24
Brennan, Richard, 26
Brigadoon, 133
Burstall, Tim, 27

Cahiers du Cinéma, 2
Camilleri, Terry, 32, 35
Cape Fear, 138, 201
Carabiniers, Les, 22
Caron, Leslie, 134
Cars That Ate Paris, The, 8, 27, 31–35, 37, 41, 46, 63
Casablanca, 1, 109, 117
Cassavetes, John, 72
Cat People, 63, 80
Chamberlain, Richard, 61, 64, 66, 67, 69, 71, 72
Charisse, Cyd, 134
Chauvel, Charles, 19
Clock, The, 186
Close, Glenn, 49
Cinesound Studios, 18
Citizen Kane, 35
City's Child, 9, 28
Coen, Joel and Ethan, 197
Commonwealth Film Unit, 18, 27, 28
Cook, Pam, 143
Cooke, Sam, 134
Cooper, Gary, 7, 131, 136
Copland, Aaron, 33
Coppola, Francis, 197, 201
Count Vim's Last Exercise, 17
Creature from the Black Lagoon, The, 103
Crossfire, 73
Cul de Sac, 26
Curtiz, Michael, 122
Cyrano de Bergerac, 193

Davies, Piers, 130
Davis, Bette, 83
Day, Doris, 186

Dead Poets Society, 5, 8, 46, 47, 55, 163–180, 182, 196, 200
Dean, James, 22, 146
Defence of the Realm, 100
Depardieu, Gérard, 40, 46, 183–197
De Niro, Robert, 138, 148, 160, 189
Dietrich, Marlene, 9
Diggers, 19
Diggers in Blighty, 19
Don's Party, 86, 93
Don't Look Now, 50, 63
Douglas, Michael, 49, 138
Dr Kildare, 68

East of Eden, 154
Easy Rider, 21
Ellis, Bob, 19
Elvira Madigan, 50, 51
Everage, Dame Edna, 21
Experimental Film Fund, 26

Falling in Love, 189
Fatal Attraction, 49
Feldman, Edward, 121
Film Australia, 27
Finney, Albert, 72
Forbidden Planet, 103
Ford, Harrison, 46, 48, 50, 93, 121–141, 143–161, 183
Ford, John, 2, 95
Fountainhead, The, 71
Friendly Persuasion, 133
Frizzell, Helen, 37, 59
Front Page, The, 103

Gallipoli, 8, 10, 47, 52, 77, 81, 83-97, 99, 100, 136, 142, 157, 158, 160, 200
Garland, Judy, 186
Georgy Girl, 21
Gibson, Mel, 1, 40, 83–97, 99–115, 13, 202
Glover, Danny, 124, 127
Go-Between, The, 39, 40
Godard, Jean-Luc, 22
Godfather, The, I, II, and III, 197

Godunov, Alexander, 137
GoodFellas, 197
Good Morning, Vietnam, 169
Good Sam, 71
Gorton, John, 19
Gow, Keith, 32
Graduate, The, 21
Graves, John, 39
Greater Union Organization, 39
Green Card, 8, 11, 24, 46, 47, 185–199, 200, 204
Green, Cliff, 38, 51, 53, 77
Greene, Graham, 146
Gregory, André, 150
Guard, Dominic, 39
Gulpilil, 46, 60, 73
Guy Named Joe, A, 201

Haas, Lukas, 124, 127
Hanna, Pat, 19
Hardcore, 147
Hatari, 2
Hawks, Howard, 2, 194
Hemingway, Ernest, 116
Hepburn, Katherine, 186, 190, 191, 192
Here We Go Round the Mulberry Bush, 21
Heyerdahl, Thor, 73
High Noon, 71, 103, 121, 131, 136
His Girl Friday, 103
Hitchcock, Alfred, 2, 53
Hoffman, Dustin, 33
Holden, William, 106
Homesdale, 25–26, 31, 33
Hopkins, Anthony, 160
HUAC, 166, 177
Hudson, Rock, 186
Humphries, Barry, 21
Hunt, Linda, 40, 46, 99–118

I Love, You Love, 18
Images in Our Souls, 41
Imitation of Life, 60
Incredible Floridas, 27
Indiana Jones series, 121
I Walked with a Zombie, 63
I Was A Male War Bride, 195

Jarre, Maurice, 127, 131, 143
Jean de Florette, 193
Jedda, 19
Jung, Carl, 8
Jungle Book, The, 85

Kants, Ivor, 46
Kavanagh, Brian, 27
Keitel, Harvey, 7, 148
Kelly, Gene, 134
Keosian, Jesse, 195
Kerr, Bill, 101
Killing Fields, The, 99, 109
King, Stephen, 80
Kipling, Rudyard, 87
Koch, C. J., 99, 104, 108, 112, 114
Kotcheff, Ted, 27
Kubrick, Stanley, 80, 94
Kurosawa, Akira, 3

Lacan, Jacques, 4, 72
Ladd, Alan, 131
La Motta, Jake, 147
Lands of the Pharaohs, 194
Lang, Fritz, 122
Last Wave, The, 7, 24, 26, 27, 46, 52, 55, 59–76, 77, 79, 80, 86, 93, 95, 97, 105, 130, 132, 140, 157, 162, 167, 190, 196, 200
Laura, 2
L'Avventura, 44, 50
Lawler, Ray, 19
Le Clos, Wayne, 24
Lee, Mark, 86
Lennon, John, 22
Leopard Man, The, 63, 80
Lester, Richard, 61
Lewis, Jerry, 2
Lewis, Joseph H., 2
Lewton, Val, 63
Life and Flight of the Rev. Buck Shotte, The, 18
Lindsay, Joan, 38, 41, 53, 54
Losey, Joseph, 39
Lovell, Pat, 35

MacDowell, Andie, 184–197
Mackenzie, Barry, 21

Mad Max, 32
Magnificent Obsession, 60, 122
Maltese Falcon, The, 105
Mamet, David, 17
Man's Favorite Sport, 2
Marvin, Lee, 123
Marx, Karl, 4
Massey, Raymond, 152
Mathews, Sue, 20, 39, 48
Mavis Branston Show, The, 18
McCullough, Colleen, 81
McElroy, Hal, 31, 32, 38, 39, 199
McElroy, Jim, 31, 32, 38, 39, 99
McFarlane, Brian, 31
McGillis, Kelly, 40, 50, 124, 133
Meet John Doe, 71
Meillon, John, 32, 35
Merchant, Vivien, 40
MGM, 61, 99
Michael, 20–25, 31, 33, 34, 46
Midnight Cowboy, 21
Midsummer Night's Dream, A, 165, 174, 178
Minnelli, Vincente, 186
Mirren, Helen, 48, 144, 159
Moffatt, Ivan, 81
Mogambo, 194
Moon in the Gutter, The, 193
Morocco, 9
Morphett, Tony, 60, 73
Mosquito Coast, The, 5, 8, 26, 46, 47, 48, 143–161, 183, 190, 200
Mr Deeds Goes to Town, 71
Murder on the Orient Express, 40
Murdoch, Rupert, 84
Murphy, Michael, 107
Music Lovers, The, 61, 67

Nanjiwara, 59
Neuwirth, Bebe, 185, 195
Newman, Paul, 166
Nolte, Nick, 100
North by Northwest, 194

213

Object of Desire, 193
On the Beach, 19
Ophuls, Max, 9, 122
Outback, 27
Out of the Past, 73
Overlanders, The, 19

Pakula, Alan, 100
Paramount Studios, 121
Paths of Glory, 94
Patterson, Les, 21
Peckinpah, Sam, 33
Petulia, 61, 67, 72
Phillips, Ethan, 195
Phoenix, River, 144, 160
Picnic at Hanging Rock, 7,
    8, 24, 28, 37–56, 47, 59,
    60, 63, 67, 68, 73, 78, 79,
    80, 86, 93, 97, 99, 112,
    132, 133, 148, 157, 163,
    167, 196, 200
Pinter, Harold, 26
Plumber, The, 27, 46, 77–81,
    190
Point Blank, 123, 129
Polanski, Roman, 26
Popescu, Petru, 61, 73
Powell, Michael, 75
Preminger, Otto, 2, 26, 122
Presumed Innocent, 138
Pretty Woman, 194
Psycho, 26, 194

Quiet American, The, 143,
    150

Raging Bull, 138, 147
Raiders of the Lost Ark, 135
Rank, J. Arthur, 19
Rats of Tobruk, The, 19
Rear Window, 194
Redford, Robert, 81
Regarding Henry, 138
Removalists, The, 84
Renoir, Jean, 122
Repulsion, 26
Revolution, 123
RKO, 63
Roberts, Rachel, 40
Robinson Crusoe, 155
Rodeo, 131

Roeg, Nicolas, 27, 50, 63
Rogers, Ginger, 133
Royce Smeal Productions,
    31
Rubes, Jan, 124
Rugged O'Riordans, The, 19
Russell, Ken, 61

Salem's Lot, 80
Salvador, 12, 17, 99, 109,
    118
Saturday Night and Sunday
    Morning, 40
Scarlet Empress, The, 9
Schepisi, Fred, 54, 123
Schrader, Paul, 143, 147,
    149, 151, 155, 159
Schulman, Tom, 163
Schwarzenegger, Arnold,
    202
Scorsese, Martin, 147, 201
Scott, George C., 147, 149,
    160
Scott, Ridley, 123, 129
Seale, John, 127, 131, 143
Searchers, The, 103
sex, lies and videotape, 193
Shane, 131
Shanghai Express, 9
Sharp, Martin, 53
Shining, The, 80
Shiralee, The, 19
Silver Screen Partners, 163
Simon and Garfunkel, 22
Siodmak, Robert, 122
Sirk, Douglas, 60, 122
Smeaton, Bruce, 52
Smith, Maggie, 163, 170
Sommer, Josef, 124
South Australian Film
    Corporation, 39, 77
Spark, Muriel, 170
Spielberg, Steven, 201
Star Wars series, 121
Steele, Jadrien, 144, 160
Stigwood, Robert, 84
Stone, Oliver, 112, 117, 138
Stork, 28
Stratton, David, 15
Straw Dogs, 33
Streep, Meryl, 189

Sukarno, President, 100
Sundowners, The, 19
Sunset Boulevard, 106
Sunstruck, 28
Swiss Family Robinson, The, 155

Tarnished Angels, The, 122
Taxi Driver, 138, 147
There's Always Tomorrow, 60
Theroux, Paul, 143, 146, 159
They're a Weird Mob, 27
This Sporting Life, 40
Thoreau, Henry, 170, 177
Thorn Birds, The, 81
Three to Go, 20, 25, 54
To Catch a Thief, 194
Tolstoy, Leo, 101
Touchstone Pictures, 163, 184
Tracy, Spencer, 186, 190
Trouble with Harry, The, 194
2000 Weeks, 27

Ulmer Edgar, 2
Under Fire, 99, 109
Union Films, 18
United Artists, 61

Valseuses, Les, 193
Vera Ellen, 134
Vertigo, 194
Von Sternberg, Josef, 9, 122

Walkabout, 27
Walker, Robert, 186
Wall Street, 138
Waltzing Matilda, 19
Warner Brothers, 80
Waterston, Sam, 100
Wayne, John, 169
Weaver, Sigourney, 1, 40, 99–118
Weinstein, Paula, 200
Weir, Peter
   birth 15
   youth 15
   European trips 16, 26–27
   career in television 17–18
Welles, Orson, 1

Westerner, The, 71
Whatever Happened to Green Valley? 27
Whitman, Walt, 165, 167, 170, 172
Widerberg, Bo, 50
Wilde, Brandon de, 131
Wilder, Billy, 106, 122
Williams, Robin, 40, 46, 163–180
Williamson, David, 19, 38, 83, 88, 93, 94, 95, 99
Wilson, Mary Louise, 195
Winer, Robert, 37, 41, 74, 83
Wings of Eagles, 194
Witness, 5, 8, 10, 24, 47, 50, 93, 121–141, 143, 147, 193, 200
Woods, James, 100
World According to Garp, The, 169
Written on the Wind, 122

Year of Living Dangerously, The, 1, 7, 8, 47, 77, 81, 93, 99–118, 126, 130, 132, 133, 135, 140, 167, 196, 200

Zamphir, Ghorghe, 52